Cite Them Right

Cite Them Right

The Essential Referencing Guide

12th edition

Richard Pears & Graham Shields

BLOOMSBURY ACADEMIC
LONDON • NEW YORK • OXFORD • NEW DELHI • SYDNEY

BLOOMSBURY ACADEMIC
Bloomsbury Publishing Inc
50 Bedford Square, London, WC1B 3DP, UK
1385 Broadway, New York, NY 10018, USA
29 Earlsfort Terrace, Dublin 2, Ireland

BLOOMSBURY, BLOOMSBURY ACADEMIC and the Diana logo are
trademarks of Bloomsbury Publishing Plc

First published in Great Britain 2004
This edition published 2022

A catalogue record for this book is available from the British Library.

Library of Congress Cataloging-in-Publication Data
Names: Pears, Richard, author. | Shields, Graham J., author.
Title: Cite them right : the essential referencing guide / Richard Pears, Graham Shields.
Description: 12th edition. | New York : Bloomsbury Academic, 2022. |
Series: Bloomsbury study skills | Includes bibliographical references and index. |
Summary: "Now in its twelfth edition, this essential resource is the go-to text for students
and authors who want to accurately reference sources and avoid plagiarism
in their work"– Provided by publisher.
Identifiers: LCCN 2021047613 (print) | LCCN 2021047614 (ebook) |
Subjects: LCSH: Bibliographical citations.
Classification: LCC PN171.F56 P43 2022 (print) | LCC PN171.F56
(ebook) | DDC 808.02/7–dc23
LC record available at https://lccn.loc.gov/2021047613
LC ebook record available at https://lccn.loc.gov/2021047614

ISBN: HB: 978-1-3509-3344-6
          PB: 978-1-3509-3345-3
          ePDF: 978-1-3509-3347-7
          eBook: 978-1-3509-3346-0

Typeset by Integra Software Services Pvt. Ltd.
Printed and bound in Great Britain by Bell and Bain Ltd, Glasgow

To find out more about our authors and books visit www.bloomsbury.com
and sign up for our newsletters.

Contents

Section F   How to reference 34

Section G   Harvard referencing style 43

Section H American Psychological Association (APA) referencing style 130

Section I   Chicago referencing style 153

Section N Vancouver referencing style 248

Foreword

Welcome to the twelfth edition of *Cite them right*. We hope that it will support and guide you in your academic work. We are grateful to the many students, teachers, researchers and librarians who send questions about referencing, and reviews of the book and *Cite them right online*. These help us to understand where clarifications and new examples are required. We hope that you will continue to send this constructive feedback to help us develop *Cite them right* for the future.

New and revised material

In response to feedback from customers, the twelfth edition goes into more detail on the basics of referencing. References appear at the end of your academic work, but, as we will show, you need to think about referencing from the first stages of research for your assignment or project. The expanded opening sections (A–F) of the book will help you to:

♦ locate and collect high-quality evidence to use in your work
♦ incorporate good information management skills in your note-taking and research
♦ paraphrase, summarise and quote from other people's work
♦ understand what plagiarism means and how to avoid it

We have included revised examples, based on new editions of guides, for the American Psychological Association (APA), Institute of Electrical and Electronic Engineers (IEEE) and the Modern Language Association (MLA) referencing styles.

There are also updated examples for the Harvard, Chicago, Modern Humanities Research Association (MHRA), Oxford Standard for Citation of Legal Authorities (OSCOLA) and Vancouver styles.

There are several ways to access a source:

♦ a film can be seen in the cinema, on television, via an internet streaming service or DVD
♦ news appears in print or online newspapers, within a database or through an app
♦ images are viewed in many formats and platforms
♦ lectures may be in person, live online through services such as Zoom or Teams, or recorded to be watched at any time
♦ some online information is freely accessible, other sources are password-restricted

We've provided examples to cite these sources in a range of media.

The COVID-19 pandemic accelerated the digital delivery of many information sources used in education, including ebooks and ejournals, digitised book chapters and archival sources. These formats existed before COVID-19, but are now even more prominent. This digital shift is shown by the many examples of online access for sources in the twelfth edition of *Cite them right*.

Cite them right online, the online institutional version, has also been expanded, with many more examples in each style than can be included in the printed book. In addition, it includes tutorials and tips to help you reference sources successfully. We will continue to provide more material online, particularly for the non-Harvard referencing styles.

How to make the best use of *Cite them right*

You are *not* expected to read this book from cover to cover, but **everyone should read Sections A–F**.

Section A explains why referencing is important and how to avoid the consequences of poor study skills such as plagiarism.

Section B provides techniques for locating academic-quality information on which to base your learning and academic work.

Section C shows you how to incorporate good information management skills in your note-taking and research.

Section D provides examples for citing sources in your text.

Section E demonstrates how to paraphrase, summarise and quote from other people's work.

Section F details how to identify which pieces of information to include in references, in a reference list or bibliography, as well as providing guidance on using non-English names, non-Roman scripts and tips for successful referencing.

Section G, the main body of the book, includes specific examples for referencing a comprehensive range of sources using the Harvard (author-date) referencing style. This originated in the USA, but has become one of the most widely used referencing styles internationally, due to its simplicity and ease of use. However, there is no single authority to define 'Harvard'; hence, there are many versions, with slight variations, of the system in use. The alternative title, 'author-date', arises from the fact that the in-text citations follow the format of using the author's surname/family name and the date of publication (where available) to link with the full reference details in the reference list/ bibliography.

You should use the **Contents** or **Index** pages to identify the type of source you need to reference (for example, ebook, web page, government publication), then follow the advice and example(s) on the relevant page(s). The Index only lists items specific to Section G, the Harvard referencing style.

Sections H–N provide examples for referencing the most commonly used sources in the APA, Chicago, IEEE, MHRA, MLA, OSCOLA and Vancouver styles.

A **Glossary** is included to explain the meaning of certain terms used in the text. These words appear in bold when they first occur within each section.

Richard Pears and Graham Shields, 2021

Acknowledgements

The authors wish to thank our editor Helen Caunce; Richard Wong, senior digital development editor; Suzannah Burywood for editing previous editions; and everyone at Bloomsbury who works on *Cite them right* and *Cite them right online*.

The publishers would like to thank the following for permission to reproduce copyright material:

artisteer/iStock, p. 7; Tom Werner/Getty Images, p. 13; PeopleImages/iStock, p. 33; DMEPhotography/iStock, p. 45; TomasSereda/iStock, p. 70; Witthaya Prasongsin/Getty Images, p. 73; AtomicSparkle/iStock, p. 99; Creative Credit/iStock, p. 104; pressureUA/iStock, p. 114; aeduard/Getty Images, p. 129; Floortje/iStock, p. 152; nata_zhekova/iStock, p.168; Phil Harrison/iStock, p. 223; dbvirago/iStock, p.227.

Section A
What is referencing?

Referencing is the process of acknowledging other people's work when you have used it as evidence in your assignments, presentations or research. It is vital that you distinguish their work from your own contribution, and you do this by referencing. It allows your reader to locate the source material easily so that they can verify the validity of your arguments.

You identify or **cite** the sources you have used by placing indicators in the text of your assignment, called **citations** or **in-text citations**. Full details of the original sources are provided in a **reference list** at the end of your work. Some styles also use either **footnotes** at the bottom of the page, or **endnotes** at the end of the work. The footnotes or endnotes (which are required in some **referencing styles** but are not used in Harvard style) and reference list only include the sources you have cited in your text. In some cases you may also need to include a **bibliography**, which includes all material used in the preparation of your work, both cited items and background reading you did not cite.

Referencing is not done as an end in itself, or meant as a chore, but as one of the integral skills used in academic and professional communications. It builds on other skills, including searching for relevant sources of information, evaluating the academic credibility of sources, distinguishing between facts and opinions in other authors' work, understanding how their work can influence and evidence your thoughts on the subject, and being able to communicate your views in writing and speaking.

Referencing in academic work

There are different approaches to education around the world. These can affect the importance attached to the referencing of sources, as there are alternative views about the ownership of information by those who created it. Some cultures have strong traditions of sharing knowledge through story and song. The original authors may have been forgotten or their individual contributions blended with later ones; in these cultures the story is more important than the author. Some educational cultures emphasise conformity, deference to experts and the community-wide sharing of knowledge that prioritises group consensus over individual views (Campbell, 2017). In these learning environments, learning by rote, repeating knowledge passed on by tutors and assessment by examinations that test retention of information are common. This emphasis on receiving knowledge from tutors may deter individual research by students, as seeking additional information or disagreeing with the tutor is considered disrespectful (Zigunovas, 2017). The sharing of information for the benefit of society also minimises the attribution of work to individual authors. In other educational systems (including the United Kingdom, Europe and North America), emphasis is placed on the verification of facts and the development of the individual to be able to question received information and contribute new knowledge through research. Assessments may be more discursive, identifying and referencing a range of opinions from different scholars and using these to mould the views of the student author. In this educational system, knowledge is viewed as the property of the person who created it.

Although rooted in different cultures, these alternative approaches to learning are not mutually exclusive and each can be seen in many countries. For example, methods of learning experienced by a UK student at school and university include rote, discussion and comparison of views, and expression of individual opinions. However, in academic writing and publishing, it is expected that information will be attributed to its creators through references in your work.

Reasons for referencing

1. To give credit to the original author/creator. Even if you create something new, such as art, works of fiction, computer code or laboratory work, there may still be guidance or inspiration from other people.
2. When you are quoting, paraphrasing or summarising other authors' text or ideas, use references to distinguish between their work and your own (see Section E). This will help you avoid plagiarism.
3. References enable the reader to locate the original material you used as evidence, so that they can form their own views on the value of your sources and how you have interpreted them.
4. To demonstrate that you have good research skills. Some readers will look at your reference list before they read your text, because they can see from your references if you have used the most up-to-date information, read the theories of the leading scholars and used a range of information sources that provide a fuller understanding of the subject. If you have relied on old data, or missed an important author, this will be revealed by your references. Conversely, you may have identified sources unknown to your reader and if you have used high-quality sources, they will begin reading your work with a positive view.
5. To achieve a better mark or grade!

Acknowledging the work of earlier authors does not mean that you must agree with their opinions. In all academic disciplines, there may be scepticism or disagreements about conclusions reached from analysing data or the evidence available; for example, in 2021 there were different views among health authorities on the use of COVID-19 vaccines. At college, university and professional levels, you are expected to critically review the information available to you, not simply to take it as read. In all subjects, it is important to think about who created the information, why they produced it and if their findings or opinions are applicable to other situations; for example, a new policy or product may appeal to one generation but not others. This questioning of sources is healthy and a fundamental part of academic work, as it spurs further investigation and leads to the discovery of new knowledge.

When should you reference?

You are expected to reference *every* time you use someone else's work or ideas in your own work. There are no exceptions to this rule and it applies to all your work, including assignments, essays, presentations, dissertations and other research or publications. This includes all material available on the **internet**. It is a common misconception that information on the internet is free from restrictions on use. Books, journals, online and audiovisual media may be *freely viewable* to students through the university or college library, but the institution pays for access: a university-wide subscription to a single science journal might cost several thousands of pounds every year, and only readers with the correct username and password can read it. Journalists use up-to-date information from around the world to produce newspaper articles, hence many newspapers charge an access fee. While websites may be freely available, their authors have spent time and possibly money to research and publish information online, for example by paying website hosting fees. The creators or authors of these sources may not expect financial rewards, but they do expect you to acknowledge and respect the work they have done by referencing. As information on the internet can be rapidly published, updated or removed, it is essential that you reference information from online sources.

It is vital to record references as soon as you begin your research, and keep these records for all the sources you used in your research, even if you did not use them in your work, until your assignment has been marked and returned to you. Start your notes with a full reference to each source you use. Do this when you are using the source, as it can be difficult (or even impossible) to locate sources again at a later date, particularly any on-line sources.

What about secondary referencing?

In some cases, you may want to refer to a source that is mentioned or quoted in the work you are reading. This is known as **secondary referencing**. In all referencing styles, you are strongly encouraged to keep this to a minimum and whenever possible you should read and cite from the original or primary source. For example, if you read about a study by Jang (primary source) in a book by Lewis (secondary source), you should try to locate and read the original work by Jang. This will enable you to check for yourself that Jang has not been misinterpreted or misquoted by Lewis. If you cannot locate the primary source (in this case Jang), you cannot include it in your reference list. You can only cite it in your text. In your essay or assignment, you should cite both sources and use the phrase 'quoted in' or 'cited in', depending on whether the author of the secondary source is directly quoting or summarising from the primary source. You should always cite the source you have actually used.

As Jang (2015, quoted in Lewis, 2018, p. 86) stated 'prices fell 30%'.

Jang's data (2015, cited in Lewis, 2018, p. 86) supported the analysis.

Lewis, T. (2018) *Retail trends*. Singapore: Clark Press.

What about referencing 'common knowledge'?

There is no need to reference information that is considered to be **common knowledge**. This is not an exact term and will depend on the context in which you are writing. It is generally defined as facts, dates, events and information that are expected to be known by someone studying a particular subject. The information can be checked in numerous publications and is not in dispute; for example, that Beijing is the capital city of China. Conversely, if you were to write 'The population of Beijing in March 2021 is 20,897,000 people', you would be expected to provide a reference for this more detailed information; for example, 'Beijing population 2021' (2021) *World population review*. Available at: https://worldpopulationreview.com/world-cities/beijing-population (Accessed: 15 June 2021). While it is generally known that Beijing is the capital city of China, its population may not be known by many people and to obtain the latest data requires you to check a published source. As a student, you may have only just started to study a particular subject and may be unaware of what is regarded as common knowledge. *If you are unsure, it is always advisable to provide a reference for the information.*

What about referencing anecdotal or personal experience?

Anecdotal sources can be compelling, particularly in the field of medicine. The primary weakness of anecdotes and personal stories is that they cannot be verified. Although, in most cases, you would not reference anecdotal sources of information, you may still use these sources, and include them as an appendix to your main text. It is important that you are aware of confidentiality and are absolutely certain that you have permission to use the material (see more about confidential information below). Clearly, if you have recorded someone recounting their story or anecdote, then you can include the transcript as an appendix to your work (with the interviewee's permission).

You can speak from personal experience in contexts like personal responses, opinion pieces or reflective papers, and in many subjects this approach is positively encouraged and expected. Experience and opinions are important in your writing because a large part of academic writing is demonstrating that you have understood the foundation of knowledge on which your contributions stand. Once again, though, to back up your opinions or responses, you should always try to support your viewpoints and experiences with substantiating scholarly material.

What about referencing confidential information?

There may be times when you need to use a source of information that is confidential, for example medical, legal or business material. This information is, by its very nature, unpublished and not in the public domain. In most cases, your tutor will offer guidance on whether you can use the information and reference it. If you decide to use confidential sources, you should always obtain permission from those who might be affected by its inclusion in your work. Similarly, it is regarded as good practice to ask for permission from the sender of information via personal communications (see Section G27).

In some cases, you may be able to anonymise the documents or sources, allowing you to refer to them for argument or statistical purposes; for example, in healthcare subjects, you could use terms such as 'Patient X' or 'Placement hospital'. See Section G30 for more details on how to reference confidential information.

So far, we have looked at why and when you should reference information you have used. One of the most important reasons is that it is clear to your reader what is your work and what you have used from other authors. This is to ensure that you are not accused of plagiarism.

What is plagiarism?

Plagiarism means the unacknowledged use of someone else's work. This includes material or ideas from any (published or unpublished) sources, whether print, electronic (even if freely available on the internet) or audiovisual. Using the words or ideas of others without citing and referencing them would be construed as plagiarism and is a very serious academic offence. It is regarded as the stealing of the author's intellectual property. There are many forms of plagiarism, and some are deliberate and others are due to poor academic skills.

Deliberate plagiarism includes:

♦ Presenting any part of someone else's work as your own. This includes the work of other students, paying for work to be written by someone else and handed in as your own work (so-called 'essay mills'), and visual material (such as photographs you obtained online and haven't given credit to the creator)
♦ Collusion: working with another person to produce an assignment and not declaring this
♦ Altering a few words of someone else's work but retaining their sentence structure (for example 'The company made a profit'/'The firm made a profit')
♦ Audio plagiarism: copying lyrics or parts of a music composition within your own work
♦ Visual plagiarism: making minor alterations to another person's images or designs without crediting the original source
♦ 'Recycling' a piece of your own work that you have previously submitted for another module or course (that is, self-plagiarism)
♦ Citing and referencing sources you have not used

Examples of plagiarism through poor academic skills include:

♦ Using a source of information word for word (without quotation marks)
♦ Paraphrasing or summarising material in your assignment without acknowledging the original source through in-text citation and reference (see Section C)
♦ Using too many quotations so that your work is little more than the work of others (even if referenced), held together by linking sentences you have written

In most cases, students plagiarise unintentionally. Poor organisation and time management, as well as a failure to understand the expected academic practices of their college or university, are often to blame. Additionally, as noted above, if a student has not experienced a learning culture that demands attribution of information to individuals, they may not appreciate the importance of referencing in an academic environment such as the UK and may be accused of plagiarism. Plagiarism happens in all countries and for range of reasons, not just cultural differences. As Simon (2019, p. 82) noted, there are many instances of plagiarism in Western politics, music and literature, not least the ghostwriting of speeches and autobiographies, practices that would be clear instances of plagiarism in academia.

How can you avoid plagiarism?

The following advice can help:

♦ Check your institution's guidance on what is expected in academic work, especially the referencing of other people's work
♦ Attend training offered by your library or study skills department

♦ Manage your time and plan your work – ensure that you give yourself enough time to prepare, read and write
♦ Use the guidance in *Cite them right* to maintain clear notes and records of all the sources you use as you use them – it can prove difficult to locate sources later
♦ Keep all your notes and references until your assignment has been graded/marked
♦ When paraphrasing an author's text, ensure that you use your own words and a sentence structure that is sufficiently different from the original text (see Section E)
♦ In your notes, highlight in colour/bold any **direct quotations** you want to use in your assignment – this will help to ensure that you use quotation marks alongside an appropriate reference when you are writing up your work
♦ Allow enough time to check your final draft for possible referencing errors or omissions: for example, check that all your in-text citations have a corresponding entry in your reference list, and vice versa

Similarity detection software

Some institutions use similarity detection software, such as Turnitin, to identify where words, phrases or sentences in a student's text are similar to or have been taken from other sources. The software compares a student's assignment against a database of the text of books, articles, websites and previous student assignments, and provides a marked-up version of the student's work showing matches with text stored in the database. This software should not alarm you if you have followed guidance from your tutors and in *Cite them right*. The software is detecting similarities, not deliberate plagiarism, and there may be good reasons for this, for example that you have quoted from other sources. The marked-up version of your text will identify where you have used quotation marks around any phrases or sentences taken directly from the original sources as quotations and provided in-text citations (or footnote numbers). It will also note in-text citations where you have paraphrased or summarised another author's work. The software will highlight in a different colour where words and phrases match text in its database but no references have been given in your text, which may be instances of plagiarism.

If the software detects a large amount of similarity, it may be that too much of your work is formed of quotations or paraphrasing from other authors, rather than your analysis or writing. You may receive a lower mark if this is the case, not because you have plagiarised, but because your tutors will usually want to read your understanding or views on a subject, not reread what they have seen in earlier sources. You should use quotations or **paraphrasing**, with references, to support what you want to say, in place of your original thinking. Although similarity detection software can be used in disciplinary proceedings where deliberate plagiarism is suspected, many institutions allow you to submit a draft of your work to Turnitin and see what level of similarity is noted. This is to help you develop your referencing and writing skills before handing in the assignment to be marked, as you have the opportunity to consider rewriting any sections of your work that are highlighted by the software.

Which sources should you use?

When looking at what you should use for academic or professional work, it's essential that you locate and use the best evidence to learn about the topic, so that the views you express in your writing are well informed, stand up to questioning and will be accepted by your readers. You should think critically about which sources to use. There are millions of sources of information available in many forms (see Section G), but not all are suitable for academic work. For example, a medical researcher would not use information or opinions from a populist magazine in determining health procedures. Instead, they would look for data, reports and comments from qualified practitioners. In all college and university work, you should try to locate information that has **academic credibility**. This means that the source is:

♦ **A**ccurate: evidenced by references that substantiate the author's findings or opinions. Ask yourself: is this fact or opinion?
♦ **C**urrent: depending on the subject, this could be medical information that is up to date, or is an older source that provides an insight into earlier historians' views on a topic

♦ **O**bjective: think about why the author created it. Some want to inform with facts and evidence, some to entertain, others to broadcast their opinions and persuade you to follow them, or to sell you a product. Is the information balanced, avoiding bias and informing you of different opinions even if these disagree with the author's views? Check for 'fake news': can you check this source against others?
♦ **R**elevant: to your research topic. For example, ensure that legal sources found online apply to the country you are writing about, and don't assume that a marketing strategy for one social group will work for everyone
♦ **N**amed: it has named authors or organisations that you check for their authority to write or speak on this subject, such as the author's experience, where they work and their scholarly or professional qualifications

We have symbolised academic credibility using ACORN as an easy-to-remember acronym, as a strong oak tree grows from an acorn. If you use reliable sources as evidence, your work will have firm foundations too.

Sources with academic credibility may vary with context and expectations in your subject. In many subjects, academic sources such as books, journal articles and conference papers, available from the library, will be **peer-reviewed** (also referred to as 'refereed' or 'scholarly'). This means that they are written by experts in their subject and then reviewed by several other experts to ensure quality and accuracy before the material is published.

All of these scholarly sources will have **references** to show you where the authors obtained their evidence. Other sources, such as lecture notes, organisation web pages, government publications, legal material and professional reports, will usually be reliable and cite sources. If a written or online source does not have references, think carefully before using it in academic work. There may be instances, such as professional or trade magazines and newspapers, where the absence of references is acceptable, but try to cross-reference information from these sources with others to check their reliability.

When using the internet, look for web pages that have .ac, .edu, or .gov as these will be from academic or government organisations. Instead of searching all of the internet, use a search engine such as Google Scholar, which will help you to locate academic-quality sources online. There is a huge amount of academic-quality open access source material available through sites such as CORE (www.core.ac.uk), PhD theses available in Open Access Theses and Dissertations (www.oatd.org) and many subject-specific collections such as Arxiv (www.arxiv.org). For sources out of copyright, look in HathiTrust Digital Library (https://www.hathitrust.org/) and Internet Archive (https://archive.org/).

When using news sources, search for balanced and impartial coverage focused on facts and produced by named reporters and commentators, rather than sensational or emotive tabloid-style articles.

Remember that there is a wide range of quality control on the internet and social media, from none, through to academic standards. In many online sources, such as blogs and tweets, people can write whatever they want and are often unaccountable for what they publish. The author may give an opinion on a topic, even if they have no expertise or academic knowledge of the subject. They may omit information that contradicts their opinions, or may publish 'fake news' or misinformation to mislead or change your views. In some subjects, you may be required to use these sources (such as giving examples of how a news story spreads online), but be clear to yourself and your readers about the author's authority and motives for what they wrote. If you are unsure about using a source, ask your tutor or librarian.

Tips to help you find sources with academic credibility

Use a search strategy that includes following up references from your tutor and in the references and bibliographies in published sources, as well as searching online using keywords and phrases for your topic.

Where to start:

♦ Check your library website for guides to high-quality online and print sources for your subject and online versions of your reading lists
♦ Wherever possible, use these recommended sources rather than taking a chance with whatever an internet search turns up
♦ When you are reading recommended sources, use **citation surfing** – look at which authors and publications were cited in the references and bibliographies,

and look for these authors too. One source helps you to identify others

- Look for other publications by recommended authors, for example journal articles, theses and conference papers
- When searching for journal articles, use library databases such as Web of Science and Scopus, publisher websites and Google Scholar; librarians will be able to recommend specific databases for your topic
- Look for book reviews in academic journals to see what experts thought of the source and how it related to existing scholarship (don't confuse these reviews by subject experts with customer reviews on retail websites!)
- Learn how to export references from library catalogues and databases

To find more relevant results (if you get a lot of results from your search):

- Think of words and phrases to describe your topic and use combinations of these in library catalogues and databases
- Use **phrase searching**, putting the required phrase into double quotation marks " ". A phrase can be the title of a source, or the name of an organisation, as well as a concept, for example "Handbook of Action Research", "World Health Organization" or "Haber process"
- If appropriate, limit the search by dates, for example sources published in the last 10 years, or information (such as newspapers articles) published within a specific date range
- Use the advanced search option in databases and search engines; this will help you to locate more relevant results

- Consider search results in library databases that include the term 'Cited by' and 'Times cited' (listing subsequent publications that referred to a source). These will guide you to newer research and more recent authors

To broaden your search (if you find too few results):

- Use truncation to broaden your search, using the common part or trunk of a word followed by a *to locate related words; for example, poli* will locate police, policy, polity, politician and political
- Use synonyms in round brackets with OR between the synonyms, for example (company OR business OR firm). This can also be used if there is a spelling variation, for example (Heracles OR Hercules)

Use search techniques in combination:

- For example, "food label" AND regulat* AND (business OR company OR firm) AND "European Union". Note that the word AND in capitals instructs the search engine or database to locate all of the words. AND may not be required in all search engines or databases

Ask for help:

- Your institution may also have librarians and study skills staff keen to teach you how to begin your research and find academic sources. Look on the library news or website for research or information literacy classes and online guides – these will give you a great start in locating the most relevant sources for your work

♦ If you are studying for a higher degree or conducting research, find out about alerting services that will save a search today then email you references to any new publications that meet your search criteria

How many references should you include?

With so many sources available in print and online, it is impossible to read every source on your subject. This is why it's important to plan a search strategy that ensures you identify major authors and sources that are relevant, not just available. The number of sources you are expected to use will depend on your level of study, the range of relevant information sources and what your subject tutors expect. It may be that in a science assignment, you need to make only one or two references if most of your work is reporting data from experiments and your analysis of this. Conversely, in the humanities and social sciences, many references may be required to represent different interpretations. In all cases, citing a reference should support or verify what you are writing, not simply add more words (Gaast, Koenders and Post, 2019, p. 105). In principle, you should reference everything that has contributed to your work, and in practice you should ask your tutor what the expectations are for the number of references in an assignment in your subject and at your level of study. You should also check if the references will be included in the word count for your assignment.

Identifying the source

When looking at information online, it can sometimes be difficult to identify what type of source you have located, as the online presentation omits the physical indications that would help you differentiate. For example, a PDF of a book chapter may look like the PDF of a journal article or a report published online by an organisation. The PDF (portable document format) is the means of access and distributing content, not the source. Help is often available in the source, as many PDFs downloaded from academic books and journals will include a citation and a timestamp, recording the publication details and also when and where it was downloaded. Note that this citation may be in the publisher's style, rather than the referencing style you are using, so check if you need to modify it to your department's referencing style.

It is important to know what type of source you are reading, because information is created for different purposes. You may have only one part of a larger work, for example part of a chapter from a longer book, and the part you have may not have all the information you need to understand the author's views – after all, they wrote the other chapters so the author thought they were important too!

All referencing systems state that it is most important to identify the author (a person or an organisation). As noted earlier, this will help you to understand how reliable the source is and the author's authority to write about the subject. If you have the author's name or the title for the source, you can search for these in a library data-base or search engine. Entering the title in quotation marks, for example "Customer segmentation in ecommerce", will help you to find the source or references to it. If there isn't a title, or if this does not locate the reference, try searching for the first few lines of the text, again in quotation marks to make your search more precise. You should also try to locate the date when the source was created. This may not be obvious, but there may be clues in the text such as references to events. In many subjects, it is essential that you have the most up-to-date information.

If you're unable to locate the full details of the source, it can still be cited, including as many elements of the reference you can establish – author, date, title, publication information and web address. However, you should think very carefully about using the source, particularly if you can't find the author. Can you locate an alternative source that provides the full reference information you need so that you can evaluate its academic credibility?

Different editions or versions of a source

You may encounter different versions or editions of a source and this can cause confusion about which one you should reference. With books, you should be able to identify which edition of the book you are using by looking at the publication information on the cover and in the first pages. Generally, you will be expected to try to use the latest edition of a book so that you have the most up-to-date research (especially in subjects like law and medicine), but in some subjects you might have to use older and newer editions to see how an author changed

their views over time, or to read specific case studies. With books, you will be expected to include the edition number in your reference, unless it was the first or only edition. With online publications, there may also be differences between versions. For example, an article in PDF format in a university research repository or a website such as Arxiv.org may be an earlier version of a journal article made available online before it was peer-reviewed and amended after the reviewer's comments (see Section G2.2). If possible, locate the latest published version and cite this, but if you cannot find a later version state where you found the source. If using visual sources, be clear to your reader about what you have seen: a painting in a gallery is seen as the painter intended, but if reproduced in a book or online it may have been cropped or digitally altered. Remember: **cite what you have used**: if you saw the image online, cite the online version, if in a book, cite the book.

Saving references and using referencing software

Many library catalogues and subscription databases have facilities for you to save bibliographic information about sources and export this to use in your assignments. Ask your library staff about this, as it will ensure that you have all of the relevant information, such as volume and page numbers, required to produce a reference at the end of your work, although you will usually need to rearrange the elements of the reference to the referencing style you are using.

If you are working on a long assignment such as a dissertation or thesis with scores of references to save, or if you are likely to use references to the same sources in several pieces of work (for example journal articles you are writing), you may wish to use referencing software. There are many reference management software tools available (some free) that can help you to manage the referencing process, including Endnote, RefWorks, Citavi, Mendeley and Zotero. Each has a range of functions in addition to storing references. Some products will convert your references into different referencing styles, if, for example, a tutor wishes you to use a different style to other tutors, or if you are writing for a journal that has its own house style. Some of the products also enable you to tag or add comments to sources and to share lists or comments with your colleagues. Your institution may have a preferred product and provide guidance to use this, or there are many guides to referencing software available online. Be aware, though, that even if you use these tools, you must still double-check your citations and references to ensure that they appear in a consistent style and follow your department's/tutor's guidelines.

There are also referencing generators available online. We advise that you use these cautiously, and ask tutors or library staff if they are good enough for academic work. The referencing software that your institution subscribes to uses bibliographic data from publishers to provide accurate information, but some of the free, online referencing generators rely on other students to input bibliographic information and do not check that this is free from errors before making these citations available to other users. In the authors' experience, this has led to some students being penalised for using incorrect references in their work.

Section C
Reading, listening and taking notes

Once you have located sources, you need to read them effectively to make notes of facts, data, opinions and other sources of information that are relevant to your topic. Before reading a source or listening to a lecture, plan how you are going to record and save the points that interest you and ensure that any text or data you want to quote or reuse in your work is attributed correctly.

Saving your work

If you are handwriting your notes, have a folder in which you can keep printouts you have annotated and any notes you have made. Try to have a separate folder for each assignment, so that your notes don't get mixed up and you can quickly go back to the information when you need it.

You could create a folder on your computer or cloud storage and ensure that all information relating to a project is saved there. This may include sources you've downloaded and annotated. If you are working on the draft of an assignment, remember to save it regularly. Do not rely on the software to do this for you. Also remember to back up your files on a regular basis!

If you are working with others on a collaborative task, you may want to save your version of the file (including your name and the date you sent it) before you pass it on to your colleagues, so that you can demonstrate your contribution and avoid problems that may occur with their computer or storage.

Scan and skim reading

Scan and skim reading are techniques for rapid assessment of a source. You can use them together when deciding if the source is relevant to your topic and worth devoting more time to analysing it (Gillett, Hammond and Martala, 2009, p. 67).

Scan reading means looking through the text quickly to locate specific information such as data, facts, names of authors or important people in the subject, or ideas, as you might if looking through a book index. You are not trying to read the text, just aiming to find those words or images that are relevant to your assignment. Do not dwell on text that is not relevant to your task. You might scan through a book or article and decide that, as there are no mentions of authors or concepts, you can leave this source and move on to others. Alternatively, the scan may show that the source has relevant information and you may look at it more closely with a first skim read of the text.

Skim reading means looking through the source to get an overview or general impression, as you might do when looking at news headlines. Skim reading will help you to identify the author's views and the scope of the work. Is it a thorough examination of a topic (as you would find in a book)? Or is it focusing on one part of a wider topic (such as a journal article that reports the results of a specific technique)?

Does it rely on your reading of more wide-ranging works to see the significance of the material in the source? For example, you may need to know the historical background before reading an article focused on a specific government policy.

For books, start at the contents page to see the overall structure. What headings or titles have been given to each chapter or section? Read the introductory paragraphs of each chapter/section, then run your eyes through the text, looking for section headings, illustrations and words and phrases relevant to your topic. These will often be presented sequentially as the author presents and discusses evidence to justify their conclusions at the end. They will help you to recall their key points. Read the concluding paragraphs to see how the author summarises the chapter/section to remind you of key points.

For articles and reports, the structure will lead you from abstract to introduction, through methodology or literature review to analysis and conclusions.

For short sources, such as news articles, space is limited so journalists will often use a catchy headline that encapsulates the information and they will embed the most important information in the first few sentences to attract your attention.

Critical reading

Once you have an overall impression of the source from skim reading, read it again and this time as you read think about the concepts or facts the author is describing. What is the purpose of each chapter or section? This should be stated in the opening paragraphs, while the closing paragraphs will **summarise** what the chapter contained. In all sources, look at the paragraph structure; generally each paragraph will focus on a key point.

As you read a source, try to do so critically (Maier, Barney and Price, 2009, p. 185). Does the author cite other authors or sources you have read, or that have been referred to in lectures, reading lists and bibliographies? Does this author agree or disagree with previous contributors? Are there new interpretations of the evidence? For example, in many humanities and social sciences subjects, researchers today are looking beyond traditional white, male, Western views to discover alternative voices among people marginalised in the past by prejudice about gender, race or socioeconomic status. Remember that readers and researchers can draw different conclusions from a piece of evidence, such as economists using the same data to propose different policies. Finally, look at the **references** and bibliography of sources used by the author. This will help you locate earlier contributors to the subject and any original source material such as archives or datasets you might wish to look at if you are undertaking more detailed research such as a dissertation or thesis. You can search library databases to locate more recent sources published after the one you are reading.

When making notes

It is important that you actually make notes, rather than highlight within a book. You should not annotate or highlight in library books – use removable coloured bookmarks to indicate important sections.

More importantly, Wood (2018, p. 69) wrote of highlighting: 'It's not learning. It's colouring in!' There is evidence to suggest that handwriting, more than typing, has a greater influence on your ability to memorise information (Magdalinski, 2013, p. 77). You should avoid copying the original text: you are creating a means through which you can remember why this source is important to you. Don't spend too much time producing detailed notes and have insufficient time for writing your assignment, or have too much information that delays you locating relevant evidence to incorporate in your work.

Ensure that you record the full reference to the lecture or the source you used, even if you don't cite it in your work. In some subjects, you may have to include in a bibliography the sources you read but did not cite. This not only identifies the breadth of your research to your reader but also recognises that reading a source may influence you.

When reading, try to identify connections between this text and others you have read, and differences of opinion between authors – why is this text different from others on the topic?

Try to **paraphrase** (Section E) in your own words the points in each paragraph. At the end of longer sections or chapters, write a summary of what you have learned. Think of how you would describe the source to someone else. Ensuring that you write your notes in your own words will help you avoid **plagiarism** (Cottrell, 2019, p. 247).

If you note facts, illustrations and data, or make **quotations** from what the author wrote or said, ensure that you copy exactly what is in the source and include a page number or other identifier, such as paragraph or section number. If you do copy words used by an author, make sure that you record them in quotation marks so you can distinguish between your work and the original author's words. You may find it useful to highlight the author's words in a different colour to your own words. This will ensure that you don't inadvertently plagiarise the original author and will help you locate quotations in your notes if you want to use them in your own work.

It may be useful to have a set of abbreviations to use for common words or frequently used names and places, to save time as you make notes (Magdalinski, 2013, p. 44). Here are some examples.

Word	Abbreviation
for example	e.g.
Equals	=
Therefore	$\therefore$
Regarding	Re:
Maximum	Max
Minimum	Min
Compare	cf
Reference	REF
Twentieth century	20C
William Shakespeare	WS

Many lectures are now recorded and made available on institutional websites or intranets, so you can use these to enhance the notes made while you listened. It is important to go back over notes from a live lecture as you may have misheard or been unable to note everything as the lecturer spoke – this is natural as very few people can type or write as fast as the lecturer speaks. Reviewing the lecture and your notes are also vital for your active learning, so that you understand and are able to recall what was said (Wood, 2018, p. 68). Play back each section of the lecture; for example, what your lecturer said for each slide of a presentation and note the important points of that section as words and phrases. Note also any references the lecturer made to other sources or data, and pause the recording if there are any important visuals such as equations or reactions you need to record exactly. You may want to take a screenshot of these to help you locate the information later instead of playing through the whole recording. If you are typing the notes, you can insert the screenshot of them into your notes, but it is also useful to practise writing or drawing the visual information by hand, as this will help you remember it and see connections (and you may have to do this in an exam).

At the end of your reading and note-taking, you will have a structured series of notes you can refer to when you are writing your own work. You might find it useful to conclude your notes with bullet points summarising the key points the author or lecturer has made.

Techniques for making notes

There are many different strategies for making notes from a source you have read, watched or heard, and you may find one more effective than others. Two common methods are linear and columned notes.

Linear notes

This is a technique whereby you make notes sequentially as you work through the pages of a book or listen to a lecture. This will retain the structure and flow of the original source, but you may need to go through and highlight important words and ideas to help you understand and memorise the information.

Columned notes

This is an adaption of the linear notes, to help you draw out the key ideas and add further information or note questions. The method is sometimes called 'Cornell Notes', after its creator Professor Walter Pauk of Cornell University (Magdalinski, 2013, p. 36). It requires some preparation in advance of a lecture or reading a source, but is a much more effective means of note-taking than linear notes. You divide your page as shown in the diagram. At the top, always begin with details of the source, either the lecture or the full reference to what you are reading. Divide the bottom of the page horizontally, for your summary. Divide the middle part of the page vertically, with a wider column on the right in which to take 'Notes' and a narrower column on the left in which to record 'Questions'. With the 'Notes' section, you are not trying to record everything spoken or printed, just the main facts and concepts. If making notes from a book or article, remember to highlight any quotations, perhaps in a different colour. With the rest of the notes, try to paraphrase what you have read by putting the author's words into your own words. This is a form of active learning and will help you remember the information. Use the 'Questions' section after the lecture or as you are making notes from a source to highlight any questions about what you have heard or read, any references cited that you want to look up, and how this source compares with others you have read. Finally, in the 'Summary' section, use bullet points and your own words to summarise what you have learned from the lecture or source.

You will find many sources of information and help to support your research, writing and presentations available from your college or university library, including guides covering searching and note-taking in more detail. Methodical research and note-taking skills will enable you to gather and effectively use relevant information, while including references for your sources will help you avoid accusations of plagiarism.

TITLE: *GEOL: 2721 Global warming*	DATE: 17/5/21

QUESTIONS	NOTES
	Intro: *to examine causes and effects of global warming*
check ref for stats	*Evidence:* *World Met Org 2020 stats show Global Surface Mean Temperature (GMST) 1.2+ 0.1C incr since 1900*
how much worse is ggm than deforesting? *Aren't aerosols reducing?* *- if so what is impact?*	*Causes:* *greenhouse gas emissions (ggms) esp. Methane and CO_2 from fossil fuel (ff) burning. Also human activity inc. deforestation for food production; aerosols and air pollution (planes)*
get evidence for land loss to sea level rise	*Impacts:* • *Temp rise: melting polar ice ->sea level rise, loss of land and habitats for ppl and anmls.* • *Also greater evapor = more weather extremes, storms, rainfall. on land droughts and desertification cause humn + anml migration, starvation etc* • *Feedback problms: ice reflects more solar radiation than sea wtr, so reduced ice leads to warming, warming also melts ice.*
examples of loss: Gt Barrier Reef etc	• *In sea, higher temp -> more CO_2 absorption, acidification of wtr, death of marine life, probls for phytoplankton and shell-based animals and coral reefs, destruction of undersea habitats.* • *On land, demand for gtr land for agric for food leads to deforestation, habitat destruction, etc. Also feedbk since forest darker than crops, more heat reflection into atmosphere whilst redctn in CO_2 absorption*
	Strtgies for ggm reduction: PTO

SUMMARY

Evidence for increased GSMT. GGMs and human activity to blame.
Impacts: temp rise -> ice melt, sea lvl rise, loss of land and droughts/desert, sea acidification + loss of marine life. Feedback probs: CO_2 and rad. reflection

Adapted from Learning Strategy Center, Cornell University (2021) *Cornell note taking system*. Available at: https://lsc.cornell.edu/how-to-study/taking-notes/cornell-note-taking-system/ (Accessed: 16 June 2021).

Section D
How to cite sources

Once you have located, read and made notes on the information sources, you can start to plan your work. The format of the work will vary between subjects, and a general guide such as *Cite them right* cannot cover the wide range of assignments from science reports to literature dissertations. Seek guidance from your department and library on how you are expected to produce academic work in your subject. However, every institution requires its students to reference in their work and your tutors will expect you to do this accurately, clearly and concisely. Before beginning your writing, you also must identify the form of referencing, called **referencing style**, used in your particular subject area.

Referencing styles

The principle of acknowledging other people's contributions in your own work through references is accepted in many countries and academic subjects, but the referencing style differs between subjects and between publishers. There are thousands of referencing styles available. Some styles are maintained by professional organisations, such as the American Psychological Association (APA) and the Institute of Electrical and Electronic Engineers (IEEE). They produce guides to writing styles and detail how sources used in books, articles and reports should be formatted and referenced. Many publishers have a preferred referencing style to be used by their authors, and academic journals will also have a favoured style and format for references. Some referencing styles are favoured in specific academic subjects, such as the Oxford University Standard for the Citation of Legal Authorities (OSCOLA) and its American equivalent *The Bluebook*, which are used in law schools and publications, or *Citing Medicine*, which is the basis of the Vancouver referencing style used in many medical, health and science schools and publications. There are also styles, such as Harvard, which have no single authority controlling the format, hence variations in what is called 'Harvard' referencing.

The huge range of referencing styles can be confusing for students and other authors. You are likely to encounter different referencing styles in the articles, books and websites you use. Although the order, formatting and punctuation in referencing styles may differ, the principles are the same: to highlight in the text where other people's work has been used, and the references provide the information on author, date, type of publication and location that the reader needs to locate these sources.

If you are writing an academic assignment, check with your department's learning handbook or with your tutor about which style of referencing they want you to use. Do this *before* you start the assignment, so you can record your references accurately while making notes and writing your assignment. It can be a lot of work to reformat all of your references if you use the wrong style.

If you are writing for a publication, check the publisher or journal website for a guide for authors, which will also give details of page formatting, use of language and abbreviations favoured by that publication. If a guide isn't available online, contact the editor of the publication to ask for a guide for authors. If you do not follow the specific referencing and writing guide, your work may be rejected or delayed until you have applied the publisher's requirements.

If you are given a choice of referencing styles to use, pick one and *use only this style – don't mix referencing styles*. There will be guides such as *Cite them right*, books by professional organisations and websites by university and college libraries to help you apply the referencing style consistently.

How to cite sources in your text

All referencing styles will use indicators in your text, called **citations** or **in-text citations**, to show your reader that you are referring to, called **citing**, someone else's work. This citation will link to full details of the sources in a list of all **references** at the end of your work, called the **reference list**, **works cited list** or **end-text citations**, or in some styles as **footnotes** at the bottom of each page. The reference list includes only the sources cited in your text. Sometimes, you may also be asked to include a **bibliography**, which uses the same referencing style, and contains the works you have cited but also any other sources you consulted, such as background reading, in the preparation of your work. Despite the many referencing styles

available, there are two general formats, based on how you cite sources in your text: **numeric** and **author-date**. When you are writing, you can use citations at the start, end and within a sentence, depending on how they can be incorporated in your writing style and to avoid repetition or disrupting the reader's concentration.

Setting out citations in numeric styles

If you are using a **numeric style**, such as Chicago (Section I), IEEE (Section J), MHRA (Section K), OSCOLA (Section M), Vancouver (Section N), place a number in your text to indicate a citation.

Example

A recent study analysed the qualifications of school-leavers.[1]

Your reader will then look for this number in the footnotes or **endnotes** to see the full reference.

Setting out citations in author-date styles

If using an **author-date style**, such as Harvard (Section G) or APA (Section H), your citations should include the following elements:

♦ Author(s) or editor(s) surname/family name
♦ Year of publication
♦ Page number(s) if required (always required for **direct quotations**)

If you are quoting directly or using ideas from a specific page or pages of a work, you should include the page number(s) in your citations. Insert the abbreviation p. (or pp.) before the page number(s).

If your citation refers to a complete work or to ideas that run through an entire work, your citation would simply use the author and date details.

The two examples above show that, with author-date in-text citations, you can incorporate the author's name in the flow of your text (the Martínez example), called narrative citation, or you can put the name in round brackets with the year and page number (Huang example), called parenthetical citation. Both are correct, but how you use them will depend on your writing style and how you wish to draw your reader's attention to the source. In some instances, it will be more important to provide a smoother flow of your thoughts and so you would use parenthetical citation. On another occasion, it might be important to emphasise which author you are citing so you could use a narrative citation.

How to cite authors in author-date styles

Citing one author/editor

Cite the author/editor.

Citing an author who has changed their name

There are occasions when an author/creator of a work has subsequently changed their name. This may be because of marriage, divorce, personal preference or gender transition. If you know that an author has changed their name and now wishes to be known by a different name, we suggest that you use the author's preferred current name for all their publications, even if this means changing a former name in a reference. For Harvard references, as long as you ensure that other details, such as article, journal or book titles and other publication details, are correct your reader will be able to locate the source. You may need to explain to your tutor why you have used a different name from that given in the source.

Citing a corporate author

Cite the name (or initials, if well known) of the corporate body. For corporate bodies with long names where you wish to make clear what its initials stand for, you should write out the name in full the first time you use it, and use the abbreviation for the citation. Be consistent in using the abbreviation each time to ensure that all your references appear correctly in your reference list.

Examples

… as shown in the BBC's annual report (2020).

… the popularity of visiting historical monuments (English Heritage, 2019).

… in claims made by the United Nations Framework Conference of Climate Change (UNFCCC, 2014) …

Citing multiple authors

Some sources have several authors. You will need to check how they should be cited in the referencing style you are using. The following examples are in Harvard style (Section G).

Citing two authors/editors

Both are listed.

Example

Recent educational research (Chounet and Zajczyk, 2021) …

Citing three authors/editors

All three are listed.

Example

Hill, Smith and Reid (2021) found …

Citing four or more authors/editors

When citing four or more authors/editors in academic assignments, you should *either* cite the first name listed followed by **et al.** (meaning 'and others') …

Example

In-text citation

Research on nanostructures by Cutler *et al.* (2011) …

Reference list

Cutler, J. *et al.* (2011) 'Polyvalent nucleic acid nanostructures', *Journal of the American Chemical Society*, 133(24), pp. 9254–9257. Available at: https://doi.org/10.1021/ja203375n

Or all the authors, if your *institution requires referencing of all named authors.*

Example

In-text citation

Research on nanostructures by Cutler, Zhang, Zheng, Auyeung, Prigodich and Mirkin (2011) …

Reference list

Cutler, J., Zhang, K., Zheng, D., Auyeung, E., Prigodich, A.E. and Mirkin, C.A. (2011) 'Polyvalent nucleic acid nanostructures', *Journal of the American Chemical Society*, 133(24), pp. 9254–9257. Available at: https://doi.org/10.1021/ja203375n

If you are writing for a publication, you should follow the editor's guidelines, as you may be required to name all the authors, regardless of the number, to ensure that each author's contribution is recognised.

Citing a source with no author/editor

Where the name of an author/editor cannot be found, use the title (in italics). Do not use 'Anon.' or 'Anonymous'.

Example

In a groundbreaking survey (*Health of the nation*, 2018) …

Citing multiple sources

If you need to refer to two or more publications at the same time, these can be separated by semicolons (;). The publications should be cited in chronological order (with the earliest date first). If more than one work is published in the same year, they should be listed alphabetically by author/editor.

Example

A number of environmental studies (Karlhofer, 2018; Town, 2018; Barkhov *et al.*, 2019; Fujiwara, 2021) considered …

Citing sources published in the same year by the same author

Sometimes you may need to cite two (or more) publications by an author published in the same year. To distinguish between the items in the text, allocate lower-case letters in alphabetical order after the publication date.

Example

In his study of the work of Rubens, Miller (2006a) emphasised the painter's mastery of drama. However, his final analysis on this subject (Miller, 2006b) argued that …

In your reference list, the publications would look like this.

Example

Miller, S. (2006a) *Rubens and his art*. London: Killington Press.

Miller, S. (2006b) *The Flemish masters*. London: Phaidon Press.

NB: In the list above, the source you cited first in your text is given the letter a, the second source cited in your text has the letter b and so on.

Citing different editions of the same work by the same author

Separate the dates of publication with a semicolon (;) with the earliest date first.

Example

In both editions (Feng, 2015; 2020) …

In your reference list, the publications would look like this.

Example

Feng S. (2015) *Chinese law*. 3rd edn. Oxford: Oxford University Press.

Feng, S. (2020) *Chinese law*. 4th edn. Oxford: Oxford University Press.

Citing multiple sources by the same author

Example

Research by one author (Singh, 2017; 2018) …

OR

Research by Singh (2017; 2018) …

In your reference list, the publications are listed by chronological date after the author's name.

Example

Singh, S. (2017) 'Sikh costume', *Indian Journal of Design*, 22, pp. 47–52.

Singh, S. (2018) *Religion in India*. Delhi: Scholars Press.

Citing sources with multiple authors

If you want to cite a book edited by Holmes and Baker, which has, for example, ten contributors and does not specify who wrote each section or chapter, follow the format of citing using the editors' names.

Example

Research (Holmes and Baker, 2019, pp. 411–428) proved …

NB: See Section G1.7 for the relevant information on citing and referencing when the author's name is given for a specific chapter or section.

Citing sources when one author has worked with other authors for some publications

For the same lead author, single author works precede works with multiple authors. Furthermore, the order of the reference list entries for works with the same lead author is determined alphabetically according to the second author's surname/family name (and so on if there are more co-authors).

Citing a source with no date

Use the phrase 'no date' or (n.d.).

Citing a source with no author or date

Use the title and 'no date'.

Citing a web page

If you are citing a web page, it should follow the preceding guidelines, citing by author and date where possible; by title and date if there is no identifiable author; or, as in the example below, by the **URL**

(Uniform Resource Locator) if neither author nor title can be identified.

NB: If you can't identify an author or title, this may not be a source with academic credibility.

For more details on how to cite and reference web pages, see Section G24.

Using illustrations in your text

In some subjects, you may be required to provide graphics or illustrations within your assignments, such as graphs in mathematics or diagrams of experiments. Your tutor or department should provide a guide, perhaps in a module handbook, for how your work is to be presented, for example fonts, referencing style, word count and how any illustrations are to be incorporated. There may also be subject-specific regulations from a professional body. *Cite them right* is not intended to replace any departmental regulations, nor can it provide guidance to cover the full range of academic subjects its readers are studying. If you are unsure about how you should present illustrations in your academic work, you should ask your tutor for guidance.

If no guidance is available from your tutor, we suggest that you number each illustration in the order they are used in your work, and provide a caption that describes the illustration, beginning the caption with 'Figure', then the number, then the description. If you have used an illustration from someone else's work, conclude the caption with, in round brackets, Source: and the details of where the illustration came from. If possible, and definitely if your work is going to be published, you should obtain written permission from the creator of the illustration to reuse their work.

Example

The magnificent ruins of Dunstanburgh Castle (Figure 1) stand on a promontory jutting out into the North Sea near Embleton in Northumberland.

Using appendices to your text

Your main text will generally be expected to be analysis or discussion of evidence leading to the statement or explanation of your views in the conclusion of your work. You may have information that is too detailed to be included in the main text, such as data or explanations of processes, and in some subjects you can present this as an appendix or appendices (if more than one is required) at the end of your assignment or research. An appendix should be clearly labelled with a letter (A) or number (1), so that your reader will know where to look for this additional information outside your main text. If an appendix contains information from other sources, these should be cited in-text in the appendix, with full references given at the end of the appendix as a separate reference list.

Figure 1 Dunstanburgh Castle, Northumberland (Source: R. Pears, 2019)

Section E
Using other people's work in your writing: quoting, paraphrasing and summarising

When you produce academic work such as assignments or presentations, your tutors are looking to see how you are developing as an author capable of independent research and making new contributions to the subject. If you are producing briefings and reports for an organisation or company, your manager wants to hear your professional views. In each case, you will need to provide evidence for how you have formed your opinions or reached your conclusions. You can incorporate this evidence in three ways: using the original author's words as **quotations**; by putting their ideas into your own words through **paraphrasing**; or noting their contribution briefly as a summary. In each case, you will need to provide an **in-text citation** and a full **reference**.

Using quotations

The most direct way of using other people's work in your own is through quotations. These should be relevant and support your arguments, and not be used to pad out your text to fill up the word count! Bear in mind that **direct quotations** will be included in your assignment's total word count, so excessive use of quotations can disrupt the flow of your writing and prevent you from demonstrating your understanding and analysis of the sources you have read. Remember also that relying too much on quotations rather than your own words will produce a high similarity result from software such as Turnitin. Your tutor will prefer to read your own interpretation of the evidence.

Short direct quotations (up to two or three lines) should be enclosed in quotation marks (single or double – be consistent) and included in the body of your text.

If you are using a numeric referencing style (e.g. Chicago, IEEE, MHRA, OSCOLA or Vancouver), place the number of the citation at the end of the quotation.

> **Examples of quotations and numeric references**
>
> It has been suggested that 'If you need to illustrate the idea of nineteenth-century America as a land of opportunity, you could hardly improve on the life of Albert Michelson'.[1]
>
> Lomotey said 'the children remained calm like professionals'.[2]

In author-date references (e.g. Harvard or APA), give the author, date and page number (if available) that the quotation was taken from. When citing direct quotations from sources without pagination (ebooks, journal articles, web pages), use the information you have to help the reader locate the quotation. For example, you may use a paragraph number if provided, or you can count down paragraphs from the beginning of the document.

Examples of quotations with author-date references

It has been suggested that 'If you need to illustrate the idea of nineteenth-century America as a land of opportunity, you could hardly improve on the life of Albert Michelson' (Bryson, 2004, p. 156).

Lomotey (2018, para. 4) said 'the children remained calm like professionals'.

NB: In these examples, the author and year can be used in parenthetical or narrative citations, depending on your writing style.

Longer quotations should be entered as a separate paragraph and indented from the main text. Quotation marks are not required.

Example

King (1997, pp. 553–554) describes the intertwining of fate and memory in many evocative passages, such as:

> So the three of them rode towards their end of the Great Road, while summer lay all about them, breathless as a gasp. Roland looked up and saw something that made him forget all about the Wizard's Rainbow. It was his mother, leaning out of her apartment's bedroom window: the oval of her face surrounded by the timeless gray stone of the castle's west wing!

Making changes to quotations

Wherever possible, you should quote exactly from the source you are using. If you need to modify the quoted text, for example to shorten it or add a clarification, you must ensure that you retain the author's original meaning and context, and don't omit words to fit your opinion.

Omitting part of a quotation

Indicate this by using three dots … called an ellipsis.

Example

'Drug prevention … efforts backed this up' (Cruz, 2017, p. 49).

Inserting your own, or different, words into a quotation

Put them in square brackets **[ ]**.

Example

'In this field [crime prevention], community support officers … ' (Jacques, 2018, p. 17).

Pointing out an error in a quotation

Do not correct the error; instead write *[**sic**]*.

Example

Williams (2008, p. 86) noted that 'builders maid [*sic*] bricks'.

Retaining/modernising historical spellings

Decide to either retain the original spelling or modernise the spelling, and note this in your text.

Examples

'Hast thou not removed one Grain of Dirt or Rhubbish?' (Kent, 1727, p. 2).

'Have you not removed one grain of dirt or rubbish?' (Kent, 1727, p. 2, spelling modernised).

Emphasising part of a quotation

Put the words you want to emphasise in italics and state that you have added the emphasis.

Example

'Large numbers of *women* are more prepared to support eco-friendly projects' (Zhang, 2019, p. 78, my emphasis).

If the original text uses italics, state that the italics are in the original source.

Example

'The dictionary is based on *rigorous analysis* of the grammar of the language' (Soanes, 2015, p. 2, original emphasis).

Quoting material not in English

You should always quote in the language that appears in the source you are reading. Cite the original author and use quotation marks (or indent for longer quotes as above).

Example

' … que nunca sabemos lo que tenemos hasta que se nos ha escapado' (Delibes, 2010, p. 47).

If necessary, for example your readers don't know the language used in the original source, add a translation in brackets after the original.

Example

As remarked by Delibes (2010, p. 47) ' … que nunca sabemos lo que tenemos hasta que se nos ha escapado' [that we never know what we have until it is gone (my translation)].

Alternatively, you could **summarise** the original source in an English translation. You should not present this as a quotation, and you must acknowledge the original source.

Example

In-text citation

Delibes (2010, p. 56) notes that you do not know what you have until it is gone.

Reference list

Delibes, M. (2010) *El camino*. Madrid: Destino.

If quoting from a translated work, you should cite the original author and quote the text in the language in which it appears in the version you are reading.

Example

In-text citation

'Daniel realised that his future was inextricably linked with his village' (Delibes, 2013, p. 82).

Reference list

Delibes, M. (2013) *The path*. Translated by Haycraft, B. and Haycraft, J. London: Dolphin Books.

Paraphrasing

When you **paraphrase**, you express someone else's writing in your own words, usually to achieve greater clarity. This is an alternative way of referring to an author's ideas or arguments without using direct quotations from their text. Used properly, it has the added benefit of fitting more neatly into your own style of writing and allows you to demonstrate that you really do understand what the author is saying. However, you must ensure that you do not change the original meaning and you must still cite and reference your source of information.

Example: original text

From 1660, several occupations were able to develop as professions in Great Britain. Among the attributes of professional status, the most important was the possession by practitioners of specialised knowledge, which they alone could reveal to the uninitiated. Such knowledge was acquired through education and vocational training, and examined by established members of the profession to ensure candidates met agreed standards. Holmes (1982, p. 7) noted that this knowledge might be expressed in specific words or language, such as the use of Latin by clergy, and professionals might also have a specialised costume, for example the gowns and wigs of barristers. Members of the profession had to persuade uninitiated potential clients that this knowledge was essential, what Corfield (1995, p. 21) called 'consumer reaction' and Prest (1987, p. 16) defined as the 'balance of authority'. Practitioners also charged some form of fee for employing this knowledge. There had to be some form of 'corporate self-awareness' (Millerson, 1964, p. 4), a consciousness between members that they were part of a profession, able to define standards of competence and so maintain the integrity of their practice, even if the practitioners were competing for employment opportunities. A profession might also be seen as a vocation for the whole of a person's life, with a hierarchy of promotion. Kaye (1960, p. 17) defined a profession as 'an occupation possessing a skilled intellectual technique, a voluntary association and a code of conduct'.

Reference list

Corfield, P.J. (1995) *Power and the professions in Britain 1700–1850.* London: Routledge.

Holmes, G. (1982) *Augustan England: professions, state and society, 1680–1730.* London: George Allen & Unwin.

Kaye, B. (1960) *The development of the architectural profession in Britain: a sociological study.* London: George Allen & Unwin.

Millerson, G. (1964) *The qualifying professions: a study in professionalization.* London: Routledge.

Prest, W.R. (1987) *The professions in early modern England.* New York: Croom Helm.

Example: paraphrased text

Pears (2013, pp. 29–30) noted that in Britain, professions developed from the mid-seventeenth century. Professionals possessed a discrete body of knowledge, which they learned and were examined on by established practitioners.

Professionals were able to persuade clients that only they could use this knowledge effectively, in return for payment of fees. Although they might compete for work, the practitioners had to see themselves as members of a group, often using specific language and costume, and had to recognise the professional status and qualifications of other members.

Reference list

Pears, R.M. (2013) *William Newton (1730–1798) and the development of the architectural profession in north-east England.* PhD thesis. Newcastle University. Available at: http://hdl.handle.net/10443/2333 (Accessed: 23 June 2021).

NB: If you are paraphrasing ideas from specific pages, you should include the page reference in your citation to help your reader find the original text, as in the Pears examples above and below.

Summarising

When you **summarise**, you provide a brief statement of the main points of your source. This brief statement is known as a **summary**. It differs from paraphrasing in that it only lists the main topics or headings, with most of the detailed information being left out.

expected to apply theories or evidence from more experienced practitioners to help with this self-analysis. You may wish to quote, paraphrase or summarise the work of other authors to show how it has influenced your practice. This evidence should be fully referenced, as in other academic writing.

Reflective writing

In many courses, and particularly those in professional or vocational subjects, you may be required to reflect on work you have done by keeping a journal, diary or learning log, or writing a reflective essay. While you might include some description, the reflection should be a constructive evaluation and is intended to support your learning and personal development (Cottrell, 2019, p. 313). Unlike other academic work, which is usually written in the third person, with reflective writing you can write as 'I', because you are the subject of the writing. The purpose of this reflection is to examine what was done, identify what you have learned about your skills, behaviours or views, and consider how you might think or act differently in future. Sometimes, the reflection involves sharing your experience with others, through **peer-review** or peer-observation, so that you can gain an understanding of how your work was received by others and can consider what worked well or where you might try alternative approaches to overcome problems.

When writing reflectively in an academic or professional capacity, you will often be their contribution to the task. This will expose any 'free riders' (Dijkstra, Latijnhouwers, Norbart and Tio, 2016, p. 675) who have not contributed to the group task.

Reference list

Dijkstra, J., Latijnhouwers, M., Norbart, A. and Tio, R.A. (2016) 'Assessing the "I" in group work assessment: state of the art and recommendations for practice', *Medical Teacher*, 38(7), pp. 675–682. Available at: https://doi.org/10.3109/0142159X.2016.1170796

Erbil, D.G. (2020) 'A review of flipped classroom and cooperative learning method within the context of Vygotsky theory', *Frontiers in Psychology*, vol. 11, article no. 1157. Available at: https://www.frontiersin.org/article/10.3389/fpsyg.2020.01157 (Accessed: 2 May 2021).

Lage, M.L., Platt, J. and Treglia, M. (2000) 'Inverting the classroom: a gateway to creating an inclusive learning environment', *Journal of Economic Education*, 31(1), pp. 30–43. Available at: https://www.jstor.org/stable/1183338 (Accessed: 2 May 2021).

Section F
How to reference

Points to note

The format of references differs between referencing styles. The examples in this section are given in Harvard style and you should consult the specific section of *Cite them right* for guidance on how to provide full references in other referencing styles.

Students often find it difficult to differentiate between the terms **reference list** and **bibliography**. The reference list is the detailed list of **references** cited in your assignment. It includes the full bibliographical information on sources, so that the reader can identify and locate the work/item. A bibliography also provides a detailed list of references but includes background reading or other material you may have consulted, but not cited, in your text.

You should always check with your tutors whether they require you to include a reference list, a bibliography, or both (where you would provide a reference list and a separate bibliography of background reading). Either way, both are located at the end of your essay/piece of work. In the Harvard system, they are always arranged in alphabetical order by the author's surname/family name or, when there is no author, by title. For **web pages** where no author or title is apparent, the **URL** should be used.

The fundamental points are that the reference links with your **citation** and includes enough information for the reader to be able to readily find the source again.

Example

In-text citation

In a recently published survey (Hill, Smith and Reid, 2021, p. 93), the authors argue that …

Reference list

Hill, P., Smith, R. and Reid, L. (2021) *Education in the 21st century.* London: Educational Research Press.

It is important that in your references you follow the format exactly for all sources, as shown in each example. This includes following the instructions consistently regarding the use of capital letters, typeface and punctuation.

Elements you may need to include in your references

Generally, the elements for inclusion for any source should be self-evident. Use the 'citation order' listed with the examples to help you identify the elements you should be looking for. When referencing some of the most commonly used sources, try the following:

For books: look on the title page or back of the title page (verso)

For printed journal articles: look at the beginning of the article or at the table of contents of the journal issue

For electronic journal articles: look at the top of the first page (before or after the article title)

For web pages: look at the top and bottom of the first page, the logos and, for the URL, in the **address bar** at the top of your screen. You may find it helpful to right-click on the mouse and select 'Properties': this will often display the date the web page was last updated/modified

Authors/editors

♦ When referencing four or more authors/ editors in academic assignments, you should reference the first name followed by *et al.* (meaning 'and others'), for example Hussein, T. *et al.* (2020), unless your institution requires you to list all authors. This replicates your citation (see Section D)
♦ If you are writing for a publication you should follow the editor's guidelines, as you may be required to name all the authors in your reference list, regardless of the number, to ensure that each author's contribution is recognised
♦ Put the surname/family name first, followed by the initial(s) of given names, for example Hill, P.L.
♦ For non-English names, see section below
♦ Some publications are written/produced by corporate bodies or organisations and you can use this name as the author, for example the National Trust. (See also the guidance given in Section D.) Note that the corporate author may also be the publisher
♦ If the publication is compiled by an editor or editors, signify this by using the abbreviation (ed.) or (eds), for example Parker, G. and Rouxeville, A. (eds)
♦ Do not use 'Anon.' if the author/editor is anonymous or no author/editor can be identified. Use the title of the work

Year/date of publication

♦ Give the year of publication in round brackets after the author's/editor's name, for example Smith, L. (2021)
♦ If no date of publication can be identified, use (no date), for example Smith, L. (no date)

Title

♦ Use the title as given, together with the subtitle (if any), for example *Studying and working in Spain: a student guide*

Edition

♦ Only include the edition number if it is not the first edition or if it is a revised edition (with or without a number). See also Section G1.1
♦ Edition is abbreviated to edn (to avoid confusion with the abbreviation ed. or eds for editor or editors), for example 3rd edn, or Rev. edn, or 4th rev. edn

Place of publication and publisher

♦ Only required for books and printed reports
♦ Separate the place of publication and the publisher with a colon, for example London: Initial Music Publishing
♦ If there is more than one place of publication, include only the most local
♦ For places of publication in the United States, add the abbreviated US state name (unless otherwise obvious), for example Cambridge, MA: Harvard University Press
♦ If a source is unpublished, please refer to Section G28

Series/volumes: for books

♦ Include series and individual volume number, if relevant, after the publisher, for example Oxford: Clio Press (World Bibliographical Series, 60)

Issue information: for journals, magazines and newspapers

♦ When provided, you need to include the following information in the order:

– volume number

– issue/part number

– date or season

♦ For example 87(3), or 19 July, or summer

Page numbers

♦ Page numbers are only required in the reference list for chapters in books, and serial (journal/magazine/newspaper) articles
♦ The abbreviation p. is used for single pages and pp. for more than one, for example London: River Press, pp. 90–99. Note that page numbers are not elided (for example pp. 90–9) but written in full

ISBNs

♦ Although ISBNs (International Standard Book Numbers) represent unique identifiers for books and eliminate confusion about editions and reprints, they are not commonly used in references

Uniform/Universal Resource Locators (URLs)

♦ When using the URL (colloquially known as a web address) for web pages, you can shorten it, as long as the route remains clear

♦ Include the date you accessed the web page or downloaded an ebook/music, for example (Accessed: 14 June 2021)

Digital Object Identifiers (DOIs)

♦ DOIs tag individual digital (online) sources. These sources can range from journal articles to conference papers and presentations. They include a number identifying the publisher, work and issue information. The following example shows how the DOI replaces the URL in the reference; note that, because the DOI is the permanent identifier for the source, it is not necessary to include an accessed date. In your reference lists, DOI is always written in lower case, as in this example.

Example

Horch, E.P. and Zhou, J. (2012) 'Charge-coupled device speckle observations of binary stars', *Astronomical Journal*, 136, pp. 312–322. Available at: http://dx.doi.org/10.1088/0004-6256/136/1/312

You or your reader can locate a source by entering its DOI in an internet search engine

Journal articles using article numbers and DOIs

♦ Some publishers now use article numbers instead of issue and page numbers
♦ The reference to the article includes the number of pages in the article
♦ To see the page numbers, you may need to open the PDF version of the article. If this is not available, you may

need to refer to the section number or even number the paragraphs and cite one of these for your reference, for example section 2.2, paragraph 3

Example

Bond, J.W. (2008) 'On the electrical characteristics of latent finger mark corrosion of brass', *J. Phys. D: Appl. Phys*, 41, 125502 (10pp). Available at: https://10.1088/0022-3727/41/12/125502

Non-English naming conventions

Across the world, there are several practices for naming individual people, including given name followed by family name (surname) (for example John Smith), family name followed by given name (for example Smith John), given name alone (for example John) and given name followed by father's name (for example John son of James). Within one country, there may be several naming conventions employed by different ethnic groups.

When referencing names of authors in your work, you may be required to use a preferred naming convention. If in doubt, ask for advice from tutors or publishers, or copy the authors' expressions of their names. The principle followed in *Cite them right* (as with other authorities) is to place the family name first in the citation, followed by the initials of given names. The following examples show the complexity of this issue.

Arabic names

The given name precedes the family name. For example, Najīb Mah.fūz would be referenced as:

Example

Mah.fūz, N. (1980) *Afrah. al-qubbah* (Wedding song). al-Fajjalah: Maktabat Mis.r.

Yusuf al-Qaradawi would be referenced as:

Example

Qaradawi, Y. (2003) *The lawful and the prohibited in Islam*. London: Al-Birr Foundation.

Tariq Ramadan would be referenced as:

Example

Ramadan, T. (2008) *Radical reform: Islamic ethics and liberation*. Oxford: Oxford University Press.

When a man has completed the Hajj pilgrimage to Mecca, he may include Hajji in his name, for example Ragayah Hajji Mat Zin. Follow the order for the person's name given in the publication. For example, Ragayah Hajji Mat Zin would be referenced as:

Example

Ragayah, H.M.Z. (2008) *Corporate governance: role of independent non-executive directors*. Bangi: Institut Kajian Malaysia dan Antarabangsa, Universiti Kebangsaan Malaysia

Burmese names

Individuals are usually referenced by the first element of their name. For example, Aung San Suu Kyi would be referenced as:

> **Example**
>
> Aung, S.S.K. (1991) *Freedom from fear and other writings*. London: Viking.

Chinese names

Traditionally, the family name is the first element of the individual's name and when citing use this first, as with Western names. For example, Hu Sen appears as Sen Hu in Western convention on the book title page, but in Chinese tradition would be referenced as:

> **Example**
>
> Hu, S. (2001) *Lecture notes on Chern-Simons-Witten theory*. Singapore and River Edge, NJ: World Scientific.

Zhang Boshu would be referenced as:

> **Example**
>
> Zhang, B. (1994) *Marxism and human sociobiology: the perspective of economic reforms in China*. Albany, NY: State University of New York Press.

If the author has adopted the convention of placing family name last, invert the elements as with Western names. For example, Sophia Tang would be referenced as:

> **Example**
>
> Tang, S. (2009) *Electronic consumer contracts in the conflict of laws*. Oxford: Hart Publishing.

Indian names

The given name precedes the family name. For example, Mohandas Gandhi would be referenced as:

> **Example**
>
> Gandhi, M.K. (1927) *An autobiography, or, the story of my experiments with truth*. Translated from the original in Gujarati by Mahadev Desa. Ahmedabad: Navajivan Press.

Japanese names

The family name precedes the given name. For example, Kenzaburo̅ O̅e would be referenced as:

> **Example**
>
> O̅e, K. (1994) *The pinch runner memorandum*. Armonk, NY: M.E. Sharpe.

Note that many Japanese authors are known by given name then family name, for example Kenzaburo̅ O̅e.

Malaysian names

Malay names may have a given name followed by a patronym or father's name, for example Nik Safiah Nik Ismail. Some names may have the family name followed by given names.

> **Example**
>
> Nik, S.N.I. (2010) *Soft skills: the what, the why, the how*. Bangi: Penerbit Universiti Kebangsaan Malaysia.

Portuguese names

In Portuguese naming conventions, individuals have a given name followed by their mother's family name and then their father's family name. Reference the father's family name first. For example, Armando Gonçalves Pereira would be referenced as:

Example

Pereira, A.G. (1949) *Algumas lições, conferências e discursos*. Lisbon: Editorial Império.

For names with particles (for example de), reference this after the initials of the given names. For example, André Luiz de Souza Filgueira would be referenced as:

Example

Souza Filgueira, A.L. de (2012) 'A utopia nacionalista de Manoel Bomfim', *Em Tempo de Histórias*, 20, pp. 153–163.

Spanish names

Traditionally, Spanish/Latin American individuals have a given name followed by their father's family name and then their mother's family name. When referencing these compound names, use the father's family name, following conventions for Western, Arabic and many other naming styles. For example, Pedro Vallina Martínez would be referenced as:

Example

Vallina Martínez, P. (1968) *Mis memorias*. México & Caracas: Tierra y Libertad.

Thai names

The given name is followed by the family name. For example, Piti Disyatat would be referenced as:

Example

Disyatat, P. (2011) 'The bank lending channel revisited', *Journal of Money, Credit and Banking*, 43(4), pp. 711–734.

Vietnamese names

Individuals are referenced by their family name, the first element of their names. For example, Võ Nguyên Giáp would be referenced as:

Example

Võ, N.G. (1975) *Unforgettable days*. Hanoi: Foreign Languages Publishing House.

Names with particles/prefixes

These are names that include, for example, d', de, de los, le, van and von. It is difficult to provide definitive examples for all names with particles/prefixes, as each language has its own rules. As mentioned above, where possible copy the authors' own expressions of their names from the publication you are viewing and, if in any doubt, use the internet or library catalogues to confirm the details.

Non-Roman scripts

You may need to reference sources that are not in Roman script as part of your work, for example Chinese and Arabic sources. It is recommended that you provide a translation of the title of the work in square brackets after the title in the original script.

You may also need to transliterate from the original language into Roman script. Chinese is transliterated into Pinyin and syllables are aggregated according to a Modern Chinese word dictionary. Arabic is transliterated according to the Library of Congress transliteration.

Example: Chinese book with Chinese script

Pu, S. (1982) 聊斋志异 [*Strange stories of Liaozhai*]. Taiyuan: Shanxi Renmin Chubanshe.

Example: Chinese book with transliterated script in Pinyin

Pu, S. (1982) *Liao zhai zhi yi* [*Strange stories of Liaozhai*]. Taiyuan: Shanxi Renmin Chubanshe.

Example: Arabic books with Arabic script

Hussein, T. (1973)
المجموعة الكاملة لمؤلفات الدكتور طه حسين
[*The complete collection of Dr. Taha Hussein's works*]. Beirut: Dār al-Kitāb al-Lubnānī.

Example: Arabic book with Romanised script

Hussein, T. (1973) al-Majmū'ah al-kāmilah li-mu'allafāt al-Duktūr Tāhā Husayn [*The complete collection of Dr. Taha Hussein's works*]. Beirut: Dār al-Kitāb al-Lubnānī.

Sample text and reference list using Harvard (author-date) referencing style

Sample text

A comparative study conducted by Bowman and Jenkins (2019), on properties built within the last twenty years and older houses, clearly illustrated the financial and environmental benefits of investing time and money in improving home insulation. A recent survey (Thermascan, 2021) and video (Norman, 2020) underlined that as much as a third of the heat generated in homes is lost through the walls or the roof as a result of poor insulation.

An article by Hallwood (2018) was fulsome in its praise of the work of organisations such as Tadea and the Energy Saving Trust in producing public information packs providing guidance on cavity wall and loft insulation. Earlier studies showed that the amount of energy needed to heat our homes can have an ever-increasing impact on both the environment and family finances (BBC, 2017; Hampson and Carr, 2017; Department of the Environment, 2018). However, Kirkwood, Harper and Jones (2017, pp. 49–58) criticised the conflicting information regarding installation costs and the subsequent savings to be made.

Energy companies have emphasised the benefits for customers to 'supply their own energy with technologies such as solar panels and ground source heat pumps' (British Gas, 2019, p. 8). However, the conflict between expensive sustainable energy and family economic constraints, have been examined by Young (2020). Strathearn (2020, p. 45) states that by finding ways to reduce our home running costs, we can simultaneously reduce our carbon footprint.

NB: This text makes extensive use of references for illustrative purposes only.

Sample reference list

This list incorporates bubble captions to identify the type of source being referenced, which are used for illustrative purposes only.

BBC (2017) *Energy use and the environment*. Available at http://www.bbc.co.uk/energy (Accessed: 18 August 2018).

(web page) see Section E8

Bowman, R. and Jenkins, S. (2019) 'Financial and environmental issues and comparisons in new and old build properties', in Harris, P. (ed.) *Studies on property improvements and environmental concerns in modern Britain.* London: Pinbury, pp. 124–145.

(chapter in edited book) see Section E1.9

British Gas (2019) *A green light to save you more*. Eastbourne: British Gas.

(company pamphlet/booklet) see Section E1.18

Department of the Environment (2018) *Energy and the environment in Britain today*. Available at: http://www.doe.gov.uk (Accessed: 18 August 2018).

(online government report) see Section E13.2

Hallwood, L. (2018) 'The good work of sustainable energy organisations continues', *The Times*, 20 June, pp. 20–21.

(electronic or print newspaper article) see Section E2.3

Hampson, P. and Carr, L. (2017) 'The impact of rising energy use on the environment: a five-year study', *Journal of Energy and Environmental Issues*, 53(5), pp. 214–231.

(electronic or print journal article) see Section E2.1

Kirkwood, L., Harper, S. and Jones, T. (2017) *The DIY culture in Britain: costs for homes and the nation*. Available at: http://www.amazon.co.uk/kindle-ebooks

(Downloaded: 8 September 2012). (signifies held on your own device) (ebook downloaded onto edevice) see Section E1.3

Norman, L. (2020) *Heat loss in houses*. Available at http://www.youtube.com/watchheatlosshouseclm (Accessed: 18 August 2021).

(YouTube video) see Section E21.9f

Strathearn, G. (2020) *Energy and environmental issues for the 21st century*. Basingstoke: Palgrave Macmillan.

(print or electronic book) see Section E1

Thermascan (2021) *A report into costs and benefits relating to heat loss in homes*. Birmingham: Thermascan.

(printed report) see Section E11

Young, L. (2020) *Sustaining our energy: challenges and conflicts*. Available at:

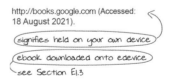

http://books.google.com (Accessed: 18 August 2021). (signifies held on your own device) (ebook downloaded onto edevice) see Section E1.3

Top 10 tips

1. *Be aware*: if you don't already know, check with your tutor which referencing style you are expected to use.
2. *Be positive*: used properly, references strengthen your writing, demonstrating that you have spent time researching and digesting material and produced your own opinions and arguments.
3. *Be decisive* about the best way to cite your sources and how you balance your use of direct quotations, paraphrasing and summarising (read about these in Section E).
4. *Be willing to ask for help*: library/ learning resource staff offer support with referencing and academic skills.
5. *Be organised*: prepare well and keep a record of all potentially useful sources as you find them.
6. *Be prepared*: read Sections A–F before you begin your first assignment.
7. *Be consistent*: once you have established the referencing style required, use it consistently throughout your piece of work.
8. *Be patient*: make time and take your time to ensure that your referencing is accurate.
9. *Be clear*: clarify the type of source you are referencing and check the appropriate section of *Cite them right* for examples.
10. *Be thorough*: check through your work and your references before you submit your assignment, ensuring that your citations all match with a full reference and vice versa.

Checklist of what to include in your reference list for the most common information sources

	Author	Year of publication	Title of article/chapter	Title of publication	Issue information (volume/ part numbers if available)	Place of publication	Publisher	Edition	Page number(s)	URL/DOI	Accessed date accessed/downloaded
Book	✓	✓		✓		✓	✓	✓			
Chapter from book	✓	✓	✓	✓		✓	✓	✓	✓		
Ebook	✓	✓		✓		✓	✓	✓		If required	If required
Journal article (print and electronic)	✓	✓	✓	✓	✓				✓	If required	If required
Web page	✓	✓		✓						✓	✓
Newspaper article (print and electronic)	✓	✓	✓	✓	✓				✓	✓	✓

Section G
Harvard referencing style

NB: Before looking at specific examples in this section, you should ensure that you have read Sections A–F.

G1   Books

G1.1   Books, including ebooks, comic and motion books and graphic novels

The increasing availability of ebooks in identical form to print has rendered the distinction between the versions unnecessary. If the online source includes all the elements seen in print versions, that is, publication details, edition and page numbers, reference in the same way as print. Use the citation order below as a template for book and ebook references.

Citation order:

♦ Author/editor
♦ Year of publication (in round brackets)
♦ Title (in italics)
♦ Edition (edition number if not the first edn and/or rev. edn)
♦ Place of publication: publisher
♦ Series and volume number (where relevant)

Example: book with one author

In-text citations

According to Cottrell (2019, p. 23) …

This thought-provoking book (Olusoga, 2016) …

Reference list

Cottrell, S. (2019) *The study skills handbook*. 5th edn. London: Red Globe Press.
Olusoga, D. (2016) *Black and British: a forgotten history*. London: Macmillan.

Example: book with an editor

In-text citation

The collection edited by Pecht and Kang (2018) …

Reference list

Pecht, M. and Kang, M. (eds) (2018) *Prognostics and health management of electronics: fundamentals, machine learning, and the internet of things*. Hoboken, NJ: John Wiley & Sons.

Examples: book with two or three authors

In-text citations

Goddard and Barrett (2016, p. 17) suggested …

Focusing on creating value (Dubois, Jolibert and Mühlbacher, 2007) …

Reference list

Dubois, P.-L., Jolibert, A. and Mühlbacher, H. (2007) *Marketing management: a value creation process.* Basingstoke: Palgrave Macmillan.

Goddard, J. and Barrett, S. (2016) *The health needs of young people leaving care.* Norwich: University of East Anglia, School of Social Work and Psychosocial Studies.

Example: book with four or more authors

In-text citation

This was proved by Petit *et al.* (2020, pp. 21–23) …

Reference list

Petit *et al.* (2020) *The anthropological demography of health.* Oxford: Oxford University Press.

OR, if your institution **requires referencing of all named authors**

Petit, V., Qureshi, K., Charbit, Y. and Kreager, P. (2020) *The anthropological demography of health.* Oxford: Oxford University Press.

Example: book with no author

In-text citation

The Percy tomb has been described as 'one of the masterpieces of medieval European art' (*Treasures of Britain and treasures of Ireland*, 1990, p. 84).

Reference list

Treasures of Britain and treasures of Ireland (1990) London: Reader's Digest Association Ltd.

Example: organisation as author

In-text citation

The new guidance from the Modern Language Association (2021) …

Reference list

Modern Language Association (2021) *MLA handbook.* 9th edn. New York, NY: Modern Language Association of America.

G1.2 Reprint and facsimile editions

For reprints and facsimile editions of older books, the year of the original publication (not the place of publication or publisher) is given, along with the full publication details of the reprint or facsimile.

Citation order:

♦ Author/editor
♦ Year of original publication (in round brackets)
♦ Title of book (in italics)
♦ Reprint or facsimile of the …
♦ Place of reprint or facsimile publication: reprint or facsimile publisher
♦ Year of reprint or facsimile

Example: reprint

In-text citation

One of the first critics of obfuscation (David, 1968) …

Reference list

David, M. (1968) *Towards honesty in public relations*. Reprint, London: B.Y. Jove, 1990.

Example: facsimile

In-text citation

… his perfect blend of adventure, magic and fantasy (Tolkien, 1937).

Reference list

Tolkien, J.R.R. (1937) *The Hobbit*. Facsimile of the 1st edn. London: HarperCollins, 2016.

G1.3   Ebooks

When an ebook looks like a printed book, with publication details and pagination, you should reference as a printed book (see Section G1.1).

On some personal electronic devices, specific ebook pagination details may not be available, so use the information you do have, such as loc, %, chapter/page/paragraph; for example (Richards, 2012, 67%), (Winters, 2011, ch. 4, p. 12).

Citation order:

♦ Author/editor
♦ Year of publication (in round brackets)
♦ Title of book (in italics)
♦ Available at: DOI *or* URL (Accessed: date)

Example

In-text citation

Arthur's argument with the council was interrupted by the Vogon Constructor Fleet (Adams, 1979, loc 876).

Reference list

Adams, D. (1979) *The hitchhiker's guide to the galaxy*. Available at: http://www.amazon.co.uk/kindle-ebooks (Accessed: 23 June 2021).

G1.4 Audiobooks

Citation order:

♦ Author/editor
♦ Year of publication/release (in round brackets)
♦ Title of book (in italics)
♦ Available at: DOI *or* URL (Accessed: date)

Example

In-text citation

A powerful narrative by Laura James (2017) …

Reference list

James, L. (2017) *Odd girl out: an autistic woman in a neurotypical world*. Available at: https://www.audible.co.uk/ (Accessed: 18 March 2021).

G1.5 Collected and multi-volume works

Citation order:

♦ Author/editor
♦ Year(s) of publication of collection (in round brackets)
♦ Title of book (in italics)
♦ Volumes (in round brackets)
♦ Place of publication: publisher

Examples

In-text citations

Butcher's (1961) guide …

His collected works (Jung, 1989–1995) provide …

Reference list

Butcher, R. (1961) *A new British flora* (4 vols). London: Leonard Hill.
Jung, C.G. (1989–1995) *Gesammelte Werke* (24 vols). Olten: Walter Verlag.

When citing a *single volume of a multi-volume work*, add the title of the relevant volume to your reference list.

Example

In-text citation

Part 3 of Butcher's work (1961) …

Reference list

Butcher, R. (1961) *A new British flora. Part 3: lycopodiaceae to salicaceae*. London: Leonard Hill.

G1.6 Chapters/sections of edited books

Citation order:

♦ Author of the chapter/section (surname followed by initials)
♦ Year of publication (in round brackets)
♦ Title of chapter/section (in single quotation marks)

- 'in' plus author/editor of book
- Title of book (in italics)
- Place of publication: publisher
- Page reference

Example

In-text citation

As recommended by Karim, Tretten and Kumar (2018, p. 562) …

Reference list

Karim, R., Tretten, T. and Kumar, U. (2018) 'eMaintenance', in M. Pecht and M. Kang (eds) *Prognostics and health management of electronics: fundamentals, machine learning, and the internet of things*. Hoboken, NJ: John Wiley & Sons, pp. 559–587.

G1.7 Anthologies

Citation order:

- Editor/compiler of anthology (surname followed by initials)
- Year of publication (in round brackets)
- Title of book (in italics)
- Place of publication: publisher

Example

In-text citation

In his collection of humorous poems, West (1989) …

Reference list

West, C. (compiler and illustrator) (1989) *The beginner's book of bad behaviour*. London: Beaver Books.

To reference *a line of a poem/section within an anthology*, use the following.

Citation order:

- Author of the poem/section (surname followed by initials)
- Year of publication (in round brackets)
- Title of poem/section (in single quotation marks)
- 'in' plus author/editor/compiler of book
- Title of book (in italics)
- Place of publication: publisher
- Page reference

Example

In-text citation

'The lion made a sudden stop

He let the dainty morsel drop' (Belloc, 1989, p. 89).

Reference list

Belloc, H. (1989) 'Jim', in West, C. (compiler and illustrator) *The beginner's book of bad behaviour*. London: Beaver Books, pp. 88–92.

G1.8 Reference sources, including encyclopedias, dictionaries and thesauri

Citation order:

- Author of the entry (surname followed by initials), if available, or use title of entry
- Year of publication (in round brackets)
- Title of entry (in single quotation marks)
- 'in' plus author/editor of book
- Title of book (in italics)
- Place of publication: publisher
- Page reference

If accessed online:

♦ Available at: DOI *or* URL (Accessed: date)
♦ Some sources may have authors, and others may have authors for individual sections as well as an editor for the whole book.

Example: with author

In-text citation

Crick's work was vital (Olby, 2014).

Reference list

Olby, R. (2014) 'Crick, Francis Harry Compton (1916–2004)', in *Oxford dictionary of national biography*. Available at: https://doi.org/10.1093/ref:odnb/93883

Example: with editor and section author

In-text citation

Byrd (2011) examined …

Reference list

Byrd, D. (2011) 'Phonetics', in P.C. Hogan (ed.), *The Cambridge encyclopedia of the language sciences*. Available at: http://search.credoreference.com/content/entry/cupelanscis/phonetics/ (Accessed: 21 April 2021).

If there is *no obvious author or editor*, cite by the title of the entry.

Example: with no authors

In-text citation

To be described as 'Spielbergian' (2018) …

Reference list

'Spielbergian' (2018) *Oxford English dictionary*. Available at: http://www.oed.com/view/Entry/69512583. (Accessed: 21 June 2021).

G1.9 Translated books

Reference the translation you have read, not the original work.

Citation order:

♦ Author/editor
♦ Year of translated publication (in round brackets)
♦ Title of book (in italics)
♦ Translated from the [original language] by …
♦ Place of publication: publisher

Example

In-text citation

Delibes (2013, pp. 4–11) vividly describes childhood in a Spanish village …

Reference list

Delibes, M. (2013) *The path*. Translated from the Spanish by G. Haycraft and R. Haycraft. London: Dolphin Books.

G1.10 Books in languages other than English

If referencing a book in its original language, give the title exactly as shown in the book.

Citation order:

♦ Author/editor
♦ Year of publication (in round brackets)
♦ Title of book (in italics)
♦ Place of publication: publisher

Example

In-text citation

Her depiction of middle-class lifestyles (Beauvoir, 1966) …

Reference list

Beauvoir, S. de (1966) *Les belles images.* Paris: Gallimard.

G1.11 Ancient texts

If citing an ancient text that existed before the invention of printing, reference the published (and translated) edition you have read, or the manuscript (see Section G32) if you used this.

Citation order:

♦ Author
♦ Year of publication (in round brackets)
♦ Title of book (in italics)
♦ Translated from the [original language] by … (if relevant, in round brackets)
♦ Edition (only include the edition number if it is not the first edition)

then

♦ Place of publication: publisher
♦ Series and volume number (where relevant)

If accessed online:
♦ Available at: DOI *or* URL (Accessed: date)

Examples

In-text citations

Classic accounts by Homer (1991) and Pliny (1969) …

Reference list

Homer (1991) *The Iliad* (Translated from the Greek by R. Fagles. Introduction and notes by B. Knox.) London: Penguin Books.
Pliny the Younger (1969) *Letters, volume II: books 8–10. Panegyricus* (Translated from the Latin by B. Radice.) Available at: https://www.loebclassics.com. (Accessed: 21 May 2021).

G1.12 Sacred texts

Citation order:

♦ Title (not in italics)
♦ Year of publication (in round brackets)
♦ Translator and edition, if required (in round brackets)
♦ Place of publication: publisher *or*
♦ Available at: DOI *or* URL (Accessed: date)

Examples

In-text citations

The Beatitudes (King James Bible, 1989, Matthew 5: 3–12) …

The reply (The Torah, 1962, Shemot 3:14) is the most profound …

'And ease for me my task' (The Qur'an, 2021, 20: 26).

Reference list

King James Bible (1989) New York: National Council of Churches.
The Qur'an (2021) (Translated by M. Khattab.) Available at: https://quran.com/20 (Accessed: 21 May 2021).
The Torah: the five books of Moses (1962) Philadelphia: Jewish Publication Society of America.

G1.13 Printed historical books in online collections

If you are reading a scanned version of the printed book, complete with publication information and page numbers, reference in the same manner as the print book (see G1.1). This includes books available in subscription collections, such as Early European Books and Eighteenth Century Collections Online, and freely available sites, including Google Books, Internet Archive and HathiTrust Digital Library.

Some early printed books do not have a publisher as they were privately printed. Record the information given in the book in your reference.

Citation order:

♦ Author/editor

♦ Year of publication (in round brackets)
♦ Title of publication (in italics)
♦ Place of publication: printing statement

Example

In-text citation

Adam's measured plans (Adam, 1764) …

Reference list

Adam, R. (1764) *Ruins of the palace of the Emperor Diocletian at Spalatro in Dalmatia.* London: Printed for the author.

G1.14 Plays

G1.14a Whole play

If you are using a modern edition, include the editor's name and any other contributors.

Citation order:

♦ Author (surname followed by initials)
♦ Year of publication (in round brackets)
♦ Title (in italics)
♦ Edition information
♦ Place of publication: publisher

Example

In-text citation

Wayne's comments on *Cymbeline* (Shakespeare, 2017, pp. 6–9) …

Reference list

Shakespeare, W. (2017) *Cymbeline.* Edited by V. Wayne. London: Bloomsbury.

G1.14b Lines within plays

Add the Act, scene and line, or if these are unavailable, add a page number to your in-text citation.

Example

In-text citation

'I prithee do not mock me fellow student' (Shakespeare, 1980, 1.2: 177).

Reference list

Shakespeare, W. (1980) *Hamlet*. Edited by T.J.B. Spencer. London: Penguin.

NB: If referencing a *live performance*, see Section G20.

G1.15 Pamphlets

Citation order:

- Author/editor
- Year of publication (in round brackets)
- Title (in italics)
- Place of publication: publisher
- Series and volume number (where relevant)

Example

In-text citation

Much revealed by Sunniside History Society (2016) …

Reference list

Sunniside History Society (2016) *Fugar, Washingwell and Watergate – a hidden heritage*. Gateshead: Sunniside History Society.

G1.16 Exhibition catalogues

Citation order:

- Author of catalogue
- Year (in round brackets)
- Title of exhibition (in italics)
- Location and date(s) of exhibition
- [Exhibition catalogue]
- Place of publication: publisher (if available)

Example

In-text citation

Urbach (2007, p. 8) noted the demands for reform …

Reference list

Urbach, P. (2007) *Reform! Reform! Reform!* Exhibition held at the Reform Club, London 2005–2006 and at Grey College, Durham University, March 2007 [Exhibition catalogue]. London: The Reform Club.

G1.17 Event programmes, including printed concert, theatre and sports programmes

Citation order:

- Author of programme (if known, or use performers)
- Year (in round brackets)
- Title of event (in italics)
- Location and date(s) of event
- [Event programme]

Example

The Avison Ensemble (2019, p. 2) were formed in 1988.

Avison Ensemble (2019) *The concerto in England – Handel and his contemporaries.* The Sage, Gateshead, 9 October [Event programme].

G1.18 Comics

Comics and graphic novels are referenced as books (see Section G1).

To reference an *entire issue of a comic*, use the following.

Citation order:

♦ Author (if available)
♦ Title of comic (in italics)
♦ Other contributors (letterer, artists, painter)
♦ Year of publication (in round brackets)
♦ Day, month, issue number (use the elements that are given)
  If accessed online (including via app): Available at: URL *or* app name (include app version number if available) (Accessed: date)

Example: print

The latest issue (*Commando, 2021*) …

Commando (2021) 25 May, no. 5442.

Example: online

Dennis and Minnie are the main characters of the Beano (2021).

Beano (2021) 29 May. Available at: *Readly* app, version 27 April 2021 (Accessed: 2 June 2021).

To reference a *comic strip*, use the following.

Citation order:

♦ Author (if available)
♦ Year of publication (in round brackets)
♦ Title of comic strip (in single quotation marks)
♦ Title of comic (in italics)
♦ Day, month, issue number, page (use the elements that are given)
♦ Available at: URL (Accessed: date)

Example

Stealing employees' ideas is seen as having 'Management potential' (Adams, 2021).

Adams, S. (2021) 'Management potential', *Dilbert*, 31 May. Available at: https://dilbert.com/strip/2021-05-31 (Accessed: 3 June 2021).

G2 Periodicals: journal, magazine and newspaper articles

G2.1 Journal articles

Citation order:

- ◆ Author (surname followed by initials)
- ◆ Year of publication (in round brackets)
- ◆ Title of article (in single quotation marks)
- ◆ Title of journal (in italics – capitalise first letter of each word in title, except for linking words such as and, of, the, for)
- ◆ Issue information: volume (unbracketed) and, where applicable, part number, month or season (all in round brackets)
- ◆ Page reference (if available) or article number

If accessed online:
- ◆ Available at: DOI *or* URL (Accessed: date)

Example: print article

In-text citation

In their review of the literature (Norrie *et al.*, 2012) …

Reference list

Norrie, C. *et al.* (2012) 'Doing it differently? A review of literature on teaching reflective practice across health and social care professions', *Reflective Practice*, 13(4), pp. 565–578.

OR, if your **institution requires referencing of all named authors**

Norrie, C., Hammond, J., D'Avray, L., Collington, V. and Fook, J. (2012) 'Doing it differently? A review of literature on teaching reflective practice across health and social care professions', *Reflective Practice*, 13(4), pp. 565–578.

Example: electronic article with doi

In-text citation

Barke and Mowl's excellent study (2016) …

Reference list

Barke, M. and Mowl, G. (2016) 'Málaga – a failed resort of the early twentieth century?', *Journal of Tourism History*, 2(3), pp. 187–212. Available at: https://doi.org/10.1080/1 755182X.2010.523145

Example: electronic article with URL

In-text citation

An example cited by Dutta and Marjit (2016, pp. 120-121) …

Reference list

Dutta, M. and Marjit, S. (2016) 'Intra-country technology transfer', *Indian Economic Review,* 51(1/2), new series, pp. 117–127. Available at: http://www.jstor.org/stable/44376239 (Accessed: 27 May 2021).

G2.2 Advanced online publication articles: preprints and in press

Digital publishing enables new research articles to be made available before they have completed peer-review and typesetting stages, or before they are allocated to a specific issue of a journal. As these stages may result in changes to the article content and pagination, state which version you have read, and, *in this instance, give the accessed date* as well as the DOI.

Citation order:

♦ Author (surname followed by initials)
♦ Year available (in round brackets)
♦ Title of article (in single quotation marks)
♦ Title of journal (in italics – capitalise first letter of each word in title, except for linking words such as and, of, the, for)
♦ (pre-proof) or (in press)
♦ Available at: DOI *and* (Accessed: date)

NB: For prepublication articles in digital repositories, see Section G8.4.

G2.3 Abstracts of articles

If you are specifically referencing the *abstract* of a journal article, your in-text citation should make this clear, for example: 'The abstract highlights … (Rodgers and Baker, 2013, p. 34).' Note that the reference would follow the same citation order for a journal article (G2.1) because the page reference would take the reader to the abstract.

G2.4 Whole journal issue

Citation order:

- Issue editor (if given)
- Year of publication (in round brackets)
- Title of issue (in single quotation marks)
- Title of journal (in italics – capitalise first letter of each word in title, except for linking words such as and, of, the, for)
- Issue information, that is, volume (unbracketed) and, where applicable, part number, month or season (all in round brackets)

If accessed online:
- Available at: DOI *or* URL (Accessed: date)

G2.5 Systematic reviews

Citation order:

- Author (surname followed by initials)
- Year of publication (in round brackets)

- The title and any subtitle (in single quotation marks)
- Database name (in italics)
- Issue number
- Article number (CD …)

If accessed online:
- Available at: DOI *or* URL (Accessed: date)

G2.6 Magazine articles

Citation order:

- Author (surname followed by initials)
- Year of publication (in round brackets)
- Title of article (in single quotation marks)
- Title of magazine (in italics – capitalise first letter of each word in title, except for linking words such as and, of, the, for)
- Issue information, that is, volume (unbracketed), part number, month or season (all in round brackets)
- Page reference (if available)

If accessed online:

♦ Available at: DOI *or* URL (Accessed: date)

Examples

In-text citations

MD (2021) and Soo Kim (2021, p. 9) quoted worrying statistics …

Reference list

Kim, S. (2021) 'Child COVID cases are highest in these states', *Newsweek* (5 May). Available at: https://www. newsweek.com/coronavirus-states- highest-child-covid-cases- children-1588815 (Accessed: 28 May 2021).
MD (2021) 'Pandemic update', *Private Eye* (1546; 30 April–13 May), pp. 8–9.

G2.7 Newspaper articles

Where the author of a newspaper article is identified, use the following citation order:

♦ Author
♦ Year of publication (in round brackets)
♦ Title of article (in single quotation marks)
♦ Title of newspaper (in italics – capitalise first letter of each word in title, except for linking words such as and, of, the, for)
♦ Edition if required (in round brackets)
♦ Day and month
♦ Section and page reference (if available)

If accessed online:

♦ Available at: DOI *or* URL (Accessed: date)

Examples

In-text citations

London property attracted major international investment (Prymm, 2019, p. 10).

Nan (2021) reported that culture has returned with the easing of restrictions.

Reference list

Nan, C. (2021) 'Musicals find their voice again', *China Daily European Edition*, 14 May. Available at: https:// www.nexis.com (Accessed: 21 May 2021).
Prymm, J. (2019) 'Surge in US tech tycoons buying London homes', *Evening Standard* (London), 19 June, p. 10.

Where *no author* is given, use the following citation order:

♦ Title of newspaper (in italics – capitalise first letter of each word in title, except for linking words such as and, of, the, for)
♦ Year of publication (in round brackets)
♦ Title of article (in single quotation marks)
♦ Day and month
♦ Page reference

Example: no author, one article

In-text citation

The article (*The Times*, 2021, p. 7) reported …

Reference list

The Times (2021) 'Bank accounts', 14 June, p. 7.

If you are citing *several articles published in the same year*, use a, b, c and so on after the year.

Examples: no author, several articles

In-text citations

The article (*The Times*, 2021a, p. 7) reported …

A second article (*The Times*, 2021b, p. 2) reported …

Reference list

The Times (2021a) 'Bank accounts', 1 June, p. 7.
The Times (2021b) 'Taxing tech corporations', 6 June, p. 2.

If you are referencing *letters*, *leading articles/editorials or sections*, you would note this in your in-text citations.

Example: letter

In-text citation

In their letter, Fells *et al.* (2021, p. 23) …

Reference list

Fells, I. *et al.* (2021) 'Energise projects', *The Times*, 1 August, p. 23.

Example: leading article

In-text citation

In the leading article (*The Independent*, 2021, p. 28) …

Reference list

The Independent (2021) 'Grace in defeat', 27 January, p. 28.

Example: section

In-text citation

Lebrun (2021) reported …

Reference list

Lebrun A.-L. (2021) 'Les rouages des troubles du comportement alimentaire' ['The inner workings of eating disorders']. *Le Figaro* (internet edn.), 5 March. Sciences section. Available at: https://www.lefigaro.fr/sciences/les-rouages-des-troubles-du-comportement-alimentaire-20210503 (Accessed: 28 May 2021).

If referencing a *whole newspaper issue*, use the following citation order:

♦ Title of newspaper (in italics – capitalise first letter of each word in title, except for linking words such as and, of, the, for)
♦ Year of publication (in round brackets)
♦ Edition if required (in round brackets)
♦ Day and month

If accessed online:
♦ Available at: DOI *or* URL (Accessed: date)

Example: whole newspaper issue

In-text citation

Yesterday's copy of the newspaper (*The Independent*, 2021) …

Reference list

The Independent (2021) 17 June.

G2.8 Press releases

Citation order:

♦ Author/organisation
♦ Date (in round brackets)
♦ Title of communication (in single quotation marks)
♦ Day and month
♦ Press release (in square brackets)
♦ Available at: URL (Accessed: date)

Example

In-text citation

President Biden changed US policy on climate change (The White House, 2021).

Reference list

The White House (2021) 'Executive Order on the establishment of the Climate Change Support Office', 7 May [Press release]. Available at: https://www.whitehouse.gov/briefing-room/presidential-actions/2021/05/07/executive-order-on-the-establishment-of-the-climate-change-support-office/ (Accessed: 23 June 2021).

G3 Conferences

G3.1 Published full conference proceedings

Citation order:

♦ Author/editor
♦ Year of publication (in round brackets)
♦ Title of conference: subtitle (in italics)
♦ Location and date of conference
♦ Place of publication: publisher

If accessed online:
♦ Available at: DOI or URL (Accessed: date)

Example

In-text citation

The conference was held online due to COVID-19 (Domenech et al., 2020) …

Reference list

Domenech, J., Merello, P., de la Poza, E. and Peña-Ortiz, R. (eds) (2020) *Proceedings of the 6th international conference on higher education advances*. Virtual conference at València (Spain), 2–5 June. València: Editorial Universitat Politècnica de València). Available at: http://dx.doi.org/10.4995/HEAD20.2020.11787

G3.2 Published conference papers or posters

Citation order:

♦ Author of paper
♦ Year of publication (in round brackets)
♦ Title of paper (in single quotation marks)
♦ Title of conference: subtitle (in italics)
♦ Location and date of conference
♦ Place of publication: publisher
♦ Page references for the paper

If accessed online:
♦ Available at: DOI or URL (Accessed: date)

Example

User experience methodology employed by Nagalingam and Ibrahim (2020) …

Nagalingam, V. and Ibrahim, R. (2020) 'Finding the right elements – user experience elements for educational games', *6th international conference on higher education advances*. Virtual conference at València (Spain), 2–5 June. València: Editorial Universitat Politècnica de València), pp. 90–93. Available at: http://dx.doi.org/10.4995/HEAD20.2020.11787

For live speeches at conferences see G25.1 and unpublished poster presentations, see G28.

G3.3 Full conference proceedings published in journals

These are often published as special issues or journal supplements and are referenced as follows.

Citation order:

♦ Title of conference, location and date (if included) (in single quotation marks)
♦ Year of journal publication (in round brackets)
♦ Title of journal (in italics – capitalise first letter of each word in title, except for linking words such as and, of, the, for)
♦ Issue information, that is, volume (unbracketed) and, where applicable, part number, month or season (all in round brackets) and page numbers

If accessed online:
♦ Available at: DOI *or* URL (Accessed: date)

Example

The quality of all the papers ('Sessions presented at the 2017 international aircraft cabin air conference', 2019) …

'Sessions presented at the 2017 international aircraft cabin air conference, Imperial College, London, 19–20 September 2017' (2019) *Journal of Health & Pollution*, 9(24), pp. S1–S144. Available at: https://doi.org/10.5696/2156-9614-9.24.191201

G3.4 Individual conference papers published in journals

Citation order:

♦ Author of paper
♦ Year of publication (in round brackets)
♦ Title of paper (in single quotation marks)
♦ From the conference title, location and date (if included) (in round brackets)
♦ Title of journal (in italics)
♦ Issue information, that is, volume (unbracketed) and, where applicable, part number, month or season (all in round brackets)
♦ Page references for the paper

If accessed online:
♦ Available at: DOI *or* URL (Accessed: date)

Example

Loraine (2019) presented …

Loraine, T. (2019) 'Origins of contaminated air' (from the Sessions presented at the 2017 international aircraft cabin air conference, Imperial College, London, 19–20 September 2017), *Journal of Health & Pollution*, 9(24), pp. S1–S144. Available at: https://doi.org/10.5696/2156-9614-9.24.191201

G4 Theses and dissertations

Citation order:

♦ Author
♦ Year of submission (in round brackets)
♦ Title of thesis (in italics)
♦ Degree statement
♦ Degree-awarding body

If accessed online:
♦ Available at: DOI *or* URL (Accessed: date)

Examples

Research by Tregear (2013) and Parsons (2011) …

Parsons, J.D. (2011) *Black holes with a twist*. PhD thesis. Durham University. Available at: http://etheses.dur.ac.uk/846 (Accessed: 14 August 2021).

Tregear, A.E.J. (2013) *Speciality regional foods in the UK: an investigation from the perspectives of marketing and social history*. Unpublished PhD thesis. Newcastle University.

G5 Reviews

Citation order:

♦ Name of the reviewer (if indicated)
♦ Year of publication of the review (in round brackets)
♦ Title of the review (in single quotation marks)
♦ Review of … (title of work reviewed – in italics)
♦ Author/director of work being reviewed
♦ Publication details (title in italics)

If accessed online:
♦ Available at: DOI *or* URL (Accessed: date)

G5.1 Book reviews

Examples

Haworth (2017) considered the book …

One online reviewer (Hauck, 2017) …

Haworth, R. (2017) Review of *Édith Piaf: a cultural history*, by D. Looseley. *Journal of European Studies*, 47(2), pp. 228–229.

Hauck, P.-G. (2017) 'It is neutron dense'. Review of *Health economics*, by F. Sloan and C.-R. Hsieh. Available at: https://www.amazon.co.uk/Health-Economics-Press-Frank-Sloan/dp/0262035111/ (Accessed: 2 June 2021).

G5.2 Drama reviews

Example

In-text citation

One reviewer (Brentley, 2019) wrote …

Reference list

Brentley, B. (2019) 'The human voice versus the internet in "Octet"'. Review of *Octet*, directed by D. Malloy. Pershing Square Signature Center, New York. *New York Times* (Theater section), 19 May. Available at: https://www.nytimes.com/2019/05/19/theater/octet-review.html (Accessed: 1 June 2021).

G5.3 Film reviews

Examples

In-text citations

Barnes (1989) and jamesjustice-92 (2021) thought it a classic film.

Reference list

Magazine review

Barnes, L. (1989) 'Citizen Kane'. Review of *Citizen Kane*, directed by O. Welles. *New Vision*, 9 October, pp. 24–25.

Internet review (IMDB)

jamesjustice-92 (2021) 'Citizen Kane and masterpiece are synonymous words'. Review of *Citizen Kane*, directed by O. Welles. Available at: https://www.imdb.com/review/rw6867005/?ref_=tt_urv (Accessed: 5 June 2021).

G5.4 Reviews of musical performances

Example

In-text citation

Hickling (2008) thought it was 'a little touch of magic'.

Reference list

Hickling, A. (2008) 'The opera'. Review of *Don Giovanni*, by Mozart. New Vic, Newcastle-under-Lyme. *The Guardian* (Review section), 5 July, p. 19.

G5.5 Author biographical information or cover blurb

Assume that this information is written by the author, unless another person is identified. The location can be given in the in-text reference, as you would a reference to a page within the book.

Citation order:

♦ Author
♦ Date (in round brackets)
♦ Title of book (in italics)
♦ Place of publication: publisher

Example

In-text citation

Margaret Atwood won the Booker Prize in 2000 (Atwood, 2009, inside back cover).

Reference list

Atwood, M. (2009) *The year of the flood*. London: Bloomsbury.

G5.6 Second-person review comments on or in a book

If reviewers' comments are published on the book cover, inner covers or flyleaves, indicate the location of these in your text, but give the reference to the author and book on or in which the comments are published.

Examples

In-text citations

Kershaw thought Mann's book (2004, back cover) was 'a brilliant and disturbing analysis'.

Philip Pullman thought it was 'magnificent' (Mantel, 2005, flyleaf).

Reference list

Mann, M. (2004) *Fascists.* Cambridge: Cambridge University Press.

Mantel, H. (2005) *Beyond black.* London: Fourth Estate.

G5.7 Product reviews

Citation order:

♦ Name of the reviewer (if indicated)
♦ Year of publication (in round brackets)
♦ Title of review (in italics)

If accessed online:
♦ Available at: DOI *or* URL (Accessed: date)

Example

In-text citation

Described as 'a great entry to the world of photography' (Hall and Wilson, 2020) …

Reference list

Hall, P. and Wilson, M. (2020) *Nikon D3500 review*. Available at: https://www.techradar.com/uk/reviews/nikon-d3500-review (Accessed: 1 June 2021).

G6 Interviews

Citation order:

♦ Name of person interviewed
♦ Year of interview (in round brackets)
♦ Title of the interview (if any) (in single quotation marks)
♦ Interview with Interviewee
♦ Interviewed by Interviewer's name
♦ for Title of publication or broadcast (in italics)
♦ Day and month of interview, page numbers (if relevant)

If accessed online:
♦ Available at: DOI *or* URL (Accessed: date)

Example: newspaper interview

In-text citation

Riley (2008) believed that 'imagination has to be captured by reality'.

Reference list

Riley, B. (2008) 'The life of Riley'. Interview with Bridget Riley. Interviewed by J. Jones for *The Guardian*, 5 July, p. 33.

Example: television interview

The prime minister avoided the question (Johnson, 2020).

Johnson, B. (2020) Interviewed by Emily Maitlis for *Newsnight*, BBC Two Television, 6 June.

Example: internet interview

The president appeared confident in the discussion (Obama, 2015).

Obama, B. (2015) Interviewed by Jon Sopel for *BBC News*, 24 July. Available at: http://www.bbc.co.uk/news/world-us-canada-33646543 (Accessed: 16 June 2021).

G7 Teaching materials, including lecture notes and VLEs, for example Blackboard, Moodle, PebblePad and MOOCs

Virtual learning environments (VLEs) and collaboration suites such as Blackboard and Moodle are used in further and higher education as stores for course documents and teaching materials, and for discussion between tutors and students and between students. Check with your tutor whether or not you are allowed to refer to course materials in your own work. It is more academically correct to refer to published sources. If you can cite these sources, you will need to distinguish what you are citing, which may include lecture notes, presentation slides, recorded lectures, journal articles and book chapters, or an item from a discussion board.

In the examples below, the URL gives the access point to the VLE because a reader would need login details to locate the item being cited. If you are citing material in a personal learning environment, eportfolio or webfolio such as PebblePad, this is also likely to have restricted access, so give the URL at which someone would log in to the site.

If you are citing something you heard in live lectures, tutorials or meetings, whether in person or live on platforms such as Zoom, Collaborate or Teams, these will also be inaccessible to anyone who was not participating at the time. Any references you make to these should provide the author of the information, title of the session, module and date, as the reader will have to rely on your reporting of the session.

If the session was recorded and is publicly available for anyone to view or listen to, it can be cited in the same format as a video or audio recording (see G22.4).

G7.1 Live lectures: in person and online via Zoom, Teams and Collaborate

Citation order:

♦ Author/speaker
♦ Year (in round brackets)
♦ Title of communication (in single quotation marks)
♦ Medium (in square brackets)

- Module code: module title (in italics) (if known)
- Institution or venue
- Day/month

Example

In-text citation

Points of interest from the lectures (Brown, 2021) …

Reference list

Brown, T. (2021) *'Banking regulation'* [Lecture]. *BUS316: BSc Economics*. Northumbria University. 21 February.

G7.2 Recorded lectures

Use this format if the lecture recording is only available to someone who can log in to the module. If the recording is publicly available for anyone to view or listen to, it can be cited in the same format as a video or audio recording (see G22.4).

Citation order:
- Author/speaker
- Year (in round brackets)
- Title of communication (in single quotation marks)
- Medium (in square brackets)
- Module code: module title (in italics) (if known)
- Institution or venue
- Day/month
- Available at: URL of VLE (Accessed: date)

Example

In-text citation

Points of interest from the lectures (Brown, 2021) …

Reference list

Brown, T. (2021) *'Bridge construction techniques'* [Recorded lecture]. *ENG1145: BEng.* Durham University. 21 March. Available at: http://duo.dur.ac.uk (Accessed: 21 April 2021).

G7.3 Tutors' handouts

Citation order:
- Tutor
- Year of distribution (in round brackets)
- Title of handout (in single quotation marks)
- Module code: module title (in italics)
- Institution
- Unpublished

Example

In-text citation

The tutor's handout (Hadley, 2021) …

Reference list

Hadley, S. (2021) 'Biomechanics: introductory readings', *BM289: Sport biomechanics*. University of Cumbria. Unpublished.

G7.4 Tutors' lecture notes in a VLE

Citation order:

♦ Author or tutor
♦ Year of publication (in round brackets)
♦ Title of item (in single quotation marks)
♦ Module code: module title (in italics)
♦ Available at: URL of VLE (Accessed: date)

Example

In-text citation

The tutor's notes (Hadley, 2021) …

Reference list

Hadley, S. (2021) 'Biomechanics: introductory readings', *BM289: Sport biomechanics*. University of Cumbria. Available at: https://mylearning. cumbria.ac.uk (Accessed: 7 April 2021).

G7.5 Presentations: PowerPoint, Prezi, etc.

Citation order:

♦ Author or tutor
♦ Year of publication (in round brackets)
♦ Title of presentation (in single quotation marks)
♦ [Presentation slides]
♦ Module code: module title (in italics)
♦ Available at: URL (Accessed: date)

Example

In-text citation

The excellent presentation (Booth, 2020) …

Reference list

Booth, L. (2020) 'History of radiography' [Presentation slides]. *MISR4004: Patient care skills: an introduction to human sciences.* University of Cumbria. Available at: https://mylearning.cumbria.ac.uk (Accessed: 7 April 2021).

G7.6 Learning support materials

Sometimes you will access, and need to reference, material from modules not produced by tutors, for example skills modules produced by learning support teams.

Citation order:

♦ Author
♦ Year of publication (in round brackets)
♦ Title of item (in single quotation marks)
♦ Title of support/skills module (in italics): subtitle (if required) (in italics)
♦ Available at: URL of VLE (Accessed: date)

Example

In-text citation

… and this module allows you to test your own skills (University of Cumbria, Library and Student Services, 2020).

Reference list

University of Cumbria, Library and Student Services (2020) 'Skills evaluation tools', *Skills@cumbria: assess your skills.* Available at: https://mylearning.cumbria.ac.uk (Accessed: 18 October 2020).

G7.7 Journal articles accessed via VLEs

For journal articles in VLEs where you have all the required elements for the reader to track the article down, you should simply cite and reference the article, as in Section G2.1.

G7.8 Extracts from books digitised for use in VLEs

You may be given an extract or chapter from a book. Cite it as a chapter from an edited book (G1.8).

G7.9 Messages from course discussion boards

Citation order:
♦ Author
♦ Year of publication (in round brackets)
♦ Title of message (in single quotation marks)
♦ Title of discussion board (in italics)
♦ 'in'
♦ Module code: module title (in italics)
♦ Available at: URL of VLE (Accessed: date)

Example

In-text citation

It is advisable to check which referencing style is required (Thomas, 2020).

Reference list

Thomas, D. (2020) 'Word count and referencing style', *Frequently asked questions discussion board*, in *SOCI2011: Housing studies.* Available at: http://duo.dur.ac.uk (Accessed: 14 January 2021).

G7.10 Publicly available online courses and MOOCs (Massive Online Open Courses)

Citation order:

♦ Producer
♦ Year of publication (in round brackets)
♦ Title of course (in italics)
♦ [MOOC]
♦ Available at: URL (Accessed: date)

Example

In-text citation

… in relation to the university's MOOC (University of Strathclyde, Glasgow, 2021).

Reference list

University of Strathclyde, Glasgow (2021) *Gender representation in the media* [MOOC]. Available at: https://www.futurelearn.com/courses/gender-and-the-media (Accessed: 10 June 2021).

G8 Digital repositories

Many academic and learned institutions maintain digital repositories of the research undertaken by their members. Repositories can also be used by authors to present their articles to readers before traditional publication processes, such as **peer-review**, have been completed. Peer-review can take many months, by which time the value and opportunities raised by the new information may be lost. Publishing in repositories is common in the sciences, where early notice and discussion of new research is essential, for example in Arxiv.org.

Items in digital repositories may be at different stages in the publication process: some may be finished sources, made freely available through open access pub-lishing. Other items may be made available before they have been peer-reviewed, or they may have been peer-reviewed but not typeset (sometimes called the author's 'final manuscript'). With this variation, it is important to cite the version of the source you have read, as it may be different to the final published version. Give the DOI or URL and accessed date and indicate the version within [ ] to show which version you read.

G8.1 Books or reports in digital repositories

Citation order:

Reference books and journal articles in repositories as you would for print versions; unless they are only available online, in which case use the URL or DOI.

Example

In-text citation

Henderson *et al.* (2020) found …

Reference list

Henderson, D. *et al.* (2020) *The digital maturity survey for Wales 2020*. [Project report]. Cardiff University. Available at: http://orca.cf.ac.uk/id/eprint/136941 (Accessed: 29 May 2021).

OR, citing all authors

Henderson, D., Jones, C., Munday, M., Roberts, A., Roche, N. and Xu, C. (2020) *The digital maturity survey for Wales 2020*. [Project report]. Cardiff University. Available at: http://orca.cf.ac.uk/id/eprint/136941 (Accessed: 29 May 2021).

G8.2 Book chapter in digital repository

Citation order:

- Author(s)
- Year (in round brackets)
- Title of chapter (in single quotation marks)
- 'in' plus author/editor of book
- Title of book (in italics)
- Version (in square brackets)
- Available at: URL (Accessed: date)

This example cites the open access ver-sion because the published version re-quires a subscription to the ebook.

Example

In the opinion of MacCarthaigh and McKeown (2021) …

MacCarthaigh, M. and McKeown, C. (2021) 'A political science perspective on fake news', in Chakraborty, T., Kumar, S., Long, C. and Padmanabhan, D. (eds), *Data science for fake news: surveys and perspectives* [Open access version]. Available at: https://pureadmin.qub.ac.uk/ws/portalfiles/portal/204845261/MacCarthaigh_and_McKeown_2020_Fake_News_and_Political_Science_final_for_PURE.pdf (Accessed: 21 May 2021).

G8.3 Conference papers in digital repositories

If the conference paper is only available online, provide the URL or DOI.

Citation order:

- Author
- Year of publication (in round brackets)
- Title of paper (in single quotation marks)
- Title of conference (in italics)
- Organisation or company (if stated)
- Location and date of conference
- Available at: DOI *or* URL (Accessed: date)

Example

As proposed in their presentation (Alamazroa and Sun, 2019) …

Alamazroa, A. and Sun, H. (2019) 'An Internet of Things (IoT) management system for improving homecare – a case study', *International symposium on networks, computers and communications (ISNCC'19)*, Istanbul, Turkey, 18–20 June 2019. Available at: https://dro.dur.ac.uk/28207/ (Accessed: 12 June 2021).

G8.4 Articles in digital repositories

Citation order:

- Author(s)
- Year (in round brackets)
- Title (in single quotation marks)
- Version (in square brackets)
- To be published in (if this is stated)
- Title of journal (in italics, if stated)
- Available at: DOI *or* URL (Accessed: date)

Example: prepublication article in repository

In-text citation

As noted by Dong and Kokotsaki (2021) …

Reference list

Dong, L. and Kokotsaki, D. (2021) 'Music achievements of being an English chorister'. To be published in *British Journal of Music Education* [Peer-reviewed accepted version]. Available at: https://dro.dur.ac.uk/33114/ (Accessed: 31 May 2021).

Example: article published only in repository

In-text citation

Lewis (2020) analysed …

Reference list

Lewis, R. (2020) 'Who is the centre of the movie universe? Using Python and NetworkX to analyse the social network of movie stars'. Available at: https://arxiv.org/abs/2002.11103 (Accessed: 31 May 2021).

Example: older item, subsequently published

In this example, you should try to read and cite the version published in *European Journal of Operational Research.*

In-text citation

Research by Ghaffarzadegan, Xue and Larson (2017) …

Reference list

Ghaffarzadegan, N., Xue, Y. and Larson, R.C. (2017) 'Work-education mismatch: An endogenous theory of professionalization' [Author's final manuscript]. Published in *European Journal of Operational Research*, 261(3), pp. 1085–1097. Available at: https://dspace.mit.edu/handle/1721.1/122922 (Accessed: 31 May 2021).

G9 Published reports, working papers and briefing papers

Sometimes referred to as 'grey literature', a huge range of information is published by governments, international organisations, companies, charities, groups and individuals.

Citation order:

♦ Name of organisation or institution
♦ Year of publication (in round brackets)
♦ Title (in italics)
♦ Reference number (if available)
♦ Place of publication: publisher

If accessed online:
♦ Available at: DOI *or* URL (Accessed: date)

Example

In-text citation

The earlier guidance (NHS England and NHS Improvement, 2016) …

Reference list

NHS England and NHS Improvement (2016) *NHS operational planning and contracting guidance 2017–2019*. Available at: https://www.england. nhs.uk/wp-content/uploads/2016/09/ NHS-operational-planning-guidance-201617-201819. pdf (Accessed: 17 October 2021).

NB For unpublished internal reports, see Section G28.

G9.1 Government publications

Many UK government publications may be accessed via https://www.gov.uk, but you should use the specific author or department as the author, if given.

Examples

In-text citations

Knife crime levels caused great concern (Ministry of Justice, 2020) as did the disparity in medical care (Public Health England, 2021).

Reference list

Ministry of Justice (2020) *Knife and offensive weapon sentencing statistics: July to September 2020*. Available at: https://www.gov.uk/ government/statistics/knife-and-offensive-weapon-sentencing-statistics-july-to-september-2020 (Accessed: 3 June 2021).

Public Health England (2021) *Health inequalities dashboard: March 2021 update*. Available at: https://www.gov. uk/government/statistics/health-inequalities-dashboard-march-2021-data-update (Accessed: 18 June 2021).

If you are *referencing government publications from more than one country*, include the country of origin (in round brackets) after the department name, unless the country is part of the name, as in the Canadian example below.

Examples

In-text citations

The three governments have published plans for greener economies (Department for Business, Energy & Industrial Strategy (UK), 2021; Department of Industry, Science, Energy and Resources (Australia), 2020; Environment and Climate Change Canada, 2020).

Reference list

Department for Business, Energy & Industrial Strategy (UK) (2021) *Industrial decarbonisation strategy*. Available at: https://www.gov.uk/government/publications/industrial-decarbonisation-strategy (Accessed: 5 June 2021).

Department of Industry, Science, Energy and Resources (Australia) (2020) *Australia's national hydrogen strategy*. Available at: https://www.industry.gov.au/data-and-publications/australias-national-hydrogen-strategy (Accessed: 5 June 2021).

Environment and Climate Change Canada (2020) *A healthy environment and a healthy economy*. Available at: https://www.canada.ca/en/services/environment/weather/climatechange/climate-plan/climate-plan-overview/healthy-environment-healthy-economy.html (Accessed: 5 June 2021).

G9.2 Publications of international organisations

Examples

In-text citations

The European Commission (2018), International Chamber of Commerce (2019) and the United Nations (2021) support climate change measures.

Reference list

European Commission (2018) *A clean planet for all: A European strategic long-term vision for a prosperous, modern, competitive and climate neutral economy.* COM/2018/773. Available at: https://eur-lex.europa.eu/legal-content/EN/TXT/?uri=CELEX:52018DC0773 (Accessed: 9 June 2021).

International Chamber of Commerce (2019) *ICC declaration on the next century of global business*. Available at: https://iccwbo.org/publication/icc-centenary-declaration/ (Accessed: 9 June 2021).

United Nations (2021) *Looking into the future: four scenarios for environmental action.* ESCAP/CED/2020/INF/2. Available at: https://digitallibrary.un.org/record/3905091?ln=en (Accessed: 9 June 2021).

G9.3 Research reports, working and briefing papers

Examples

In-text citations

Looking at New Zealand's plans (Casalini, Bagherzadeh and Gray, 2021, pp. 7–11) …

A survey by Hann and Nash (2020) …

Proposals by Basu and Getachew (2017, p. 23–25) …

Reference list

Basu P. and Getachew, Y. (2017) *Redistributive innovation policy, inequality and efficiency*. Durham University Business School working paper 2017.2. Available at: https://www.dur.ac.uk/resources/business/working-papers/RD_2017_02.pdf (Accessed: 1 July 2021).

Casalini, F., Bagherzadeh. M. and Gray. E. (2021) *Building the resilience of New Zealand's agricultural sector to floods*. OECD Food, Agriculture and Fisheries Papers, No. 160. Paris: OECD Publishing. Available at: https://doi.org/10.1787/dd62d270-en

Hann, D. and Nash, D. (2020) *Disputes and their management in the workplace.* Advisory Conciliation and Advisory Service (ACAS) report. Available at: https://www.acas.org.uk/disputes-and-their-management-in-the-workplace (Accessed: 14 May 2021).

G9.4 Company reports

Examples

In-text citations

The company's operations are extensive (Sky Group Ltd, 2021).

Elon Musk stated that 'the hardest thing is scaling production' (Tesla, 2021, 28:30 mins).

Reference list

Sky Group Ltd (2021) *Year at Sky 2020–2021*. Available at: https://www.skygroup.sky/year-at-sky (Accessed: 8 June 2021).

Tesla (2020) *Annual meeting of stockholders and battery day livestream report*. 22 September. Available at: https://www.tesla.com/en_gb/2020shareholdermeeting (Accessed: 13 June 2021).

G9.5 Market research reports from online databases

Example

In-text citation

Mintel (2021) noted opportunities …

Reference list

Mintel (2021) *Tea drinks – China – May 2021*. Available at: https://clients-mintel-com/ (Accessed: 5 June 2021).

G9.6 Financial reports from online databases

Example

In-text citation

Skoda's turnover in 2019 was $20.9bn (Bureau van Dijk, 2021).

Reference list

Bureau van Dijk (2021) *Skoda Auto, A.S. company report*. Available at: https://orbis4.bvdinfo.com/ip (Accessed: 5 June 2021).

G9.7 Financial reports from terminal-based databases

As these databases are not available through the internet, give the name of the database instead of an URL.

Citation order:

♦ Publishing organisation
♦ Year of publication/last updated (in round brackets)
♦ Title of extract (in italics)
♦ Available at: Title of database (in italics) (Accessed: date)

Examples

In-text citations

Comparing the company data from Datastream (2020) and Bloomberg (2020) …

Reference list

Bloomberg (2020) *BT share prices 2015-2020*. Available at: *Bloomberg*. (Accessed: 5 April 2021).

Datastream (2020) *BT Group plc company report*. Available at: *Datastream*. (Accessed: 5 April 2021).

G10 UK legal sources using the Harvard (author-date) style

Many UK law schools use the OSCOLA referencing system (Section M), and each country's law schools may recommend a specific style for legal sources (for example *The Bluebook* in the USA). However, many other disciplines use legal sources in their research and do not apply the same conventions for publication abbreviations and punctuation as the law schools. Here, we provide examples for citing legal sources in author-date (Harvard) format.

The author-date format uses the elements of references common to other sources as the in-text and reference list documentation: speakers recorded in *Hansard* are treated as authors; law reports are treated as journal articles, with the case name used as the article title.

UK legislation is available on BAILII (http://www.bailii.org/), Legislation.gov.uk (http://www.legislation.gov.uk/) and subscription services including LexisLibrary and Westlaw.

G10.1 Papers: House of Commons and House of Lords

Citation order:

♦ Parliament. House of …
♦ Year of publication (in round brackets)
♦ Title (in italics)
♦ Paper number (in round brackets). For House of Lords papers, the paper number is also in round brackets to distinguish it from identical House of Commons paper numbers (see examples below)
♦ Place of publication: publisher

If accessed online:

♦ Available at: URL (Accessed: date)

Examples

In-text citations

Parliamentary reports for the year included the criminal justice system (Parliament. House of Commons, 1999) and renewable energy (Parliament. House of Lords, 1999).

Reference list

Parliament. House of Commons (1999) *Criminal justice: working together, session 1999–2000*. (HC 1999–2000 29). London: The Stationery Office.

Parliament. House of Lords (1999) *Electricity from renewables: first report from the Select Committee on the European Union*. (HL 1999–2000 (18)). London: The Stationery Office.

G10.2 House of Commons Library briefing papers

Citation order:

♦ Author or organisation
♦ Year of publication (in round brackets)
♦ Title of report (in italics)
♦ Title of publication series and number (in round brackets)
♦ Place of publication: publisher

If accessed online:
♦ Available at: URL (Accessed: date)

Example

In-text citation

Brown (2021) outlined …

Reference list

Brown, J. (2021) *Coronavirus: enforcing restrictions*. (House of Commons Library briefing paper 9024). Available at: https://commonslibrary.parliament.uk/research-briefings/cbp-9024/ (Accessed: 31 May 2021).

G10.3 Official records: House of Commons and House of Lords

G10.3a Hansard

Hansard is the official record of debates, speeches, oral and written answers/statements, petitions and Westminster Hall discussions in the Houses of the UK Parliament. A fully searchable version of *Hansard* from 1803 to the present is available online at http://www.parliament.uk/business/publications/hansard/.

Citation order:

- ◆ Name of speaker/author
- ◆ Year of publication (in round brackets)
- ◆ Subject of debate or speech (in single quotation marks)
- ◆ Hansard: Name of House of Parliament (in italics)
- ◆ Debates/written statement/Westminster Hall or petitions (in italics)
- ◆ Day and month
- ◆ Volume number, column number or page number
- ◆ Available at: URL (Accessed: date)

Example

In-text citation

Hywell Williams MP (2015) questioned the impact of sanctions in Wales.

Reference list

Williams, H. (2015) 'Benefit sanctions', *Hansard: House of Commons debates*, 16 September, 599, c.1032. Available at: https://publications. parliament.uk/pa/cm201516/ cmhansrd/chan45.pdf (Accessed: 17 May 2021).

G10.3b Written questions, answers and statements in Parliament

Before September 2014, written questions and answers and written statements were recorded in *Hansard*.

Citation order:

- ◆ Name of author
- ◆ Year of publication (in round brackets)

- ◆ Subject of question, answer or statement (in single quotation marks)
- ◆ Hansard: Name of House of Parliament (in italics)
- ◆ Debates/written statement/Westminster Hall or petitions (in italics)
- ◆ Day and month
- ◆ Volume number, column number or page number
- ◆ Available at: URL (Accessed: date)

Example

In-text citation

Mr Lansley (2012) welcomed the forum.

Reference list

Lansley, A. (2012) 'NHS future forum', *Hansard: House of Commons written ministerial statements*, 10 January, 7WS. Available at: http://www. publications.parliament.uk/pa/ cm201212/cmhansrd/cm120110/ wmstext/120110m0001. htm#12011044000132 (Accessed: 23 May 2021).

Since 12 September 2014, written questions and answers have been published in the *Written questions and answers* database (http://www.parliament.uk/business/publications/written-questions-answers-statements/written-questions-answers/) instead of *Hansard*. This means that the column reference is no longer used. Questions and answers in the database are given a number to include in their citation.

Citation order:

- Name of author
- Year of publication (in round brackets)
- Subject of question, answer or statement (in single quotation marks)
- UK Parliament: written questions, answers and statements (in italics)
- Day and month
- Question, answer or statement number
- Available at: URL (Accessed: date)

Example

In-text citation

In her statement Chloe Smith (2021) stated …

Reference list

Smith, C. (2021) 'Empowering British citizens overseas to participate in our democracy', *UK Parliament: written questions, answers and statements*, 27 May, Statement UIN HCWS62. Available at: https://questions-statements.parliament.uk/written-statements/detail/2021-05-27/hcws62 (Accessed: 7 June 2021).

G10.4 Bills: House of Commons and House of Lords

Citation order:

- Title (in italics)
- Year of publication (in round brackets)
- Parliament: House of Commons or Lords
- Bill number
- Place of publication: publisher

If viewed online:

- Available at: URL (Accessed: date)

Example

In-text citation

On 12 May, the government introduced the *Advanced Research and Invention Agency Bill* (2021).

Reference list

Advanced Research and Invention Agency Bill (2021). Parliament: House of Commons. Bill no. 1. Available at: https://bills.parliament.uk/bills/2836 (Accessed: 5 June 2021).

G10.5 UK statutes (Acts of Parliament)

Before 1963, an Act was cited according to the regnal year, that is, the number of years since the monarch's accession. You may see references to legislation in this format in early publications, for example *Act of Supremacy 1534* (26 Hen 8 c1). However, for all Acts (including pre-1963), you should use the short title of the Act, with the year in which it was enacted. Most Acts and parts of Acts are now available as PDFs or web pages to be viewed online, so reference the website where you located the Act. As the date appears in the title of the Acts, there is no need to repeat the date in round brackets after the title.

Citation order:

♦ Title of Act including year and chapter number (in italics)
♦ Country/jurisdiction (only if referencing more than one country's legislation)
♦ Available at: URL (Accessed: date)

Example: whole Act

In-text citation

The legislation (*Fire Safety Act 2021*) was too late to prevent the Grenfell disaster.

Reference list

Fire Safety Act 2021, c. 7. Available at: https://www.legislation.gov.uk/ukpga/2021/24/contents/enacted (Accessed: 17 May 2021).

Example: section of an Act

In-text citation

As defined in section 10(2) of the Act (*Children Act 2004*) …

Reference list

Children Act 2004, c. 31. Available at: http://www.legislation.gov.uk/ukpga/2004/31/contents (Accessed: 17 September 2018).

G10.6 Statutory Instruments (SIs)

Citation order:

♦ Name/title and year (in italics)
♦ SI year and number (in round brackets)
♦ Available at: URL (Accessed: date)

Example

In-text citation

Referring to the *General Dental Council (Constitution) (Amendment) Order 2012* …

Reference list

General Dental Council (Constitution) (Amendment) Order 2012 (SI 2012/1655). Available at: https://www.legislation.gov.uk/uksi/2012/1655/contents/made (Accessed: 17 May 2021).

G10.7 Legislation from the UK devolved legislatures

Legislation from UK devolved legislatures is available online at http://www.legislation.gov.uk and in subscription databases such as Westlaw and LexisLibrary. Note in the examples below that the part of the UK to which the legislation applies is part of the title and so is italicised.

G10.7a Acts of the Scottish Parliament

For Acts of the post-devolution Scottish Parliament, replace the chapter number with 'asp' (meaning Act of the Scottish Parliament).

Citation order:

♦ Title of Act and year (in italics)
♦ asp number (in round brackets)
♦ Available at: URL (Accessed: date)

Example

In-text citation

In the legislation (*Budget (Scotland) Act 2015*) ...

Reference list

Budget (Scotland) Act 2015 (asp 2). Available at: http://www.legislation. gov.uk/asp/2015/2/contents (Accessed: 17 May 2021).

G10.7b Scottish Statutory Instruments (SSIs)

Citation order:

♦ Title of SSI and year (in italics)
♦ SSI year/number (in round brackets)
♦ Available at: URL (Accessed: date)

Example

In-text citation

As stated in the regulations (*The Social Security Information-sharing (Scotland) Regulations 2021*) ...

Reference list

The Social Security Information-sharing (Scotland) Regulations 2021 (SSI 2021/178). Available at: https:// www.legislation.gov.uk/ssi/2021/178/ contents/made (Accessed: 17 May 2021).

G10.8 Acts of the Northern Ireland Assembly

Citation order:

♦ Title of Act (Northern Ireland) and year (in italics)
♦ Available at: URL (Accessed: date)

Example

In-text citation

... which was discussed in the legislation (*Domestic Abuse and Civil Proceedings Act (Northern Ireland) 2021*).

Reference list

Domestic Abuse and Civil Proceedings Act (Northern Ireland) 2021. Available at: https://www. legislation.gov.uk/nia/2021/2/contents (Accessed: 17 May 2021).

G10.8a Statutory Rules of Northern Ireland

The Northern Ireland Assembly may pass Statutory Instruments. These are called Statutory Rules of Northern Ireland.

Citation order:

♦ Title of Rule (Northern Ireland) and year (in italics)
♦ SSI year/number (in round brackets)
♦ Available at: URL (Accessed: date)

Example

In-text citation

The rules relating to flavourings (*Smoke Flavourings Regulations (Northern Ireland) 2005*) ...

Reference list

Smoke Flavourings Regulations (Northern Ireland) 2005 (SR 2005/76). Available at: https://www.legislation.gov. uk/nisr/2005/76/contents/made (Accessed: 17 May 2021).

G10.9 Welsh legislation

Legislative devolution in Wales has evolved since 2006. From 2007 to 2011, the National Assembly for Wales passed Assembly Measures (nawm). From 2012 to 2020, the National Assembly passed Acts of the National Assembly for Wales (anaw). From 6 May 2020, the National Assembly was renamed the Welsh Parliament or Senedd Cymru, passing Acts of the Senedd Cymru (asc).

G10.9a National Assembly for Wales Measures

Citation order:

- Title of Assembly Measure and year (in italics)
- (nawm number)
- Available at: URL (Accessed: date)

Example

In-text citation

The *NHS Redress (Wales) Measure 2008* …

Reference list

NHS Redress (Wales) Measure 2008 (nawm 1). Available at: http://www.legislation.gov.uk/mwa/2008/1/2008-07-09 (Accessed: 17 May 2021).

G10.9b Acts of the National Assembly for Wales

Citation order:

- Title of Act of the National Assembly for Wales and year (in italics)
- (anaw number)
- Available at: URL (Accessed: date)

Example

In-text citation

The *Legislation (Wales) Act 2019* provided …

Reference list

Legislation (Wales) Act 2019 (anaw 4). Available at: https://www.legislation.gov.uk/anaw/2019/4/contents (Accessed: 17 May 2021).

G10.9c Acts of the Senedd Cymru

Citation order:

- Title of Act of the Senedd Cymru and year (in italics)
- (asc number)
- Available at: URL (Accessed: date)

Example

In-text citation

The Senedd passed the *Health and Social Care (Quality and Engagement) (Wales) Act 2020*.

Reference list

Health and Social Care (Quality and Engagement) (Wales) Act 2020 (asc 1). Available at: https://www.legislation.gov.uk/asc/2020/1/contents (Accessed: 17 May 2021).

G10.9d Welsh Statutory Instruments

As well as the SI number and year, Welsh Statutory Instruments have a W. number.

Citation order:

- Title of Order (Wales) and year (in italics)

- SI number (W. number)
- Available at: URL (Accessed: date)

Example

In-text citation

The Sennedd approved the *Additional Learning Needs (Wales) Regulations 2021*.

Reference list

Additional Learning Needs (Wales) Regulations 2021 No. 401 (W. 130). Available at: https://www.legislation. gov.uk/wsi/2021/401/contents/made (Accessed: 17 May 2021).

G10.10 Citing different jurisdictions

If you are citing legislation from more than one jurisdiction, include the country or authority after the title in the reference list. However, the titles of legislation from the UK's devolved assemblies already include the jurisdiction, so this is not necessary. In the UK and Singapore examples, the name of the country or jurisdiction is not part of the title, so is not italicised.

Examples

In-text citations

In the legislation (*Budget (Scotland) Act 2015*) ...

... which was discussed in the legislation (*Domestic Abuse and Civil Proceedings Act (Northern Ireland) 2021*).

The Sennedd passed the *Health and Social Care (Quality and Engagement) (Wales) Act 2020*.

The UK Parliament passed the *Fire Safety Act 2021* ...

In Singapore, the *Vulnerable Adults Act 2018* ...

Reference list

Budget (Scotland) Act 2015 (asp 2). Available at: http://www.legislation. gov.uk/asp/2015/2/contents (Accessed: 17 May 2021).

Domestic Abuse and Civil Proceedings Act (Northern Ireland) 2021. Available at: https://www. legislation.gov.uk/nia/2021/2/contents (Accessed: 17 May 2021).

Health and Social Care (Quality and Engagement) (Wales) Act 2020 (asc 1). Available at: https://www. legislation.gov.uk/asc/2020/1/ contents (Accessed: 17 May 2021).

Fire Safety Act 2021, c.24 (United Kingdom). Available at: https://www. legislation.gov.uk/ukpga/2021/24/ contents/enacted (Accessed: 17 May 2021).

Vulnerable Adults Act 2018, no. 27 (Singapore). Available at: https://sso. agc.gov.sg/Act/VAA2018 (Accessed: 17 May 2021)

G10.11 Law Commission reports and consultation papers

Citation order:

♦ Law Commission
♦ Year of publication (in round brackets)
♦ Title of report or consultation paper (in italics)
♦ Number of report or consultation paper, Command Paper number (if given) (in round brackets)
♦ Place of publication: publisher

If accessed online:
♦ DOI *or* Available at: URL (Accessed: date)

Examples

In-text citation

The report (Law Commission, 2001) recommended that retrial after acquittal should be permitted in cases of murder, if new evidence became available.

Reference list

Law Commission (2001) *Double Jeopardy and Prosecution Appeals.* (Law Com No 267, Cm 5048). London: The Stationery Office.

Or

Law Commission (2001) *Double Jeopardy and Prosecution Appeals.* (Law Com No 267, Cm 5048). Available at: https://www.lawcom.gov. uk/project/double-jeopardy-and-prosecution-appeals/ (Accessed: 17 May 2021).

G10.12 Command Papers, including Green and White Papers

Citation order:

♦ Department
♦ Year of publication (in round brackets)
♦ Title of report or consultation paper (in italics)
♦ Command Paper number (in round brackets)
♦ Place of publication: publisher

If accessed online:
♦ DOI *or* Available at: URL (Accessed: date)

Examples

In-text citations

In her essay she cited proposals on the minimum wage (Department for Business Innovation & Skills, 2015) and Trade Practices (Secretary of State for Prices and Consumer Protection, 1979).

Reference list

Department for Business, Innovation & Skills (2015) *Regulations implementing the National Minimum Wage – a report on the apprentice rate* (Cm 9061). Available at: https://www.gov.uk/ government/publications/national-minimum-wage-report-on-the-2015-apprentice-rate (Accessed: 17 May 2021).

Secretary of State for Prices and Consumer Protection (1979) *Review of restrictive trade practices policy* (Cmnd. 7512). London: HMSO.

G10.13 Law reports

G10.13a Law reports (cases) up to 2002

Citation order:

♦ Name of case (in single quotation marks)
♦ Year (in round brackets)
♦ Title of law report (in italics)
♦ Volume number
♦ Page numbers

Example

In-text citation

The earlier case ('R v. Edward (John)', 1991) ...

Reference list

'R v. Edward (John)' (1991) *Weekly Law Reports*, 1, pp. 207–208.

G10.13b Law reports (cases) from 2002 with neutral citations

From 2002, cases have been given a neutral citation that identifies the case without referring to the printed law report series in which the case was published. This helps to identify the case online, for example through the freely available transcripts of the British and Irish Legal Information Institute (www.bailii.org) and databases including Westlaw and LexisLibrary. Check with your tutor if you should include the neutral citation in addition to the publication in which the case was reported or the database or website you used.

Citation order:

♦ Name of parties involved in case (in single quotation marks)
♦ Year (in round brackets)
♦ Court and case no.
♦ Database *or* website (in italics)
♦ Available at: DOI *or* URL (Accessed: date)

Example

In-text citation

The case of *'Humphreys v. Revenue and Customs'* (2012) ...

Reference list

'Humphreys v. Revenue and Customs' (2012) United Kingdom Supreme Court, case 18. *BAILII*. Available at: http://www.bailii.org/uk/cases/UKSC/2012/18.html (Accessed: 17 May 2021).

G10.13c Case analyses

In addition to law reports, legal chambers or publishers may publish comments or analyses of cases. It is important to be clear that these are opinions by individual or organisation authors, and are different to law reports.

Citation order:

♦ Author or organisation
♦ Year of publication (in round brackets)
♦ Title of case (in single quotation marks)
♦ Title of website or database (in italics)
♦ Available at: URL (Accessed: date)

Examples

Two analyses of the case (Essex Chambers, 2018; Thomson Reuters, 2018) …

Essex Chambers (2018) 'CH v A Metropolitan Council'. *Essex Chambers*. Available at: https://www.39essex.com/cop_cases/ch-v-metropolitan-council/ (Accessed: 17 May 2021).

Thomson Reuters (2018) 'CH v A Metropolitan Council'. *Westlaw*. Available at: http://www.westlaw.com (Accessed: 17 May 2021).

G10.14 Inquiries

Public and independent inquiries may be published by order of Parliament, and if so are given a Parliamentary or Command Paper number.

Citation order:

♦ Author
♦ Year of publication (in round brackets)
♦ Title of inquiry (in italics)
♦ Parliamentary or Command Paper number (in round brackets)
♦ Place of publication: publisher

If accessed online:
♦ Available at: DOI *or* URL (Accessed: date)

Examples

The Hillsborough (2012) and Francis (2013) inquiries …

Francis, R. (2013) *Report of the Mid Staffordshire NHS Foundation Trust public inquiry*. (HC 898). London: The Stationery Office.

Hillsborough. Report of the Hillsborough Independent Panel (2012) (HC 581). Available at: https://www.gov.uk/government/publications/the-report-of-the-hillsborough-independent-panel (Accessed: 27 May 2021).

G11 European Union (EU) legal sources

Legal documents from the EU include legislation, directives, decisions and regulations. The most authoritative source is the *Official Journal of the European Union*.

G11.1 EU legislation

Citation order:

♦ Legislation title (in italics)
♦ Year (in round brackets)
♦ Official Journal (in italics)
♦ Series initial issue
♦ Page numbers

Example

In-text citation

All signatories to the Treaty (*Consolidated Version of the Treaty on European Union*, 2008) …

Reference list

Consolidated Version of the Treaty on European Union (2008) *Official Journal* C 115, 9 May, pp.13–45.

G11.2 EU directives, decisions and regulations

Citation order:

♦ Legislation type (in single quotation marks)
♦ Number and title (in single quotation marks)
♦ Year (in round brackets)
♦ Official Journal (OJ) series (in italics)
♦ Issue
♦ Page numbers

or
♦ Available at: DOI *or* URL (Accessed: date)

Examples

In-text citations

The minister highlighted the terms of 'Council directive 2008/52/EC' (2008), 'Council regulation (EU) 2015/760' (2015) and 'DS Smith/Duropack' (2015) …

Reference list

Directives:

'Council directive 2008/52/EC on certain aspects of mediation in civil and commercial matters' (2008) *Official Journal* L136, p. 3.

Regulations:

'Council regulation (EU) 2015/760 on European long-term investment funds' (2015) *Official Journal* L123, p. 98.

Commission decisions are cited as cases:

'Case M.7558 – DS Smith/Duropack' (2015) Commission decision. *Eur-Lex*. Available at: https://ec.europa.eu/competition/mergers/cases/decisions/m7558_497_2.pdf (Accessed: 27 May 2021).

G11.3 Judgements of the European Court of Justice (ECJ) and General Court (GC)

Citation order:

♦ Case name (in single quotation marks)
♦ Year (in round brackets)
♦ Case number
♦ European Case Law Identifier – ECLI
♦ Publication title (in italics)
♦ Section, page numbers

Example

Consideration of the Swedish view ('Commission of the European Communities v Kingdom of Sweden', 2005) …

'Commission of the European Communities v Kingdom of Sweden' (2005) Case no. C-111/03; ECLI:EU:C:2005:619. *European Court Reports,* I, 08789.

G12 United Nations resolutions

For General Assembly resolutions, place A/RES/ before the resolution number, for example A/RES/62/24.

For Security Council resolutions, place S/RES/ before the resolution number, for example S/RES/1801.

Citation order:

♦ Organisation
♦ Year (in round brackets)
♦ Title (in italics)
♦ Resolution no.
♦ Available at: DOI *or* URL (Accessed: date)

Example

The climate change resolution (United Nations General Assembly, 1994) …

United Nations General Assembly (1994) *United Nations framework convention on climate change.* Resolution A/RES/48/189. Available at: https://unfccc.int/sites/default/files/resource/docs/1994/un/eng/ares48189.pdf (Accessed: 15 May 2021).

G13 International treaties, conventions and accords

If possible, cite from the United Nations Treaty Series.

Citation order:

♦ Title of treaty (in italics)
♦ Year (in round brackets)
♦ Treaty number
♦ Publication title (in italics)
♦ Volume and page numbers

If accessed online:
♦ Available at: DOI *or* URL (Accessed: date)

Example

The UK supported the *Convention Relating to the Status of Refugees* (1951) …

Convention relating to the status of refugees (1951) Treaty no. 2545. *United Nations Treaty Series*, 189, pp. 137–221. Available at: https://treaties.un.org/doc/Publication/UNTS/Volume%20189/volume-189-I-2545-English.pdf (Accessed: 17 May 2021).

G14 International Court of Justice (ICJ) cases

Documentation produced in hearing cases at the ICJ includes merits, written and oral proceedings, orders, judgements, press releases and correspondence.

Citation order:

♦ Case name (in single quotation marks)
♦ Year (in round brackets)
♦ International Court of Justice cases (in italic)
♦ Publication type and date (if required)
♦ Available at: DOI *or* URL (Accessed: date)

Examples

The cases of 'East Timor (Portugal v. Australia)' (1991) and 'Maritime Dispute (Peru v. Chile)' (2014) considered …

'East Timor (Portugal v. Australia)', (1991) *International Court of Justice cases*. Available at: https://www.icj-cij.org/en/case/84 (Accessed: 14 May 2021).

'Maritime Dispute (Peru v. Chile)' (2014) *International Court of Justice cases.* Judgement of 27 January. Available at: https://www.icj-cij.org/en/case/137 (Accessed: 14 May 2021).

G15 US legal material

For information on citing and referencing US legal material, see *The Bluebook: A Uniform System of Citation* (2020) 21st edn. Cambridge, MA: Harvard Law Review Association. A useful online guide is P.W. Martin (2020) *Introduction to Basic Legal Citation*. Available at: http://www.law.cornell.edu/citation/ (Accessed: 26 May 2021).

G16 Protocols, regulations and guidelines

These often relate to official procedures, rules and guidance from health, government and other corporate bodies (for example NICE, National Institute for Health and Care Excellence).

NB: For scientific and technical standards, see Section G17.1.

Citation order:

♦ Author
♦ Year of publication (in round brackets)
♦ Title (in italics)
♦ Series or publication number (if given)
♦ Place of publication: publisher

If accessed online:
♦ Available at: DOI *or* URL (Accessed: date)

Examples

In-text citations

The hospital's guideline (Great Ormond Street Hospital for Children, 2020) and the updated guidance (National Institute for Health and Care Excellence [hereafter NICE], 2021) …

Reference list

Great Ormond Street Hospital for Children (2020) *Ciclosporin after bone marrow transplant*. 2020F0542. Available at: https://media.gosh.nhs.uk/documents/Ciclosporin_after_BMT_F0542_FINAL_May20_0.pdf (Accessed: 30 May 2021).

National Institute for Health and Care Excellence [NICE] (2021). *Postnatal care*. NG194. Available at: https://www.nice.org.uk/guidance/ng194 (Accessed: 18 May 2021).

G17 Scientific and technical information

G17.1 Technical standards

Citation order:

♦ Name of authorising organisation
♦ Year of publication (in round brackets)
♦ Number and title of standard (in italics)
♦ Place of publication: publisher

If accessed online:
♦ Available at: DOI *or* URL (Accessed: date)

Example

In-text citation

Checking for compliance with the regulations (British Standards Institution, 2021) …

Reference list

British Standards Institution (2021) *BS EN IEC 60068-2-13:2021: Environmental testing. Tests. Test M: Low air pressure*. Available at: https://bsol-bsigroup-com (Accessed: 30 June 2021).

G17.2 Patents

Citation order:

♦ Inventor(s)
♦ Year of publication (in round brackets)
♦ Title (in italics)
♦ Authorising organisation
♦ Patent number
♦ Available at: DOI *or* URL (Accessed: date)

Example

In-text citation

Padley (2015) proposed a solution.

Reference list

Padley, S. (2015) *Radiator isolating valve*. UK Intellectual Property Office Patent no. GB2463069. Available at: https://worldwide.espacenet.com/ (Accessed: 24 May 2021).

G17.3 Research datasets

Reference where you located the data, for example journal article/book/online.

Citation order:

♦ Author
♦ Date (in round brackets)
♦ Title of data (in single quotation marks)
♦ Available at: DOI *or* URL (Accessed: date)

Example

In-text citation

The dateset by Le *et al.* (2021) provided …

Reference list

Le, T. *et al.* (2021) 'SyntheticFur dataset for neural rendering'. Available: https://arxiv.org/abs/2105.06409 (Accessed: 2 August 2021).

G17.4 Requests for Comments (RFCs)

Citation order:

♦ Author/editor
♦ Year (in round brackets)
♦ Title (in italics)
♦ Document number

If accessed online:
♦ Available at: DOI *or* URL (Accessed: date)

Example

In-text citation

A number of comments were made relating to the document (Hoffman and Harris, 2015).

Reference list

Hoffman, P. and Harris, S. (2006) *The Tao of IETF: a novice's guide to the Internet Engineering Task Force.* Nos: FYI 17 and RFC 4677. Available at: https://datatracker.ietf.org/doc/html/rfc4677 (Accessed: 20 May 2021).

G17.5 Mathematical equations

Reference where you located the equation, for example online journal article.

Citation order:

♦ Author
♦ Year of publication (in round brackets)
♦ Title of article (in single quotation marks)
♦ Title of journal (in italics – capitalise first letter of each word in title, except for linking words such as and, of, the, for)
♦ Volume, issue, page numbers

If accessed online:
♦ Available at: DOI *or* URL (Accessed: date)

Example

Fradelizi and Meyer (2008, p. 1436) noted that for $z > 0$

$$P(K) \geq \frac{e^{n+1-z} Z^{n+1}}{(n!)^2}$$

Fradelizi, M. and Meyer, M. (2008) 'Some functional inverse Santaló inequalities', *Advances in Mathematics*, 218(5), pp. 1430–1452. Available at: https://10.1016/j.aim.2008.03.013

G17.6 Graphs

Reference where you located the graph, for example in a book (give book details).

Citation order:

♦ Author
♦ Year of publication (in round brackets)
♦ Title of book (in italics)
♦ Place of publication: publisher
♦ Page number or figure number for graph
♦ Graph

Example

The effects of the compounds (Day and Gastel, 2016, p. 95) …

Day, R. and Gastel, B. (2016) *How to write and publish a scientific paper*. Cambridge: Cambridge University Press, p. 95, graph.

G18 Maps

G18.1 Ordnance Survey maps

Citation order:

♦ Ordnance Survey
♦ Year of publication (in round brackets)
♦ Title (in italics)
♦ Sheet number, scale
♦ Place of publication: publisher
♦ Series (in round brackets)

Example

Archaeological sites are italicised (Ordnance Survey, 2002).

Ordnance Survey (2002) *Preston and Blackpool*, sheet 102, 1:50,000.

Southampton: Ordnance Survey (Landranger series).

G18.2 Geological Survey maps

Citation order:

♦ Corporate author and publisher
♦ Year of publication (in round brackets)
♦ Title (in italics)
♦ Sheet number, scale
♦ Place of publication: publisher
♦ Series (in round brackets)

Example

In-text citation

The landscape has undergone profound changes since the map (Ordnance Survey, 1980) was printed.

Reference list

Ordnance Survey (1980) *Bellingham (solid)*, sheet 13, 1:50,000. Southampton: Ordnance Survey. (Geological Survey of Great Britain [England and Wales]).

G18.3 Online maps

Citation order:

♦ Map publisher
♦ Year of publication (in round brackets)
♦ Title of map section (in italics)
♦ Sheet number or tile, scale
♦ Available at: DOI *or* URL (Accessed: date)

Examples

In-text citations

The leisure centre is close to Tiddenfoot Lake (Ordnance Survey, 2021).

The dock layout and road network can be seen using *Google Maps* (Google, 2021).

Reference list

Google (2018) *Cardiff Bay*. Available at: http://maps.google.co.uk (Accessed: 5 July 2021).

Ordnance Survey (2021) *Tiddenfoot Lake*, Tile sp92sw, 1:10,000. Available at: http://edina.ac.uk/digimap/ (Accessed: 3 May 2021).

G18.4 GIS maps

Citation order:

♦ Corporate author and publisher
♦ Year of publication (in round brackets)
♦ Map title (in italics)
♦ Scale
♦ Datafile title (in italics)
♦ Using: software (name in italics)
♦ Place of publication: publisher

Example

In-text citation

The decline of woodland is evident (Natural England, 2017).

Reference list

Natural England (2017) *Map of deciduous woodland in North Yorkshire*. Scale 1cm = 1km. *Deciduous woodland BAP priority habitat (England) datafile*. Using: *Explorer for ArcGIS*. Redlands, CA: Esri.

G18.5 Map dataset, including LIDAR

Citation order:

♦ Corporate author/publisher
♦ Year of publication (in round brackets)
♦ Datafile title (in italics)
♦ Format (in square brackets)
♦ Available at: DOI *or* URL (Accessed: date)

Examples

Examining brownfield use in Birmingham (Ordnance Survey, 2021) and Scotland (Environment Agency, 2021) …

Environment Agency (2021) *2m LIDAR composite DSM and DTM for Scotland* [Dataset]. Available at: https://data.gov.uk/dataset/95df1b2b-dc6a-479c-9685-40291a46ec2c/2m-lidar-composite-dsm-dtm-for-scotland (Accessed: 21 June 2021).

Ordnance Survey (2021) *Birmingham city centre* [Dataset]. Available at: http://edina.ac.uk/digimap (Accessed: 21 January 2021).

G18.6 Atlases

Citation order:

♦ Author/editor (if available, if not use title)
♦ Year of publication (in round brackets)
♦ Title (in italics)
♦ Place of publication: publisher

Example

The Korean border with China (*The Times Comprehensive Atlas of the World*, 2011, p. 201) …

The Times comprehensive atlas of the world (2011) 13th edn. London: Times Books.

G19 Visual and artistic sources

Visual sources are available in many different formats and the same image might be viewed in physical form, such as a painting in a gallery, in a printed book or online. The key principle is: *cite what you have seen and in the format in which you viewed them*. See also Section G22.

G19.1 Exhibitions

G19.1a Whole exhibitions: venue and online

Citation order:

♦ Title of exhibition (in italics)
♦ Year (in round brackets)
♦ [Exhibition]
♦ Location. Date(s) of exhibition

If it is an online exhibition, add:

♦ Available at: URL (Accessed: date)

If the artist is known, use:

♦ Artist (if known, or use title of exhibition)
♦ Year (in round brackets)
♦ Title of exhibition (in italics)
♦ [Exhibition or Online exhibition]
♦ Location. Date(s) of exhibition

If it is an online exhibition, add:

♦ Available at: URL (Accessed: date)

Examples

The highly praised exhibition in Koln (*Andy Warhol Now* (2020–2021)) and Tuulikki's (2021) online exhibition were most memorable.

Andy Warhol now (2020–2021) [Exhibition]. Museum Ludwig, Koln, Germany. December 12, 2020 – June 13, 2021.

Tuulikki, H. (2021) *SING SIGN: a close duet* [Online exhibition]. National Galleries of Scotland, Edinburgh. 3 May–13 June 2021. Available at: https://www.nationalgalleries.org/exhibition/hanna-tuulikki-sing-sign-close-duet (Accessed: 3 June 2021).

G19.1b Installations/exhibits

Citation order:

♦ Artist
♦ Year (in round brackets)
♦ Title of installation or exhibit (in italics)
♦ [Installation] or [Exhibit]
♦ Gallery or location
♦ (Viewed: date)

Example

My Bed by Tracey Emin (1999) …

Emin, T. (1999) *My bed* [Installation]. Tate Gallery, London (Viewed: 31 October 2000).

G19.2 Works of art in original media: paintings, sculptures, monuments and installations

Citation order:

♦ Artist (surname followed by initials)
♦ Year of production (in round brackets)
♦ Title of work (in italics)
♦ [Medium]
♦ Location of the work
♦ (Viewed: date)

Examples

Her favourite pieces were by Gormley (1998); Rodin (1882); and Martin (1817).

He photographed several monuments (Melton, 2000; Leong Swee Lim (1967) …

Gormley, A. (1998) *Angel of the North* [Sculpture]. Low Fell, Gateshead (Viewed: 2 March 2021).

Lim L.S. (1967) *Civilian War Memorial*, War Memorial Park, Beach Road, Singapore (Viewed: 4 February 2002).

Martin, J. (1817) *The bard* [Painting]. Laing Art Gallery, Newcastle upon Tyne (Viewed: 21 February 2020).

Melton, S. (2000) *Admiral Sir Bertram Home Ramsey* [Statue]. Dover Castle, Kent (Viewed: 8 August 2018).

Rodin, A. (1882) *The kiss* [Sculpture]. Musee Rodin, Paris, France (Viewed: 7 July 2019).

G19.3 Online images of works of art

If you want to reference the work as seen on a website, you would use the website as the location element of your reference.

Examples

In-text citations

The *Angel* is a welcoming sight by the motorway (Gormley, 1998).

A favourite painting is the *Madonna* by Dalí (1958).

Reference list

Dalí, S. (1958) *Madonna* [Oil on canvas]. Available at: http://www.oxfordartonline.com (Accessed: 9 June 2021).

Gormley, A. (1998). *Angel of the North* [Sculpture]. Available at: https://newcastlegateshead.com/business-directory/things-to-do/angel-of-the-north (Accessed: 6 June 2021).

G19.4 Digital art, including non-fungible token (NFT) artwork

Example

In-text citation

Ludy's work *Sky Lapis* (2021) is to be auctioned at Sotheby's.

Reference list

Ludy, S. (2021) *Sky lapis* [Digital art]. Available at: https://www.saraludy.com/skylapis (Accessed: 6 June 2021).

G19.5 Book and article illustrations, figures, diagrams and tables

If you are citing an illustration, figure, diagram or table, start with the source in which it appeared. In your in-text citation, give the page number and any caption number that will help to identify the illustration, using the terminology in the book or article (for example illus./fig./diagram/logo/table). The reference list entry will be for the whole article or book.

Citation order:

♦ Author
♦ Year of publication (in round brackets)
♦ Publication information for book or article

Examples

In-text citations

Holbein's painting illustrated the prelate's ornate mitre (Strong, 1990, p. 62. Fig. 12).

The GDP data for the UK (James, 2021, p. 12, Table 2) …

Reference list

James. T. (2021) 'UK economic forecasts 2020–21', *Business Insider*, 6(2), pp. 9–14.

Strong, R. (1990) *Lost treasures of Britain*. London: Viking.

G19.6 Photographs/images

G19.6a Prints or slides

Citation order:

♦ Photographer
♦ Year (in round brackets)
♦ Title of photograph (in italics)
♦ [Photograph]
♦ Place of publication: publisher (if available)

Example

In-text citation

The seasonal and architectural changes were captured on film (Thomas, 2017).

Reference list

Thomas, T. (2017) *Redevelopment in Byker* [Photograph]. Newcastle upon Tyne: Then & Now Publishing.

G19.6b Images available online

There are many means to view images online, including library databases such as ArtStor and Bridgeman, and websites and social media sites, including Facebook, Flickr, Instagram, Pinterest or Tumblr. Cite where you viewed or uploaded the image or video.

Citation order:

♦ Photographer (if available)
♦ Year of publication (in round brackets)
♦ Title of photograph/video (or collection) (in italics)
♦ Available at: DOI *or* URL (Accessed: date)

Examples

In-text citations

Photos on the theme of dancing from Barnes and Barnes (1969), vincentemendez (2008), Fotofling Scotland (2014) and stanitsa_dance (2021) …

Reference list

Barnes, R.H. and Barnes, R. (1969) *Baha Kewa Payong Amun Toda dancing in Lèu Tuan*. Available at:// library-artstor-org.ezphost.dur.ac.uk/ asset/YALE__1027_22789691 (Accessed: 13 June 2021).

Fotofling Scotland (2014) *Atholl Highlanders – Highland dancing*. Available at: https://www.tumblr.com/ blog/view/fotoflingscotland (Accessed: 13 June 2021).

stanitsa_dance (2021) *Cossack dance ensemble*. Available at: https://www. instagram.com/p/COI_slphWJ_/ (Accessed: 13 June 2021).

vicentemendez.com (2008) *Dogon group of dancers, Nombori*. Available at: https://www.pinterest.co.uk/ pin/313633561557214364/ (Accessed: 13 June 2021).

G19.6c Images with no creator

Citation order:

♦ Title (in italics)
♦ Year (in round brackets)
♦ Available at: DOI *or* URL (Accessed: date)

Example

In-text citation

The dancers circled the maypole (*Kernewek Lowender – Copper Coast Cornish Festival* 2021).

Kernewek Lowender – Copper Coast Cornish festival (2021) Available at: https://www.facebook.com/kernewekcc/photos/a.539234689495962/4033810613371668 (Accessed: 13 June 2021).

G19.7 Word clouds/infographics

Citation order:

♦ Creator (if available)
♦ Year of publication (in round brackets)
♦ Title of image (in italics)
♦ Available at: DOI *or* URL (Accessed: date)

Examples

Newberry Effective Solutions (2015) and the Health Foundation (2021) offered advice visually.

Health Foundation (2021) *What does the pandemic mean for health and health inequalities?* Available at: https://www.health.org.uk/sites/default/files/2021-02/hf_covid_infographic_blue.png (Accessed: 21 May 2021).

Newberry Effective Solutions (2015) *What does influence mean to you?* Available at: https://www.newberrysolutions.com/the-edge-blog/2015/04/13/what-does-influence-mean-to-you (Accessed: 21 May 2021).

G19.8 Clip art

Note that some citation order details may not always be available.

Citation order:

♦ Producer
♦ Year of publication (in round brackets)
♦ Title of clip art (in italics)
♦ Available at: URL (Accessed: date)

Example

The new 'wellness at work' logo (*Benefits Cliparts* #27587, no date) …

Benefits Cliparts #27587 (no date) Available at: http://clipart-library.com/clipart/4250.htm (Accessed: 15 June 2021).

G19.9 Medical images

Many kinds of medical/anatomical images can be viewed and downloaded from the internet (for example MRI, PET, CT and ultrasound scans, and X-rays) for use in supporting your arguments or demonstrating particular aspects of anatomical or medical information. These would simply be referenced as images available online (see Section G19.3).

Other images may be found in online databases such as *Anatomy TV*. For these, use the following format.

Citation order:

♦ Image title (in italics)
♦ Year (in round brackets)
♦ Medium (in square brackets)
♦ Available at: DOI *or* URL (Accessed: date)

Example

In-text citation

The X-ray and scan (*The Spine*, 2013) clearly showed …

Reference list

The spine (2013) [X-ray and MRI scan]. Available at: http://www.anatomy.tv/new_home.aspx (Accessed: 28 June 2021).

If you have to reference *confidential images*, such as patients' medical scans, anonymise them (as shown in Section G30), and ensure that you have the patients' and hospital's permission to use the images in your text/appendices. In these circumstances, use the following format.

Citation order:

♦ Anonymised patient's name (in square brackets)
♦ Year image produced (in round brackets)
♦ Image title (in italics)
♦ Medium (in square brackets)
♦ Location
♦ Institution

Example

In-text citation

Patient Y's X-ray (2018) …

Reference list

[Patient Y] (2018) *Left knee joint* [X-ray]. Bradford: Bradford Royal Infirmary.

G19.10 Inscriptions

G19.10a Inscriptions on monuments

Provide as much information as possible for another person to locate the gravestone or memorial. In some instances, the plot number of a grave will be obtainable and can be referenced; if not, try to give an indication of the location from a landmark.

Citation order:

♦ Name of deceased (in single quotation marks)
♦ Year of death/event (in round brackets)
♦ [Monument inscription]
♦ Location
♦ (Viewed: date)

Example

In-text citation

The gravestone of the railway engineman ('Oswald Gardiner', 1840) compares him to one of the locomotives he drove: 'My engine now is cold and still. No water does my boiler fill.'

Reference list

'Oswald Gardiner' (1840) [Monument inscription]. St Mary the Virgin Churchyard (5m northwest of church), Whickham, Tyne and Wear (Viewed: 12 August 2018).

G19.10b Inscriptions on structures

Referencing inscriptions on structures can be difficult, as the author may not be identified and the wording may be a quotation from an earlier source. Give as much information as you are able to.

Citation order:

♦ Author (if known); if not, use title of statue/building (in italics)
♦ Year of inscription (in round brackets)
♦ Inscription on (in italics)
♦ Location
♦ (Viewed: date)

Example

In-text citation

Lewis's inscription (2004) is inspirational.

Reference list

Lewis, G. (2004) *Inscription on Wales Millennium Centre*, Cardiff Bay, Cardiff, Wales (Viewed: 8 August 2012).

G19.11 Graffiti

By its nature, graffiti is anonymous, even when the graffitist includes their signature tag. It is usually short-lived artistic expression (or vandalism, depending on one's perspective). As it may be removed at any time, it is essential to include as much information as possible to describe the content, location and date viewed. Be careful if citing offensive language or imagery in graffiti.

Citation order:

♦ Artist (if known, or use title)
♦ Year (in round brackets)
♦ Title or description (with graffitist's tag, if present) (in italics)
♦ [Graffiti]
♦ Location
♦ (Viewed: date)

Example

In-text citation

Banksy (2021) modified his earlier image in tribute to the NHS.

Reference list

Banksy (2020) *The girl with the pierced eardrum with blue face mask (Covid-19)* [Graffiti]. Albion Dockyard, Hanover Place, Bristol, United Kingdom. (Viewed: 20 September 2020).

G19.12 Silhouettes

Citation order:

♦ Artist
♦ Year (in round brackets)
♦ Title of work (in italics)
♦ Medium (in square brackets)
♦ Location
♦ Reference number

If accessed online:

♦ Available at: DOI *or* URL (Accessed: date)

Example

In-text citation

The silhouette (Leslie, 1926) captured the 1920s dress.

Reference list

Leslie, H. (1926) *Doreen Graham* [Silhouette]. National Portrait Gallery, London. NPG D46674. Available at: https://www.npg.org.uk/collections/search/portrait/mw269357 (Accessed: 14 June 2021).

G19.13 Collages

A collage is a new artwork created by mixing material from photography, painting, printed text and artefacts. As with any image, cite what you have seen, for example a photograph on a website, or an original piece of work in a gallery.

Citation order:

♦ Artist
♦ Year (in round brackets)
♦ Title (in italics)
♦ Medium (in square brackets)
♦ Exhibited at
♦ Location and date(s) of presentation

If accessed online:
♦ Available at: DOI *or* URL (Accessed: date)

Examples

In-text citations

His blending of newspaper, photos and paint (Schwitter, 1942; 1947) …

Reference list

Schwitter, K. (1942) *The proposal* [Collage]. Available at: https://www. tate.org.uk/art/artworks/schwitters-the-proposal-t12398 (Accessed: 12 June 2021).

Schwitter, K. (1947) *Big fight.* [Collage]. Exhibited at Victoria & Albert Museum, London.

G19.13a Digital collages

With digital technology, it is possible to modify any image or video to incorporate material from other sources, for example blending photographs, cartoons and paintings to create a new image.

Citation order:

♦ Artist
♦ Date (in round brackets)
♦ Title
♦ Medium (in square brackets]
♦ Location
♦ Available at: DOI *or* URL (Accessed: date)

Examples

In-text citations

The mystical image (Jasmine, no date) …

Hughes's satire (2021) on holidaying at home …

Reference list

Hughes, R. (2020) *Staycation* [Digital collage]. Available at: https://www. rachelhughesfineart.com/work (Accessed: 21 August 2021).

Jasmine (no date) *Wolf girl* [Digital collage]. Available at: https://pixabay. com/en/wolf-girl-large-mystical-fog-mood-2082333/ (Accessed: 21 August 2021).

G19.14 Cinemagraphs

These are still images that incorporate short movements within the frame. They are used in advertising to hold viewers' attention longer than a still image does.

Citation order:

♦ Artist
♦ Year (in round brackets)
♦ Title (in italics)

- Medium (in square brackets)
- Available at: DOI *or* URL (Accessed: date)

In-text citation

mrjonkane (2017) reversed the movement between the hummingbird and its background.

Reference list

mrjonkane (2017) *Summer hummmer in Sonoma, California* [Cinemagraph]. Available at: https://flixel.com/cinemagraph/f1y9e6dsund1ixdnoalm/ (Accessed: 21 May 2021).

G19.15 Body art, including tattoos and Mehndi (henna)

Tattoos are visible in several formats and you should use the citation order for the format in which you saw the image.

For a *photograph of body art in a book*, use the following citation order:

- Author of book
- Year (if available)
- Title of the image, including the figure number (in single quotation marks)
- Title of the book (in italics)
- Place of publication: publisher

Example

In-text citation

The tattoos of a Marquesan warrior (Kuwuhara, 2005, p. 92) …

Reference list

Kuwuhara, M. (2005) *Tattoo: an anthropology*. Oxford: Berg.

For an *online photograph of body art:*

Citation order:

- Photographer (if known)
- Year (if available, in round brackets)
- Title of the image (in single quotation marks)
- Title of the website (in italics)
- Available at: URL (Accessed: date)

Example

In-text citation

The bride's vibrant robes and elaborate Mehndi decoration (NY wedding and events, 2018) …

Reference list

NY wedding and events (2018) 'Flowers', *Latest bridal Mehndi designs*. Available at: https://www.pinterest.co.uk/pin/605874956094393915/ (Accessed: 27 June 2021).

For *body art on a person*, if you have seen the tattoo in person, put the title in italics as you would for a work of art.

Citation order:

- Tattoo artist (if known)
- Year (if available, in round brackets)
- Title of the image (in italics)
- [Tattoo]
- On [name of person]
- Viewed: date (in round brackets)

Example

In-text citation

The image of the eagle (Riley, 2017) …

Reference list

Riley, K. (2017) *Eagle* [Tattoo]. On Kiara James (Viewed: 28 July 2020).

G19.16 Packaging

Citation order:

- Manufacturer
- Year seen (in round brackets)
- Product name (in italics)
- Medium (in square brackets)

Example

In-text citation

A bar of *Toblerone* has 2209kJ of energy per 100g (Mondelez International, 2021).

Reference list

Mondelez International (2021) *Toblerone* [Wrapper].

G19.17 Cartoons

Citation order:

- Artist
- Date (if available)
- Title of cartoon (in single quotation marks)
- [Cartoon]
- Title of publication (in italics)
- Day and month

If accessed online:

- Available at: URL (Accessed: date)

Example

In-text citation

Peter Brookes paid tribute to Captain Sir Tom Moore (2021).

Reference list

Brookes, P. (2021) 'A statue that will last … ' [Cartoon]. *The Times*, 3 February. Available at: https://twitter.com/BrookesTimes/status/1356938191933210624/photo/1 (Accessed: 2 July 2021).

G19.18 Posters

Citation order:

- Artist (if known, or use title)
- Year (in round brackets)
- Title (in italics)
- [Poster]
- Exhibited at
- Location and date(s) of exhibition
- Dimensions (if relevant and available)

Example: poster copy of painting

In-text citation

The image (Chagall, no date) …

Reference list

Chagall, M. (no date) *Le violiniste* [Poster]. 84cm x 48cm.

Example: poster for exhibition

In-text citation

Smith's poster (2003) …

Reference list

Smith, K. (2003) *Prints, books and things* [Poster]. Exhibited at New York, Museum of Modern Art. 5 December 2003 to 8 March 2004.

G19.19 Mood boards

Citation order:

- ◆ Designer (if known)
- ◆ Year (in round brackets)
- ◆ Title (in italics)
- ◆ [Mood board]
- ◆ Presented at
- ◆ Location and date(s) of presentation

If accessed online:

- ◆ Available at: URL (Accessed: date)

Example

In-text citation

His highly effective mood board (Weitzel, 2018) …

Reference list

Weitzel, L. (2018) *Say cheese* [Mood board]. Available at: http://flickr.com/photos/daisies7/5857970176/ (Accessed: 12 June 2021).

G19.20 Postcards

Citation order:

- ◆ Artist (if available)
- ◆ Year (in round brackets if available)
- ◆ Title (in italics)
- ◆ [Postcard]
- ◆ Place of publication: publisher

Example

In-text citation

The flat sandy beach (Corrance, no date) …

Reference list

Corrance, D. (no date) *Gairloch, Wester Ross* [Postcard]. Scotland: Stirling Gallery.

G19.21 Logos

Citation order:

- ◆ Artist/organisation
- ◆ Date (if available)
- ◆ Title of logo (in italics)
- ◆ [Logo]

If accessed online:

- ◆ Available at: URL (Accessed: date)

Example

In-text citation

Twitter's logo (Bowman, 2012) features a blue bird.

Reference list

Bowman, D. (2012) *Twitter bird* [Logo]. Available at: https://about.twitter.com/en/who-we-are/brand-toolkit (Accessed: 23 May 2021).

G19.22 Sewing/knitting patterns

Citation order:

- Producer
- Year (if available)
- Title of the pattern (in italics) with (pattern/design number), if available
- Medium [in square brackets]
- Place of publication: publisher

If accessed online:
- Available at: URL (Accessed: date)

Examples

In-text citations

The two detailed patterns (UK Hand Knitting Association, no date; Simplicity NewLook, 2021) …

Reference list

Simplicity NewLook (2018) *Men's costume coat and hat* (S9096) [Sewing pattern]. Available at: https://www.sewdirect.com/product/s9096/ (Accessed: 22 May 2021).

UK Hand Knitting Association (no date) *Double knitting: cardigans, hat and blanket* (UKHKA 110) [Knitting pattern]. Bingley: UK Hand Knitting Association.

G20 Live performances

G20.1 Concerts

Citation order:

- Composer
- Year of performance (in round brackets)
- Title (in italics)
- Performed by … conducted by …
- [Location. Date seen]

Examples

In-text citations

The Kings of Leon (2008) wowed the crowd …

A wonderful premiere (Lord, 2007) …

Reference list

Kings of Leon (2008) [Glastonbury Festival. 27 June].

Lord, J. (2007) *Durham Concerto*. Performed by the Royal Liverpool Philharmonic Orchestra, conducted by Mischa Damev [Durham Cathedral, Durham. 20 October].

G20.2 Dance

Citation order:

- Name of choreographer or composer
- (chor.) or (comp.)
- Year of performance (in round brackets)
- Title (in italics)
- Directed by (if available)
- Produced by (if available)
- Performed by (dance company, if available)
- [Location. Date seen]

Example

In-text citation

The performance was true to the intentions of its creator (Ashton, 1937).

Reference list

Ashton, F. (chor.) (1937) *A wedding bouquet*. Performed by The Royal Ballet [Royal Opera House, London. 22 October 2004].

G20.3 Plays

Citation order:

♦ Title (in italics)
♦ by Author
♦ Year of performance (in round brackets)
♦ Directed by …
♦ [Location. Date seen]

Example

In-text citation

One innovation was the use of Sellotape for the fairies' webs (*A midsummer night's dream,* 1995).

Reference list

A midsummer night's dream by William Shakespeare (1995) Directed by I. Judge [Theatre Royal, Newcastle upon Tyne. 26 February].

G20.4 Musicals

Citation order:

♦ Composer and choreographer
♦ Year of performance (in round brackets)
♦ Title (in italics)
♦ Other attributions (e.g. Lyrics by … ; directed by …
♦ [Location. Date seen]

Example

In-text citation

Parker and Nicholaw's irreverent comedy (2018) …

Reference list

Parker, T. and Nicholaw, C. (2018) *The book of Mormon*. Lyrics and music by T. Parker, R. Lopez and M. Stone; choreography by C. Nicholaw. [Prince of Wales Theatre, London. 4 May].

G20.5 Circuses

Citation order:

♦ Name of circus
♦ Year of performance
♦ Title of circus (if available, in italics)
♦ Presented by … (if relevant)
♦ [Location. Date seen]

Example

In-text citation

The spectacular circus (Zippos Circus, 2018) …

Reference list

Zippos Circus (2018) *Legacy*. Presented by N. Barrett [London, Gladstone Park, 22 May 2018].

G21 Audio sources

Cite the format for the media you used to listen to audio sources. If available, include the date of the original broadcast as well as the date you accessed the recording. To refer to a specific time within the recording, use a timestamp in the format 'minutes: seconds', as in example G22.1a.

G21.1 Radio

G21.1a Radio programmes

Citation order:

♦ Title of programme (in italics)
♦ Year of transmission (in round brackets)
♦ Transmission channel
♦ Date of transmission (day/month), time of transmission

Example

In-text citation

The minister's response was challenged (*Today*, 2021, 08:40) …

Reference list

Today (2021) BBC Radio 4, 15 August, 06:00.

G21.1b Radio programmes heard online

Radio programmes may be heard live online, or after the original transmission through radio catch-up services, such as the BBC's iPlayer Radio. If available, specify the full date of the original broadcast as well as the date you accessed the programme. See also G22.7.

Citation order:

♦ Title of programme (in italics)
♦ Year of original transmission (in round brackets)
♦ Transmission channel
♦ Day and month of original transmission (if available)
♦ Available at: DOI *or* URL (Accessed: date)

Example

In-text citation

Throughout the show, Jack Dee had the audience in stitches (*I'm Sorry I Haven't a Clue*, 2021) …

Reference list

I'm sorry I haven't a clue (2021) BBC Radio 4, 14 June. Available at: https://www.bbc.co.uk/programmes/m000wz2p (Accessed: 21 June 2021).

G21.2 Podcasts

Citation order:

♦ Author/presenter
♦ Year that the site was published/last updated (in round brackets)
♦ Title of podcast (in italics)
♦ [Podcast]
♦ Day/month of posted message
♦ Available at: URL (Accessed: date)

Example

In-text citation

Professor Baliga's research (Hussain, 2021) highlighted ...

Reference list

Hussain, M. M. (2021) *IEEE EDS podcasts with luminaries: episode 2: Prof. Jayant Baliga* [Podcast]. 25 January. Available at: https://www.podbean.com/media/share/pb-vu8en-f88e6e. (Accessed: 18 April 2021).

G21.3 Music streaming services

Music downloads are available from a range of different websites, including Spotify, YouTube Music, Tidal, Qobuz, Primephonic, Amazon Music, Apple Music, SoundCloud, Deezer and iTunes.

Citation order:

♦ Artist name (individual, band, orchestra etc.)
♦ Year of release (in round brackets)
♦ Title of song/track title (if required, in single quotation marks)

♦ Title of album (if required, in italics)
♦ Available at: name of streaming service
♦ (Accessed: date)

Example: track from an album

In-text citation

The exceptional track (Girl in Red, 2021) ...

Reference list

Girl in Red (2021) 'Apartment 402', *If I could make it go quiet*. Available at: Spotify (Accessed: 5 May 2021).

Example: whole albums

In-text citation

Girl in Red's new album (2021) ...

Reference list

Girl in Red (2021) *If I could make it go quiet*. Available at: Spotify (Accessed: 12 May 2021).

G21.4 Recordings on CD, audio cassettes or vinyl

If you are citing a single track on an album, add this before the title of the album.

Citation order:

♦ Artist/composer
♦ Year of publication (in round brackets)
♦ Title of song/track (if required, in single quotation marks)

- Title of album (in italics)
- [format]
- Additional notes if required
- Place of distribution: distribution company

Examples

In-text citations

She chose contrasting music from Mahler (1994) and Mary Carpenter (2004).

Reference list

Carpenter, M.C. (2004) 'My heaven', *Between here and gone* [CD]. New York: Columbia Records.

Mahler, G. (1994) *Symphony No. 10* [Audio cassette]. BBC National Orchestra of Wales, conducted by M. Wigglesworth. 26 November 1993. London: BBC.

G21.5 Musical scores and librettos

Citation order:

- Composer or librettist
- Year of publication (in round brackets)
- Title of publication (in italics)
- [Medium]
- Notes (if required)
- Place of publication: publisher

Examples

In-text citations

Mendelssohn's evocation of the sea in *The Hebrides* (1999) …

Sterbini's libretto (1962) added …

Reference list

Mendelssohn, F. (1999) *The Hebrides* [Musical score]. Edited from composer's notes by J. Wilson. London: Initial Music Publishing.

Sterbini, C. (1962) *The barber of Seville: a comic opera in three acts* [Libretto]. Music composed by G. Rossini. English version by R. Martin and T. Martin. New York: G. Schirmer.

G21.6 Lyrics from songs/hymns

Citation order:

- Lyricist
- Year of release (in round brackets)
- Title of song (in italics)
- Place of distribution: distribution company

Example

In-text citation

Lennon and McCartney (1966) expressed the frustration of every new author: 'Dear Sir or Madam, will you read my book? It took me years to write, will you take a look?'

Reference list

Lennon, J. and McCartney, P. (1966) *Paperback writer*. Liverpool: Northern Songs Ltd.

G21.7 Liner notes

Citation order:

- Author
- Year (in round brackets)
- Title of liner notes text (in single quotation marks)
- 'In'
- Title of recording (in italics)
- [CD liner notes]
- Place of distribution: distribution company

Example

In-text citation

Thrills (1997, p. 11) described Weller's lyrics as 'sheer poetry'.

Reference list

Thrills, A. (1997) 'What a catalyst he turned out to be'. In *The very best of The Jam* [CD liner notes]. London: Polydor.

G22 Audiovisual recordings, including broadcasts, streaming/sharing services, DVDs and videos

G22.1 Television

For television programmes viewed via video streaming (catch-up TV or subscription) services, e.g. Netflix, (Amazon) Prime Video, BBC iPlayer, Box of Broadcasts, see Section G22.2.

G22.1a Television programmes

Citation order:

- Title of programme (in italics)
- Year of transmission (in round brackets)
- Transmission channel
- Date of transmission (day/month), time of transmission

Example: individual programme

In-text citation

The embarrassing corporate wannabes (*The Apprentice*, 2017) …

Reference list

The Apprentice (2017) BBC One Television, 23 September, 21:00.

Example: to quote something a character/presenter has said

In-text citation

'You're fired!' (Sugar, 2017) …

Reference list

Sugar, A. (2017) *The Apprentice*. BBC One Television, 23 June, 21:00.

G22.1b Episodes of a television series

Citation order:

- Title of episode (in single quotation marks) if known; if not, use series title
- Year of transmission (in round brackets)
- Title of programme/series (in italics)
- Series and episode numbers
- Transmission channel
- Date of transmission (day/month), time of transmission

Example

In-text citation

The brilliantly crafted episode ('Don't forget the sea', 2020) …

Reference list

'Don't forget the sea' (2020) *I may destroy you*, series 1, episode 3. BBC One Television. 15 June, 21:00.

G22.1c Television programmes/series on DVD/Blu-ray

Citation order:

♦ Title of episode (in single quotation marks)
♦ Year of distribution (in round brackets)
♦ Title of programme/series (in italics)
♦ Series and episode numbers (if known)
♦ Date of original transmission (if known)
♦ [DVD, catalogue number] *or* [Blu-ray, catalogue number]
♦ Place of distribution: distribution company

Example

In-text citation

The origins of the Doctor's most fearsome foe were revealed in 'Genesis of the Daleks' (2006).

Reference list

'Genesis of the daleks' (2006) *Doctor Who*, episode 1. First broadcast 1975 [DVD]. London: BBC DVD.

G22.1d Separate episodes from DVD/Blu-ray box sets

Citation order:

♦ Title of episode (in single quotation marks)
♦ Year of distribution (in round brackets)
♦ Title of programme/series (in italics)
♦ 'In'
♦ Title of compilation or box set (in italics)
♦ [Medium]
♦ Place of distribution: Distributor

Example

In-text citation

Close attention was paid to period details ('Episode 8', 2014) …

Reference list

'Episode 8' (2014) *Downton Abbey* In *Downton Abbey series 5* [DVD]. London: Universal Pictures UK.

G22.2 Programmes viewed through streaming services

These can include catch-up services like Box of Broadcasts, BBC iPlayer, ITV Hub, All 4, My5 and subscription services such as Netflix, (Amazon) Prime Video, Disney+ and Now TV. You do not need to refer to the device you have used to view the video; the examples below illustrate the elements required to reference this material correctly and consistently.

G22.2a Programmes

Citation order:

♦ Title of programme (in italics)
♦ Year of original broadcast (in round brackets)
♦ Production company
♦ Available at: name of streaming service
♦ (Accessed: date)

Example: single programme

In-text citation

The industry was crippled by the pandemic (*Billion Pound Cruises: All at Sea*, 2021).

Reference list

Billion pound cruises: all at sea (2021) ITV. Available at: ITV Hub (Accessed: 5 June 2021).

G22.2b Episode from a series

Citation order:

♦ Title of episode (in single quotation marks) if known; if not, use series title
♦ Year of original broadcast (in round brackets)
♦ Title of series/season (in italics)
♦ Series/season and episode numbers, or day month (if available)
♦ Production company
♦ Available at: name of streaming service
♦ (Accessed: date)

Example: Amazon Prime

In-text citation

The brilliantly paced episode ('God sees', 2017) highlighted …

Reference list

'God sees' (2017) *Bosch*, series 3, episode 3. Amazon Studios. Available at: Amazon Prime Video (Accessed: 5 March 2021).

Example: NowTV

In-text citation

Moss's heart-breaking performance ('The last ceremony', 2018) …

Reference list

'The last ceremony' (2018) *The handmaid's tale,* season 2, episode 10. MGM Television. Available at: NowTV (Accessed: 16 February 2021).

Example: Netflix

In-text citation

Princess Margaret's love life was exposed in 'Gloriana' (2016).

Reference list

'Gloriana' (2016) *The Crown*, season 1, episode 10. Netflix. Available at: Netflix (Accessed 24 May 2021).

Example: BBC iPlayer

In-text citation

In 'Space: how far can we go?' (2018) Cox stated …

Reference list

'Space: how far can we go?' (2018) *Brian Cox's adventures in space and time*, 30 May. BBC One. Available at: BBC iPlayer (Accessed: 5 June 2021).

Example: Box of Broadcasts

In-text citation

Simon Schama's exploration of the Renaissance ('The Triumph of Art', 2018) …

Reference list

'The triumph of art' (2018) *Civilisations*, episode 5, BBC Two, 1 March. Available at: Box of Broadcasts (Accessed 5 June 2021).

G22.3 Films

G22.3a Films viewed at the cinema

Citation order:

♦ Title of film (in italics)
♦ Year of distribution (in round brackets)
♦ Directed by …
♦ [Feature film]
♦ Place of distribution: distribution company

Example

In-text citation

Movies were used to attack President Bush's policies (*Fahrenheit 9/11*, 2004).

Reference list

Fahrenheit 9/11 (2004) Directed by M. Moore. [Feature film]. Santa Monica, CA: Lions Gate Films.

G22.3b Films viewed via streaming services

Citation order:

♦ Title of film (in italics)
♦ Year of distribution (in round brackets)
♦ Directed by …
♦ Available at: DOI *or* name of service *or* URL (Accessed: date)

Example

In-text citation

The hero (*Black Panther*, 2018) …

Reference list

Black panther (2018) Directed by R. Coogler. Available at: Netflix (Accessed: 5 June 2021).

G22.3c Films on DVD/Blu-ray and video cassette

Citation order:

♦ Title of film (in italics)
♦ Year of distribution (in round brackets)
♦ Directed by …
♦ [Medium]
♦ Place of distribution: distribution company

Examples

Besson's film *La Femme Nikita* (1990) and *The Fifth Element* (1997) have strong female leads.

La femme Nikita (1990) Directed by J. Besson. [Video cassette]. Culver City, CA: Columbia TristarWarner Bros.

The fifth element (1997) Directed by J. Besson. [DVD]. Los Angeles, CA: Twentieth Century Fox.

For *films that have been reissued*, use the following format.

Citation order:

♦ Title of film (in italics)
♦ Year of original film distribution (in round brackets)
♦ Directed by …
♦ [Medium]
♦ Reissued
♦ Place of distribution: distributor company
♦ Year of reissue

Example

… in this breathtaking, poetic film (*Pink Narcissus*, 1971).

Pink narcissus (1971) Directed by J. Bidgood. [DVD, BFIVD620]. Reissued. London: BFI, 2007.

Thus, just the year of the original film distribution is given in-text. The reference list also includes the date of reissue.

Many films on DVD/Blu-ray come with additional material on other disks, such as interviews with actors and directors and outtakes. Sections G22.3d–e give examples for referencing some of this material.

G22.3d Directors' commentaries on DVD/Blu-ray

Citation order:

♦ Name of commentator
♦ Year (in round brackets)
♦ Director's commentary (in single quotation marks)
♦ Name of film (in italics)
♦ Directed by …
♦ [Medium]
♦ Place of distribution: distribution company

Example

The director enjoyed making the film (Besson, 1997).

Besson, J. (1997) 'Director's commentary', *The fifth element*. Directed by J. Besson [DVD]. Los Angeles, CA: Twentieth Century Fox.

G22.3e Interviews with film directors

Citation order:

♦ Name of person interviewed
♦ Year of interview (in round brackets)

- Title of the interview (if any) (in single quotation marks)
- Interview with/interviewed by
- Interviewer's name
- Title of film (in italics)
- [Medium]
- Place of distribution: distribution company

If accessed online:
- Available at: DOI *or* name of service *or* URL (Accessed: date)

Example

In-text citation

Besson (1997) praised Jojovich's performance.

Reference list

Besson, L. (1997) Interviewed by L. Jones. *The fifth element* [DVD]. Los Angeles, CA: Twentieth Century Fox.

G22.4 Online video sharing platforms, including YouTube, Vimeo, IGTV, Dailymotion, TED

Citation order:

- Name of person or organisation posting video
- Year video posted (in round brackets)
- Title of film or programme (in italics)
- Date uploaded (if available)
- Available at: DOI *or* name of streaming service/app *or* URL (Accessed: date)

Example: whole video

In-text citation

Professor González inspired her audience (Cambridge Cosmology, 2021).

Reference list

Cambridge Cosmology (2021) *Professor Gabriella González: Black holes and gravitational waves.* 12 January. Available at: https://www.youtube.com/watch?v=Txuq1sO8fkY (Accessed: 5 May 2021).

To *highlight a specific place in the recording*, use a timestamp in the in-text citation. The reference list entry will be the same as above.

Example: specific part of video

In-text citation

The professor described 'Gravity's symphony' (Cambridge Cosmology, 2021, 27:45).

G22.5 Online presentations

Citation order:

- Author
- Year (in round brackets)
- Title of communication (in italics)
- Medium (in square brackets)
- Available at: URL (Accessed: date)
- If you wish to cite the contents of a specific slide, do this in the in-text citation.

Example

The fifteen endangered species listed by Mahindrakar (2013, slide 22) …

Mahindrakar, R. (2013) *Biodiversity of India* [PowerPoint presentation]. Available at: https://www.slideshare.net/RameshMahindrakar/biodiversity-of-india (Accessed: 16 August 2020).

G22.6 Vodcasts/vidcasts

Vodcasts include video as well as audio in the recording.

Citation order:

♦ Author
♦ Year that the site was published/last updated (in round brackets)
♦ Title of vodcast (in italics)
♦ [Vodcast]
♦ Available at: URL (Accessed: date)

Example

Chopra and Barnett (no date) gave advice in their vodcast.

Chopra, A. and Barnett, C. (no date) *Making SEN appeals* [Vodcast]. Available at: https://cpotential.org.uk/services/making-sen-appeals/ (Accessed: 19 June 2021).

G22.7 Screencasts

These are digital recordings of computer screen activity that provide instructions for using software applications.

Citation order:

♦ Author/narrator
♦ Year of production (in round brackets)
♦ Title of screencast (in italics)
♦ [Screencast]
♦ Available at: URL (Accessed: date)

Example

An online video demonstrated how to add bookmarks (Holmes, 2021).

Holmes, R.K. (2021) *Installing the bookmarking tool* [Screencast]. Available at: https://durham.cloud.panopto.eu/Panopto/Pages/Viewer.aspx?id=a299efa8-924d-4bd6-a91f-ad0a010556f3 (Accessed: 16 June 2021).

G23 Computer/video games, computer programs and mobile apps

G23.1 Computer/video games

Citation order:

♦ Company/individual developer
♦ Release year (in round brackets)
♦ Title of game (in italics and capitalise initial letters – include edition if relevant)

♦ [Video game]
♦ Publisher

If accessed online:

♦ Available at DOI *or* URL (Accessed: date)

Example

The launch of *Halo: the Master Chief Collection* (2020) …

343 Industries (2020) *Halo: the master chief collection* [Video game]. Microsoft Studios. Available at: https://www.xbox.com/en-GB/ games/halo-the-master-chief-collection (Accessed: 28 May 2021).

G23.2 Computer programs

Citation order:

♦ Author (if given)
♦ Date – if given (in round brackets)
♦ Title of program (in italics and capitalise initial letters)
♦ Version (in round brackets)
♦ [Computer program]
♦ Availability, that is, distributor, address, order number (if given)

If accessed online:

♦ Available at: DOI *or* URL (Accessed: date)

Example

Camtasia 2020 (TechSmith, 2021) can be used to record tutorials.

TechSmith Corporation (2021) *Camtasia 2020* (Version 2021.0.0) [Computer program]. Available at: https://www.techsmith.com/video-editor.html (Accessed: 21 June 2021).

G23.3 Mobile apps

Use the name of the producer of the app if available. If not, use the title of the app as the first element.

Citation order:

♦ Developer
♦ Year of release/update (in round brackets)
♦ Title of app (in italics and capitalise initial letters)
♦ Edition and/or version number (in round brackets)
♦ [Mobile app]
♦ Available at: URL (Accessed: date)

Example

With the *NHS COVID-19 app* (NHS Digital, 2020) you can check in to a venue …

NHS Digital (2020) *NHS COVID-19 app* (Version 4.9 (185)) [Mobile app]. Available at: https://play.google.com/store/apps/details?id=uk.nhs.covid19.production (Accessed: 26 May 2021).

G24 Organisation and personal websites, blogs and wikis

When referencing information you have retrieved from the internet, *you must distinguish what you are referring to*. The internet is made up of organisation and personal websites, government publications, ebooks and journal articles, images, company data, presentations – a vast range of material. Examples of how to reference individual sources, such as journal articles, ebooks and images, are given with the entries for those sources. In this section, you will find examples of how to cite and reference websites and web pages produced by individuals and organisations.

The nature of what you are referring to will govern how you cite or reference it. You should aim to provide sufficient information for a reader to be able to locate your information source. As material on the internet can be removed or changed, you should also note the date when you accessed/viewed the information – it might not be there in a few months' time.

Remember to evaluate all internet information for Accuracy, Currency, Objectivity, Relevance and Named authors (ACORN, see Section B). The ability to publish information on the internet bears no relation to the author's academic abilities.

The defining element in referencing a web page is its Uniform Resource Locator (URL). This should be included in your reference list, but do not include the URL in your in-text citation, unless this is the only piece of information you have.

Generally, web pages do not have page numbers. To help your reader locate where you have quoted or paraphrased from a website, you can number the paragraphs on the page and include the paragraph in your in-text citation.

Example

Lomotey (2018, para. 4) said 'the children remained calm like professionals'.

Lomotey, D. (2018) *Behind the scenes of one girl's journey*. Available at: https://www.actionaid.org.uk/blog/news/2018/10/22/behind-the-scenes-of-one-girls-journey (Accessed: 27 May 2021).

G24.1 Websites and web pages with individual authors

Citation order:

♦ Author
♦ Year the site was published/last updated (in round brackets)
♦ Title of website or web page (in italics)
♦ Available at: URL (Accessed: date)

Example: whole website

In-text citation

Professor Verlet's (2021) research profile …

Reference list

Verlet, J.R.R. (2021) *GroupVerlet*. Available at: http://www.verlet.net/ (Accessed: 14 May 2021).

Example: specific web page within website

In-text citation

He researches anion formation (Verlet, 2021).

Reference list

Verlet, J.R.R. (2021) *Dynamics of anion formation*. Available at: http://www.verlet.net/edc.html (Accessed: 14 May 2021).

G24.2 Websites with organisations as authors

Example

In-text citation

After identifying symptoms (National Health Service, 2021) …

Reference list

National Health Service (2021) *Coronavirus (COVID-19)*. Available at: https://www.nhs.uk/conditions/coronavirus-covid-19/ (Accessed: 17 May 2021).

G24.3 Websites with no authors

Use the title of the web page.

Example

In-text citation

Illustrations of the houses can be found online (*Palladio's Italian Villas*, 2005).

Reference list

Palladio's Italian villas (2005) Available at: http://www.boglewood.com/palladio/ (Accessed: 23 August 2018).

G24.4 Websites with no dates

If the web page has no obvious date of publication/revision, use the author (no date) and the date you accessed the page. You might question how useful undated information is to your research as it may be out of date.

Example

In-text citation

Compression may be required (Flixel, no date).

Reference list

Flixel (no date) *Magical tools for visual storytelling*. Available at: https://flixel.com/company/ (Accessed: 1 June 2021).

G24.5 Websites with no authors or titles

If no author or title can be identified, you should use the web page's URL. It may be possible to shorten a very long URL, as long as the route remains clear, but it may be necessary to give the full URL even in your citation. *If a web page has no author or title, it is unlikely to be suitable for academic work.*

Example

In-text citation

A site of dubious information (http://www.unknownprovenance.com, 2018) …

Reference list

http://www.unknownprovenance.com (2018) (Accessed: 14 May 2021).

G24.6 Blogs/vlogs

Blogs (weblogs) and vlogs (video logs) are produced by individuals and organisations to provide updates on issues of interest or concern. Be aware that, because blogs/vlogs are someone's opinions, they may not provide objective, reasoned discussion of an issue. Use blogs/vlogs in conjunction with reputable sources. Note that, due to the informality of the internet, many authors give first names or aliases. Use the name they have used in your reference.

Citation order:

♦ Author of message
♦ Year the site was last updated (in round brackets)
♦ Title of blog post (in single quotation marks)
♦ Title of internet site (in italics)
♦ Day/month of posted message
♦ Available at: URL (Accessed: date)

Example

In-text citation

The appraisal of Greta by Davies (2019) …

Reference list

Davies, C. (2019) 'Inspiring thursday: Greta Thunberg', *Wave blog*, 24 October. Available at: https://blog.wave-network.org/inspiring-thursday-greta-thunberg (Accessed: 11 May 2021).

G24.7 Wikis

Wikis are collaborative websites in which several (usually unidentified) authors can add and edit the information presented. What you read today may have changed by tomorrow. There have also been instances of false information being presented, although wiki editors try to ensure that the information is authentic. Wikis can be useful to get an overview of a topic, but check with your tutor if you are permitted to cite information in wikis. If you are going to use information from a wiki, *make sure that it is thoroughly referenced*. As with other websites, if no references are given, the information is unlikely to be suitable for academic work. Evaluate wiki information against sources of proven academic quality such as books and journal articles.

Citation order:

♦ Title of article (in single quotation marks)
♦ Year the entry was published/last updated (in round brackets)
♦ Title of wiki site (in italics)
♦ Available at: URL (Accessed: date)

Example

In-text citation

Telford introduced new techniques of bridge construction ('Thomas Telford', 2021).

Reference list

'Thomas Telford' (2021) *Wikipedia*. Available at: http://en.wikipedia.org/wiki/Thomas_Telford (Accessed: 2 June 2021).

G25 Public communications

These include lectures, seminars, webinars, PowerPoint presentations, videoconferences/electronic discussion groups, bulletin boards/press releases, announcements/leaflets, advertisements/display boards and RSS feeds.

NB: For communications in VLEs, see Section G7.

G25.1 Live lectures

Use this format for lectures, seminars, conference speeches and poster presentations you saw live, either in person or virtually via Zoom/Teams/Skype etc., which are unavailable in a published source you can direct your reader to.

NB: For live and recorded lectures as part of your course, see Section G7.1 and G7.2. For lectures that were recorded and are publicly available as videos, see Section G22.4.

Citation order:

♦ Author/speaker
♦ Year (in round brackets)
♦ Title of communication (in italics)
♦ Medium (in square brackets)
♦ Institution or venue
♦ Day/month

Examples

Stanton (2018) illustrated …

The keynote address by Professor Miklos Vasarhelyi (2019) …

Stanton, J. (2018) *Wordsworth's imagination* [Lecture]. Durham Book Festival, Gala Theatre, Durham. 18 September.

Vasarhelyi, M. (2019) *Disruption in (accounting) education* [Lecture]. British Accounting and Finance Association Accounting Education Special Interest Group Conference, Brighton, Sussex, 2 May.

G25.2 Electronic discussion groups and bulletin boards

The examples in Sections G25.2–3 deal with email correspondence made public in electronic conferences, discussion groups and bulletin boards.

NB: For personal email correspondence, see Section G27.

Citation order:

♦ Author of message
♦ Year of message (in round brackets)
♦ Subject of the message (in single quotation marks)
♦ Discussion group or bulletin board (in italics)
♦ Date posted: day/month
♦ Available email: email address

Example

Debt cancellation was discussed by Peters (2021) …

Peters, W.R. (2021) 'International finance questions', *British Business School Librarians Group discussion list*, 11 March. Available email: lisbusiness@ jiscmail.com.

G25.3 Entire discussion groups or bulletin boards

Citation order:

♦ List name (in italics)
♦ Year of last update (in round brackets)
♦ Available email: email address
♦ (Accessed: date)

Example

The *Photography News List* (2021) …

Photography news list (2021). Available email: pnl@btinfonet (Accessed: 3 April 2021).

G25.4 Leaflets

By their nature, leaflets are unlikely to have all the citation/reference elements, so include as much information as possible. It may also be useful to include a copy of the leaflet in an appendix to your assignment.

Citation order:

♦ Author (individual or corporate)
♦ Date (if available – in round brackets)
♦ Title (in italics)
♦ [Leaflet]
♦ Date obtained

Example

In-text citation

Shared Interest (no date) campaign for fair trade farmers.

Reference list

Shared Interest (no date) *Make your money count*. [Leaflet]. 4 June 2021.

G25.5 Advertisements

If referencing information in an advertisement, you will need to specify where it was seen. This might be online, in a newspaper, on television or in a location. Advertisements are often short-lived, so it is important to include the date you viewed them.

Citation order:

♦ Cite and reference according to the medium in which the advertisement appeared (see examples)

Examples

In-text citations

Advertisements by QuickBooks (2021), Rightmove (2021) and Northern Electric (2021) and in *The Guardian* (2021) …

Reference list

Television advertisement

QuickBooks (2021) [Advertisement on ITV1 television]. 23 May.

Internet advertisement

Rightmove (2021) *Selling your house?* [Advertisement]. Available at http://www.hotmail.com (Accessed: 13 February 2021).

Billboard advertisement

Northern Electric plc (2021) *Green energy* [Billboard at Ellison Road, Dunston-on-Tyne]. 14 January.

Newspaper advertisement

The Guardian (2021) 'Can't get decent broadband where you live? Try konnect' [Advertisement]. 1 May, p. 33.

G25.6 Display boards, for example in museums

It is rare for an author to be given for information on display boards, so the example uses the title first.

Citation order:

♦ Title (in italics)
♦ Year of production (if available – in round brackets)

- Display board at
- Name of venue, city
- Date observed

Example

In-text citation

Martin's vivid colours are a noted feature of his work (*Paintings of John Martin*, 2017).

Reference list

Paintings of John Martin (2017) Display board at Laing Art Gallery exhibition, Newcastle upon Tyne, 23 June 2021.

G26 Social media

You should apply the ACORN criteria (Section G24) to decide if social media content is suitable for your academic work. If in doubt, ask your tutor.

Some social media information is publicly accessible, while other sources are private and can only be seen by message recipients or group members. If you are citing these restricted sources, you may wish to include a copy of the communication as an appendix to your work, so that readers without access to the original can read it. You should seek permission from other parties in the correspondence before quoting them in your work.

For sites that are publicly accessible, you can cite the whole site, or an individual post.

G26.1 Whole social media sites

Citation order:

- Author (if available; if not use title)
- Year site was last updated (in round brackets)
- Title of site (in italics)
- [Name of platform]
- Available at: URL (Accessed: date)

Example

In-text citation

Facebook and other social media are used in university communications (*University of Canberra*, 2021).

Reference list

University of Canberra (2021) [Facebook]. Available at: https://www.facebook.com/UniversityOfCanberra (Accessed: 6 June 2021).

G26.2 Social media posts: Facebook, Twitter, Weibo, TikTok

Citation order:

- Author of post
- Year posted (in round brackets)
- Title or description of post (in single quotation marks)
- [Name of platform]
- Day/month posted
- Available at: URL (Accessed: date)

Example: Facebook post

In-text citation

Marina Martiniello (2021) spoke of her experiences as an Aboriginal woman.

Reference list

Martiniello, M. (2021) 'I learnt very early on that there's only power to words, if you give power to those words' [Facebook] 27 February. Available at: https://www.facebook.com/UniversityOfCanberra (Accessed: 6 June 2021).

Example: Twitter

In-text citation

Stephen Fry (2021) tweeted his support for young people's mental health.

Reference list

Fry, S. (2021) 'Mental health services for children & young people are struggling to meet the need for help.' [Twitter] 1 June. Available at: https://twitter.com/stephenfry/status/1399667041250906121 (Accessed: 5 June 2021).

Example: Weibo

In-text citation

Durham University Physics Department (2021) posted an image of galaxies merging.

Reference list

Durham University Physics Department (2021) '之天文学 ——星系合并可能会限制恒星的形成' [Weibo] 14 January. Available at: https://www.weibo.com/durhamuni (Accessed: 5 June 2021).

Example: TikTok

In-text citation

Students give peer-to-peer revision advice (University of Melbourne, 2021).

Reference list

University of Melbourne (2021) 'Biomed student @felicitynotes shares this awesome study hack – spaced repetition!' [TikTok]. 28 April. Available at: https://www.tiktok.com/@unimelb/video/6956096029867412738. (Accessed: 2 June 2021).

G27 Personal communications, including private messaging services and unrecorded conversations

If the information is not publicly accessible, cite it as a personal communication. This includes verbal conversations in person, by phone, Skype, FaceTime, unrecorded conversations via Zoom or Teams, email, text message, letter or fax, and any service that requires registration or invitation before the information can be accessed, such as Snapchat/WhatsApp/Signal/Threema/WeChat/Telegram/Wire.

Citation order:

♦ Sender/speaker/author
♦ Year of communication (in round brackets)
♦ Medium of communication
♦ Receiver of communication
♦ Day/month of communication

Examples

In-text citation

This was suggested by Walters (2021).

Reference list

Walters, F. (2021) Facebook/Snapchat/WhatsApp/Signal/Threema/WeChat/ Telegram/Wire message to John Stephens, 6 June.

Walters, F. (2021) Conversation with John Stephens, 13 August.

Walters, F. (2021) Letter to John Stephens, 23 January.

Walters, F. (2021) Email to John Stephens, 14 August.

Walters, F. (2021) Telephone conversation with John Stephens, 25 January.

Walters, F. (2021) Skype conversation with John Stephens, 21 June.

Walters, F. (2021) FaceTime conversation with John Stephens, 21 June.

Walters, F. (2021) Text message to John Stephens, 14 June.

Walters, F. (2021) Fax to John Stephens, 17 December.

G28 Unpublished documents, including hard copy, on intranets and files shared online between group members

'Unpublished' is generally understood as meaning 'not in the public domain'. This section includes a number of the most commonly used unpublished documents. Documents that are available only in hard copy, or held on an organisation's intranet, or distributed only to certain members of a group or organisation in print or online, should be treated as unpublished sources as they are inaccessible to anyone outside the organisation (or even within the organisation if they do not have permission to access it). This includes documents such as minutes of meetings shared through online services such as Sharepoint, Onedrive, Dropbox and WeTransfer. Although these are online, it would be difficult for anyone outside the organisation or group to read the document. If you have permission from other group members, these sources could be included at the end of your work as an appendix.

NB: For published reports, see Section G9.

Citation order:

♦ Author or organisation
♦ Year produced (in round brackets)
♦ Title of report, document or file (in single quotation marks)
♦ Name of organisation
♦ Unpublished

Examples

In-text citations

Jones (2020, item 3.1) suggested work shadowing.

The editor sent the proofs through Dropbox (Fern, 2021).

Reference list

Fern, R.W. (2021) 'Article 10, 2021'. Society of Antiquaries of Newcastle upon Tyne. Unpublished.

Jones, T. (2020) 'Minutes of staff development committee meeting 23 February 2020'. Western Health Trust, Shrewsbury. Unpublished.

G29 Student assignments

You should check with your tutor if it is acceptable to cite your own or other students' assignments.

For theses, see Section G4.

Citation order:

♦ Student name
♦ Year of submission (in round brackets)
♦ Title of essay/assignment (in single quotation marks)

♦ Assignment for
♦ Module and degree (in italics)
♦ Institution
♦ Unpublished

Example

In-text citation

The topic of the essay (Sanders, 2021) …

Reference list

Sanders, M. (2021) 'An examination of the factors influencing air routes and the siting of international airports'. Assignment for *GEM1092, BSc. Geography and environmental management,* City University. Unpublished.

G30 Confidential information

In many cases, you will need to anonymise the person or institution involved. In medical situations, for example, you may use terms such as 'Subject 1', 'Patient X' or 'Baby J' instead of real names; or 'Placement school', 'Placement hospital' or 'Placement agency' instead of actual institutions. These documents are likely to be unpublished.

Citation order:

♦ Anonymised institution/agency (in square brackets)
♦ Year produced (in round brackets)
♦ Anonymised title (in italics) (use square brackets for the anonymised part)
♦ Location
♦ Anonymised producer (in square brackets)
♦ Unpublished

If providing the town or city name is likely to identify a specific institution, you can simply insert the county, for example Lancashire: [Placement hospital].

You may be asked by your tutor to supply them with the agency/employer name if there is any doubt about the authenticity of your reference.

NB: See Section G19.9 for information relating to using and referencing medical images.

G31 Genealogical sources

Many archive and genealogical sources are available online, but the majority of these unique sources exist only in physical form in archives and record offices.

G31.1 Birth, marriage and death certificates

Citation order:

♦ Name of person (in single quotation marks)
♦ Year of event (in round brackets)
♦ Certified copy of … certificate for … (in italics)

♦ Full name of person (forenames, surname) (in italics)
♦ Day/month/year of event (in italics)
♦ Application number from certificate
♦ Location of register office

If you retrieved the certificate online, add:

♦ Year of last update (in round brackets)
♦ Available at: URL (Accessed: date)

G31.2 Wills

Citation order:

♦ Title of document (in italics)
♦ Year of will (in round brackets)
♦ Name of archive or repository
♦ Reference number

If accessed online:

♦ Available at: URL (Accessed: date)

If the exact URL is behind a paywall or password control, give the general URL of the website.

Examples

Michael inherited the estate from his father (*Will of John Doubleday of Alnwick Abbey, Northumberland*, 1752) and bequeathed it to his nephews (*Will of Michael Doubleday of Alnwick Abbey, Northumberland*, 1797).

Reference list

Will of John Doubleday of Alnwick Abbey, Northumberland (1752) Durham University Library & Collections. Catalogue reference: DPR/I/1/1752/D3/1-6. Available at: https://www.familysearch.org (Accessed: 6 June 2021).

Will of Michael Doubleday of Alnwick Abbey, Northumberland (1797) The National Archives: Public Record Office. Catalogue reference: PROB/11/1290.

G31.3 Censuses

Citation order:

♦ Name of person (in single quotation marks)
♦ Year of census (in round brackets)
♦ Census return for (in italics)
♦ Street, place, registration subdistrict, county (in italics)
♦ Public Record Office:
♦ Piece number, folio number, page number

If you retrieved the information online, add:

♦ Year of last update (in round brackets)
♦ Available at: URL (Accessed: date)

Example

In-text citation

Thomas Wilson moved to Willington in the 1850s ('Thomas Wilson', 1861).

Reference list

'Thomas Wilson' (1861) *Census return for New Row, Willington, St Oswald subdistrict, County Durham.* Public Record Office: PRO RG9/3739, folio 74, p. 11 (2008). Available at: http://www.ancestry.co.uk (Accessed: 23 July 2021).

G31.4 Parish registers

Citation order:

♦ Name of person(s) (in single quotation marks)
♦ Year of event (in round brackets)
♦ Baptism, marriage or burial of
♦ Full name of person(s) (forenames, surname)
♦ Day/month/year of event
♦ Title of register (in italics)

If you retrieved the certificate online, add:

♦ Year of last update (in round brackets)
♦ Available at: URL (Accessed: date)

Example

Mary and Edward's wedding ('Edward Robson and Mary Slack', 1784) …

'Edward Robson and Mary Slack' (1784) Marriage of Edward Robson and Mary Slack, 6 May 1784. *St Augustine's Church Alston, Cumberland marriage register 1784–1812* (2004). Available at: http://www.genuki.org.uk/big/eng/CUL/Alston/MALS1701.html (Accessed: 13 July 2021).

G31.5 Military records

Citation order:

♦ Name of person (in single quotation marks)
♦ Year of publication (in round brackets)
♦ Title of publication (in italics)
♦ Publication details

If accessed online:

♦ Available at: URL (Accessed: date)

Example

Private Wakenshaw fought on even after losing his arm ('Adam Herbert Wakenshaw VC', 2008).

'Adam Herbert Wakenshaw VC' (2008) *Commonwealth War Graves Commission casualty details*. Available at: https://www.cwgc.org/find-records/find-war-dead/casualty-details/2212745/ADAM%20HERBERT%20WAKENSHAW/ (Accessed: 21 June 2021).

G32 Manuscripts and archive sources

G32.1 Individual manuscripts

If *the author of a manuscript is known*, use the following.

Citation order:

♦ Author
♦ Year (in round brackets)
♦ Title of manuscript (in italics)
♦ Date (if available)
♦ Name of collection containing manuscript and reference number
♦ Location of manuscript in archive or repository

Example

The architect enjoyed a close relationship with his patron (Newton, 1785).

Newton, W. (1785) *Letter to William Ord, 23 June*. Ord Manuscripts 324 E11/4, Northumberland Archives, Woodhorn.

Where *the author of a manuscript is not known*, use the following.

Citation order:

♦ Title of manuscript (in italics)
♦ Year (if known, in round brackets)
♦ Name of collection containing manuscript and reference number
♦ Location of manuscript in archive or repository

Example

Expenditure was high in this period (*Fenham Journal*, 1795).

Fenham journal (1795) Ord Manuscripts, 324 E12, Northumberland Archives, Woodhorn.

G32.2 Collections of manuscripts

To refer to a whole collection of manuscripts (MS), use the name of the collection.

Citation order:

♦ Location of collection in archive or repository
♦ Name of collection
♦ No date is given for a collection in the text or the reference list as the collection contains items of various dates.

Example

Consulting the family records (British Library, Lansdowne MS), the author discovered …

British Library, Lansdowne MS.

G32.3 Manuscripts in digital collections

Citation order:

♦ Author (if known; if not, use title)
♦ Year (in round brackets)
♦ Title of manuscript (in italics)
♦ Date (if available)
♦ Name of collection containing manuscript and reference number
♦ Available at: name of digital collection
♦ (Accessed: date)

Example

In-text citation

The Queen consulted her advisers about the Spanish Ambassador's request (*Consultation at Greenwich*, 1561)

Reference list

Consultation at Greenwich (1561) 1 May. Calendar of State Papers, Domestic Series, Elizabeth I, vol. 17(1), p. 175. Document Ref.: SP 12/17 f.1. Available at: State Papers Online (Accessed: 6 June 2021).

G32.4 Manuscripts on microform: microfiche and microfilm

Citation order:

♦ Author
♦ Year of publication (in round brackets)
♦ Title of microform (in italics)
♦ Medium (in square brackets)
♦ Place of publication: publisher

Example

In-text citation

Data from Fritsch (1987) …

Reference list

Fritsch, F.E. (1987) *The Fritsch collection: algae illustrations on microfiche* [Microfiche]. Ambleside: Freshwater Biological Association.

Section H
American Psychological Association (APA) referencing style

The APA referencing style is used in some social science subjects. Like Harvard, it uses an author-date format to identify the citation in the text. Full details are given in an alphabetical Reference list at the end of your work. For more information on the APA referencing style, see:

American Psychological Association. (2019). *Publication Manual of the American Psychological Association.* 7th ed.; American Psychological Association. (2021). *APA Style Blog.* https://apastyle.apa.org/blog; and Purdue University. (2021). *Online Writing Lab* (OWL). https://owl.purdue.edu/owl/research_and_citation/apa_style/apa_style_introduction.html

Conventions when using the APA referencing style

In-text citations

♦ Use the author's family or surname and the year of publication in your text. This can be a narrative citation: Khan (2020), or a parenthetical citation: (Khan, 2020)

Organisation as author

♦ Cite the organisation name in full, for example Princeton University (2021) or (Princeton University, 2021)

♦ If the name is usually abbreviated, give the abbreviation in square brackets in the first citation, then use the abbreviation in subsequent in-text citations

Examples

First in-text citations

National Health Service [NHS] (2021) or (National Health Service [NHS], 2021)

Subsequent in-text citations

NHS (2021) or (NHS, 2021)

Two authors

♦ Separate the authors' names with an ampersand &:

Examples

In-text citations

Brooks & Gibbons (2021) or (Brooks & Gibbons, 2021)

Three or more authors

♦ For works with more than two authors, abbreviate to the first author name plus et al. (not italicised) for all in-text citations

Examples

Winner et al. (2020) or (Winner et al., 2020)

If there are other sources with the same citation, add a further name to differentiate them:

Winner, Reyes et al. (2021) or (Winner, Reyes et al., 2021)

No authors identified

♦ If no authors or editors are listed, use the title of the source

Examples

In-text citation

Referring to the *3D Printing Manual* (2021) …

As defined (*3D Printing Manual* (2021) …

Page numbers

♦ Include page numbers with in-text references where you have quoted, paraphrased or highlighted a specific part of the source

Examples

In-text citations

Zhang (2020, p. 45) or (Zhang, 2020, p. 45) …

Reference list layout

♦ All lines after the first line of each reference list entry should be indented half an inch from the left margin. This is called 'hanging indentation'
♦ In your reference list, sources are listed in alphabetical order by the authors' names

Example

Reference list

Rippe, J. M. (2019). *Lifestyle medicine* (3rd ed.). CRC Press. https://doi.org/10.1201/9781315201108

Authors/editors

♦ Give the last name (surname/family name) and initials of given names
♦ Full stops are used after each of the author initials and spaces are inserted between initials
♦ Full stops are used after corporate names
♦ For editor or editors, use the abbreviation Ed. or Eds., respectively, in round brackets

Examples

Reference list

Brooks, G. J. (Ed.). (2021) …

Hernández, G. (2019) …

Oxfam. (2021) …

Multiple authors

♦ For your reference list, list all authors *up to twenty*, with the last author name preceded by an ampersand (&)

Example: work with up to twenty authors

In-text citation

Games can assist recovery (Weathers et al., 2014) …

Reference list

Weathers, L., Bedell, J. R., Marlowe, H., Gordon, R. E., & Adams, J. (2014). Using psychotherapeutic games to train patients' skills. In R. E. Gordon and K. K. Gordon (Eds.), *Systems of treatment for the mentally ill* (pp. 109–124). Grune & Stratton.

♦ Where you have *more than twenty authors*, you should list the *first nineteen* then use an ellipsis … and list the name of the last author of the work (no ampersand is required)

Example: work with more than twenty authors

In-text citation

Johnson et al. (2020) argue that …

Reference list

Johnson, P., Peters, S. T., Ahmed, J., Schmidt, P., Stein, L. H., Nunes, A., Siete, P., Oito, D., Iva, L., Toban, G., Juichi, G., Tolv, E. G., Treiz, E., Fjorte, N., Funfzeh, N., Sol, A., Sibce, D., Achttie, N., Dicianno, V. E., … Scorsa, O. (2020). Electromagnetic theory. *Nature*, *3*(1), 25–32.

♦ If *no authors or editors are listed*, use the title of the source

Example

Reference list

3D printing manual. (2021). Innovations Ltd.

Year of publication

♦ In brackets, followed by a full stop, for example (2021).

Titles

♦ The titles of sources are italicised, as are volume numbers of journal articles, but not issue or page numbers
♦ For a book, only the first letter of the first word of the title and subtitle (if there is one) and any **proper nouns** are capitalised
♦ Full stops are inserted after book titles

Example

Psychoanalysis: Its image and its public in China.

♦ Titles of articles within journals, or chapters within books, are not enclosed in quotation marks
♦ For *journal titles*, each major word of the title is capitalised and followed by a comma

Example

Journal of Comparative and Physiological Psychology,

Editions

♦ Edition is abbreviated to ed. and enclosed in round brackets, with a full stop after the brackets (6th ed.)
♦ With the exception of first editions, include the edition number after the title in round brackets. There is no full stop after the title before the round brackets

Example

Ramage, P. L. (2016). *History in the making* (4th ed.). Harvest Press.

Publication details

♦ Give the name of the publisher for books, ebooks, chapters in books, reports and computer software and apps
♦ For audiovisual sources, publication details may include the production, distribution or broadcast organisation
♦ Do not include place of publication, but do give a location when this is relevant, for example as part of conference references
♦ If the author is the same as the publisher, omit the publisher from the reference

Example

American Psychological Association. (2019). *Publication manual of the American Psychological Association* (7th ed.).

Volume and issue information for periodicals

♦ Volume numbers are italicised. Issue numbers are included in round brackets, for example *31*(2)

Page numbers

♦ Page numbers for book chapters and journal articles are given immediately after the title of the book in round brackets and before publication details (see H2.2 and H5). In the reference list, include p. or pp. for chapters in edited books and anthologies, but omit p. or pp. for journal article entries

Internet sources

♦ The word Internet is always capitalised, whereas website is not
♦ Internet sources should be indicated by including the Digital Object Identifier (DOI) as https://doi.org/ or a URL if no DOI is available
♦ Generally, you do not need to include a retrieval date for online sources, unless the content is meant to change over time
♦ You do not need to include the name of the library database when referencing online journals or ebooks
♦ No punctuation marks are added after DOIs or URLs in reference list entries

Footnotes

♦ Footnotes may be used in APA style, but should be used only where they provide additional information that supports your work, for example when a detailed explanation would distract your reader if it was included in the main text, or a link to further information online. Each footnote should relate to only one idea. You should use a **superscript number** following almost any punctuation marks. Footnote numbers should not follow hyphens, and if they appear in a sentence in brackets, the footnote number should be inserted within the brackets

Example

Researchers believe that the occurrence of dementia in England points to a number of highly pertinent facts.[1] (These have now been published separately.[2])

Secondary (indirect) sources

Read and cite the original source whenever you can, but if you are relying on another author to represent the original source, indicate this by citing the author or title of the original source in your text and including the secondary source in round brackets. Provide a full reference for the secondary source in the reference list.

Example

Hislop (as cited in Ridley, 2019, p. 56) argued that …

Thus, only the details for Ridley's work would appear in your reference list.

How to reference common sources

H1 Books

H1.1 Printed books and ebooks in academic databases without a unique DOI

Citation order:

♦ Author/editor (surname followed by initials)
♦ Year of publication (in round brackets)
♦ Title (in italics)
♦ Edition (if it is not the first edition)
♦ Publisher

Example

In-text citation

As discussed by Milton et al. (2011, p. 106) …

Reference list

Milton, J., Polmear, C., & Fabricius, J. (2011). *A short introduction to psychoanalysis* (2nd ed.). Sage.

H1.2 Books with DOIs

Citation order:

♦ Author/editor (surname followed by initials)
♦ Year of publication (in round brackets)
♦ Title (in italics)
♦ Edition (if it is not the first edition)
♦ Publisher
♦ https://doi.org/

Example

Rippe (2019, p. 54) stated …

Rippe, J. M. (2019). *Lifestyle medicine* (3rd ed.). CRC Press. https://doi.org/10.1201/9781315201108

H1.3 Mobile ebook, e.g. Kindle, KOBO

Ebooks often lack page numbers, although PDF versions may have them. There may be 'location' numbers and % marks that are static, but these are of little use to anyone who does not have the same device, or is using a different font-size display. To cite a quotation or section in text, use the major sections (chapter, section and paragraph number; abbreviate if titles are long). Provide as much information as the reader needs to locate the material you are using.

Example

Bregman's view of this (2020, Chapter 1, Section 2, para. 2) …

Serafino, E. P., & Smith, T. W. (2020). *Health psychology: Biopsychosocial interactions* (9th ed.). Wiley. https://www.amazon.co.uk/gp/product/B01N0TLF2I/

H2 Edited books, including anthologies

H2.1 Whole book with editor

Citation order:

- Name of editor of book (Ed.)
- Year of publication (in round brackets)
- Title of book (in italics)
- Edition (if it is not the first edition)
- Publisher
- https://doi.org/ *or* URL (if required)

Example

A comprehensive study by Helman (2018) …

Helman, C. (Ed.). (2018). *Doctors and patients: An anthology*. CRC Press. https://doi.org/10.1201/9781315375939

H2.2 Chapters/sections of edited books and encyclopedias

Citation order:

- Author of the chapter/section (surname followed by initials)
- Year of publication (in round brackets)
- Title of chapter/section
- In
- Name of editor of book (Ed.)
- Title of book (in italics)
- Edition (if it is not the first edition)
- Page numbers of chapter/section (in round brackets)
- Publisher
- https://doi.org/ *or* URL (if required)

Examples

The view proposed by Leites (2013, p. 444) …

Crick's career (Olby 2014) …

Leites, N. (2013). Transference interpretations only? In A. H. Esman (Ed.), *Essential papers on transference* (pp. 434–454). New York University Press.

Olby, R. (2014). Crick, Francis Harry Compton (1916–2004). In *Oxford dictionary of national biography* (Online ed.). Oxford University Press. https://doi.org/10.1093/ref:odnb/93883

H3 Translated works

Citation order:

♦ Author/editor (surname followed by initials)
♦ Years of publication (in round brackets)
♦ Title (in italics)
♦ Name of translator, Trans. (in round brackets)
♦ Publisher
♦ https://doi.org/ *or* URL (if required)

Example

Zola (1873/1969) …

Zola, É. (1969). *The belly of Paris*. (D. W. Harris, Trans.). Grant & Cutler. (Original work published 1873).

H4 Multi-volume works

Citation order:

♦ Author/editor (surname followed by initials)
♦ Year(s) of publication (in round brackets)
♦ Title of book (in italics)
♦ Edition (if it is not the first edition)
♦ Volumes (in round brackets)
♦ Publisher
♦ https://doi.org/ *or* URL (if required)

Example

Butcher's (1961–1963) comprehensive work …

Butcher, R. (Ed.). (1961–1963). *A new British flora* (4 vols.). Leonard Hill.

H5 Journal articles

H5.1 Print and online articles

Citation order:

♦ Author (surname followed by initials)
♦ Year of publication (in round brackets)
♦ Title of article
♦ Title of journal (in italics)
♦ Volume number (in italics)
♦ Issue (in round brackets)
♦ Page numbers *or* Article number
♦ https://doi.org/ *or* URL

Examples

In-text citations

Research by Erbil (2020), Frosch (2012) and King (1993) …

Reference list

Erbil, D. G. (2020). A review of flipped classroom and cooperative learning method within the context of Vygotsky theory. *Frontiers in Psychology, 11*, Article 1157. https://www.frontiersin.org/article/10.3389/fpsyg.2020.01157

Frosch, A. (2012). Transference: Psychic reality and material reality. *Psychoanalytic Psychology, 19*(4), 603–633.

King, A. (1993). From sage on the stage to guide on the side. *College Teaching, 41*(1), 30–35. https://doi.org/10.1080/87567555.1993.9926781

H5.2 Advance online publications

Citation order:

♦ Author (surname followed by initials)
♦ Year of posting (in round brackets)
♦ Title of the article
♦ Journal title (in italics)
♦ Advance online publication
♦ https://doi.org/ *or* URL

Example

In-text citation

The latest research (Madan et al., 2021) …

Reference list

Madan, C., Spetch, M. L., Machado, F. M. D. S., Mason, A., & Ludvig, E. A. (2021). Encoding context denotes risky choice. *Psychological Science*. Advance online publication. https://doi.org/10.1177/0956797620977516

H5.3 Articles in press

Citation order:

♦ Author (surname followed by initials)
♦ in press (in round brackets)
♦ Title of the article
♦ Journal title (in italics)

Example

In-text citation

This new research (Hastings, in press) …

Reference list

Hastings, P. L. (in press). Combined therapy: Medication, talking therapies and self-help in the treatment of anxiety and depression. *Mental Illness Quarterly*.

H5.4 Articles in systematic reviews

Citation order:

- ♦ Author (surname followed by initials)
- ♦ Year of publication (in round brackets)
- ♦ Title of review
- ♦ Database name (in italics)
- ♦ https://doi.org/ or URL

Example

In-text citation

Following a systematic review (Pasquali et al., 2018) …

Reference list

Pasquali, S., Hadjinicolaou, A. V., Chiarion Sileni, V., Rossi, C. R., & Mocellin, S. (2018) Systemic treatments for metastatic cutaneous melanoma. *Cochrane Database of Systematic Reviews*. https://doi.org/10.1002/14651858.CD011123.pub2

H5.5 Book reviews

Citation order:

- ♦ Reviewer (surname followed by initials)
- ♦ Year of publication (in round brackets)
- ♦ Title of book review or
- ♦ [Review of the book *Title of book*, by Author of book]
- ♦ Title of source where the review appears (in italics)
- ♦ Volume number (in italics)
- ♦ Issue (in round brackets), page numbers
- ♦ https://doi.org/ or URL (if required)

Example

In-text citation

The favourable review by Darden (2007) …

Reference list

Darden, L. (2007) New cell research. [Review of the book *Discovering cell mechanisms: The creation of modern cell biology*, by W. Bechtel]. *Journal of the History of Biology, 40*(1), 185–187. https://doi.org/10.1007/s10739-006-9121-5

Use this format for any reviews; simply indicate the medium being reviewed in the brackets (film, DVD, television programme).

If the reviewed item is a film, DVD or other medium, include the year of release after the title of the work, separated by a comma.

H6 Magazine and newspaper articles

Citation order:

- ♦ Author (surname followed by initials) or pseudonym
- ♦ Year and date of publication (in round brackets)
- ♦ Title of article
- ♦ Title of magazine/newspaper/newsletter (in italics)
- ♦ Volume number (in italics) – if available
- ♦ Issue (in round brackets) – if available
- ♦ Page numbers – if available
- ♦ https://doi.org/ or URL

Examples: magazine articles

In-text citations

MD (2021) and Kim (2021) gave examples from the UK and USA.

Reference list

Kim, S. (2021, May 5). Child COVID cases are highest in these states. *Newsweek*. https://www. newsweek.com/coronavirus-states-highest-child-covid-cases-children-1588815

MD. (2021, April 30–May 13). Pandemic update. *Private Eye*, (1546), 8–9.

Examples: newspaper articles

In-text citations

Articles by Anne-Laure Lebrun (2021) and Bentham (2019) …

Reference list

Bentham, M. (2019, June 19). Homelessness rises to a record high. *Evening Standard*, 8.

Lebrun, A.-L. (2021, March 5). Les rouages des troubles du comportement alimentaire [The inner workings of eating disorders]. *Le Figaro*. https://www.lefigaro.fr/sciences/les-rouages-des-troubles-du-comportement-alimentaire-20210503

H7 Reports and working papers

Citation order:

♦ Author (surname followed by initials) or name of organisation
♦ Year of publication (in round brackets)
♦ Title of report (in italics)
♦ Series and report number (in round brackets)
♦ Publisher (if different from the author; omit if they are the same)

If available online, add:
♦ https://doi.org/ *or* URL

Examples

In-text citations

Nissan's financial report (2020) …

Policy proposals by Basu and Getachew (2017) …

Reference list

Basu, P., & Getachew, Y. (2017). *Redistributive innovation policy, inequality and efficiency* (DUBS Working Paper 2017.2). Durham University Business School. Available from: https://www.dur.ac.uk/resources/business/working-papers/RD_2017_02.pdf

Nissan Motor Company. (2020). *FY2020: 3rd quarter financial results*. https://global.nissannews.com/en/channels/investor-relations

NB: Publisher omitted in Nissan example as same as the author.

H8 Conferences and symposia

H8.1 Full conference proceedings: print or electronic

Citation order:

- Author/editor (surname followed by initials)
- Year of publication (in round brackets)
- Title of conference: subtitle of conference (in italics)
- Location, date of conference (in italics)
- Publisher

If viewed online:
- https://doi.org/ or URL

Example

In-text citation

… in the full conference proceedings (Hewlett & Carson, 2019).

Reference list

Hewlett, P., & Carson, L. (Eds.). (2019). *Preparing nurses for the next decade: Proceedings of the 2019 National Conference on Education in Nursing, University of Cumbria*. Greendale Press.

H8.2 Conference presentations, papers and posters

Citation order:

- Author of paper or presenter
- Year and month/days span of conference (in round brackets)
- Title of paper or presentation (in italics)
- Type of contribution (in square brackets)
- Title of conference: subtitle of conference
- Location of conference or online conference
- https://doi.org/ or URL

Examples

In-text citations

The research of Jomantas (2019), Mendes and Romão (2018) and Zador (2020) …

Reference list

Jomantas, S. (2019, June 28). *Interethnic enjoyment, myth and materialism*. [Poster presentation]. SALSA XII Sesquiannual Conference, Vienna, Austria. https://i1.wp.com/www.salsa-tipiti. org/wp-content/uploads/2018/11/ sarunas-jomantas-poster-small.png

Mendes, L., & Romão, T. (2018, November 8–11). *Children as teachers*. [Conference paper]. 8th International Conference on Advances in Computer Entertainment Technology, Lisbon, Portugal. https://doi. org/10.1145/2071423.2071438

Zador, A. M. (2020, December 6–12). *The genomic bottleneck: A lesson from biology*. [Paper presentation]. 34th Conference on Neural Information Processing Systems. Online conference. https://nips.cc/ virtual/2020/public/invited_16167. html

H9 Theses and dissertations

Citation order:

♦ Author (surname followed by initials)
♦ Year of submission (in round brackets)
♦ Title of dissertation/thesis (in italics)
♦ Degree statement (in square brackets)
♦ Degree-awarding body

If available online, add:
♦ Database *or* website name and URL

Examples

In-text citations

Research by Medac (2015) and Brodie (2013) …

Reference list

Brodie, L. M. (2013). *Speciality regional foods in the UK: An investigation from the perspectives of marketing and social history* [Doctoral thesis, Newcastle University]. Newcastle University Theses. http://hdl.handle.net/10443/434

Medac, N. (2015). *Food for thought: Examining the neural circuitry regulating food choices* [Unpublished doctoral thesis]. University of Cambridge.

H10 Research datasets

Citation order:

♦ Author or name of organisation
♦ Year of publication (in round brackets)
♦ Title (in italics)
♦ Version (in round brackets)
♦ [Dataset]
♦ Publisher (if different from the author; omit if they are the same)
♦ https://doi.org/ *or* URL

Example

In-text citation

Data from the Department for Environment, Food & Rural Affairs (2021) …

Reference list

Department for Environment, Food & Rural Affairs. (2021). *UK chick and poultry placings – monthly dataset.* (Data for June 2021) [Dataset]. https://www.gov.uk/government/statistics/poultry-and-poultry-meat-statistics

H11 Government publications

Citation order:

♦ Author
♦ Year of publication (in round brackets)
♦ Title (in italics)
♦ Report series and number (in round brackets)
♦ Publisher (if different from the author; omit if they are the same)
♦ https://doi.org/ *or* URL

Example

Government policy on combatting extremism (Department for Education, 2015) …

Department for Education. (2015). *Government response to the education select committee report: Extremism in schools – the Trojan Horse affair.* (Cm. 9094). Her Majesty's Stationery Office. https://www.gov.uk/government/publications/extremism-in-schools-response-to-education-select-committee

If you are referencing government publications from more than one country, add the country after the department name, for example Department of Energy (USA) and Department for Education (UK).

H12 Legal information

The citation orders below are adapted from examples in the *Publication manual of the American Psychological Association* (7th edn.), pp. 355–368, as the *Manual* only provides examples of US and United Nations legal sources.

H12.1 Legislation

Citation order:

♦ Title of the legislation (including year)
♦ Number (if applicable)
♦ URL

If you need to cite a specific part of the legislation, do this in your text. The title of the legislation is in italics for the in-text citation, but not for the reference list entry.

Example

Under Section 7(7) of the *Human Rights Act 1998* …

Human Rights Act 1998, c42. https://www.legislation.gov.uk/ukpga/1998/42/contents

If you are citing *legislation from more than one jurisdiction*, clarify this with your in-text citation.

Examples

The UK Parliament passed the *Fire Safety Act 2021* …

In Singapore, the *Vulnerable Adults Act 2018* …

Fire Safety Act 2021, c.24. https://www.legislation.gov.uk/ukpga/2021/24/contents/enacted
Vulnerable Adults Act 2018, no. 27. https://sso.agc.gov.sg/Act/VAA2018

H12.2 Cases

The name of the case report is abbreviated in accordance with the *Cardiff Index to Legal Abbreviations* (2012) Available at: http://www.legalabbrevs.cardiff.ac.uk/ (Accessed: 12 June 2021). Since 2002, cases have been given a neutral citation using the abbreviated name of the court that heard the case, the year the case was heard and the number of the case within that year.

Citation order:

♦ Title of the case (italicised in text but not in reference list)
♦ Year of publication (in round brackets)
♦ Neutral citation (for cases since 2002)
♦ Year [in square brackets], volume number, abbreviated name of case report, first page number of the case

Note that legal cases do not use p. or pp. before page numbers.

Examples: with and without neutral citations

In-text citations

The cases of *R v. Edwards (John)* (1991) and *R v. Dunlop* (2006) …

Reference list

R v. Dunlop (2006) EWCA Crim 1354, [2007] 1 All ER 593
R v. Edwards (John) (1991) 93 Cr App R 48

H13 Organisation or personal web pages and websites

Citation order:

♦ Author
♦ Date the site was published/last updated (in round brackets) or use (n.d.) if no date
♦ Title of web page (in italics)
♦ Website name (if different to the author)
♦ https://doi.org/ *or* URL (use Retrieved from URL and date if the content is meant to change over time)

Examples

In-text citations

There are several career paths (British Psychological Association, 2021) …

According to Keefe et al. (2021) …

Reference list

British Psychological Association. (2021). *Become a psychologist*. https://www.bps.org.uk/public/become-psychologist
Keefe, J., Ramirez, R., & Fritz, R. (2021, August 5) *The West's historic drought in 3 maps*. CNN. Retrieved August 8, 2021, from https://edition.cnn.com/2021/06/17/weather/westcalifornia-drought-maps/index.html

H14 Blogs

Citation order:

- ♦ Author (surname followed by initials)
- ♦ Year and date of post (in round brackets)
- ♦ Title of post
- ♦ Title of site (in italics)
- ♦ https://doi.org/ *or* URL

Example

In-text citation

The appraisal of Greta by Davies (2019) …

Reference list

Davies, C. (2019, October 24). Inspiring thursday: Greta Thunberg, *Wave blog*. https://blog.wave-network.org/inspiring-thursday-greta-thunberg

H15 Social media: Twitter, Facebook, Instagram, Tumblr and Reddit

Citation order:

- ♦ Author or organisation and/or [@username]
- ♦ Year, month day (in round brackets)
- ♦ Title or first twenty words of description (in italics)
- ♦ [Type of post]
- ♦ Site name
- ♦ https://doi.org/ *or* URL

Examples

In-text citations

Laura Kuenssberg (2021) tweeted on ministerial integrity.

AI offers great opportunities for business (Confederation of Indian Industry, 2021).

Surf on a turquoise sea (Australia News Today, 2021).

Reference list

Australia News Today [@australianews]. (2021, April 5). *No words can describe the beauty* [Photograph]. Instagram. https://www.instagram.com/p/CNQyOB-FqoG/

Confederation of Indian Industry. (2021, May 4). *Did you know by 2035 #AI is expected to boost India's annual growth rate by 1.3%?* [Image attached] [Status update]. Facebook. https://www.facebook.com/FollowCII/posts/4389646397736448

Kuenssberg, L. [@bbclaurak]. (2021, April 28). *Matt Hancock refuses to answer a question on whether ministers who break party funding rules or the law should resign* [Tweet]. Twitter. https://twitter.com/bbclaurak/status/1387445378375639045

H16 Television programmes

H16.1 Television series

Citation order:

♦ Creators (including writer, director, producer, host, presenter) and roles (in round brackets)
♦ Date
♦ Title of work (in italics)
♦ Description (in square brackets)
♦ Publisher/production company/museum name and location/department and university name
♦ URL (if viewed online)

Example

In-text citation

Nikki Wilson (2014–2017) produced series eight to ten of *Doctor Who*.

Reference list

Wilson, N. (Producer). (2014–2017). *Doctor Who* [TV series]. BBC.

H16.2 Episode in a television series

Citation order:

♦ Creators (including writer, director, producer, host, presenter) and roles (in round brackets)
♦ Date of broadcast (in round brackets)
♦ Title of episode
♦ Series/season and episode number (in round brackets)
♦ [TV series episode]
♦ In
♦ Producer (initials then surname) (Producer)

♦ Series title (in italics)
♦ Production company
♦ URL (if viewed online)

Example

In-text citation

… of their intriguing script (Roberts & Moffat, 2014).

Reference list

Roberts, G., & Moffat, S. (Writers), & Murphy, P. (Director). (2014, September 27). The caretaker (season 8, episode 6) [TV series episode]. In N. Wilson (Producer), *Doctor Who*. BBC.

H16.3 Stand-alone programme

Citation order:

♦ Creators (including writer, director, producer, host, presenter) and roles (in round brackets)
♦ Date
♦ Title of work (in italics)
♦ Description (in square brackets)
♦ Publisher/production company/museum name and location/department and university name
♦ URL (if viewed online)

Example

The powerful presentation (Attenborough and Davies, 2019) …

Attenborough, D. (Presenter), & Davies, S. (Director). (2019, May 18). *Climate change – the facts* [TV programme]. BBC. https://www.bbc.co.uk/iplayer/episode/m00049b1/climate-change-the-facts

H17 Radio programmes

Citation order:

♦ Name of presenter/host
♦ Date of broadcast (in round brackets)
♦ Title of radio programme (in italics)
♦ [Radio broadcast]
♦ Broadcaster
♦ If heard online, add https://doi.org/ *or* URL

Example

Sean Farrington (2021) examined plans for working from home.

Farrington, S. (Host). (2021, May 6). *All in a hybrid day's work* [Radio broadcast]. BBC Radio 5 Live. https://www.bbc.co.uk/programmes/m000vqsk

H18 Film or video recordings

The director is treated as the author of the film. You do not need to include how you watched the film (such as Amazon Prime, HULU, Disney+, Netflix, Kanopy, Box of Broadcasts) but include the medium where this is relevant (such as a DVD with director's commentary).

Citation order:

♦ Name of director (surname followed by initials)
♦ (Director)
♦ Year of distribution (in round brackets)
♦ Title (in italics)
♦ [Medium]
♦ Distributor/publisher

Examples

Last month I watched films by Besson (1997) and Coogler (2018).

Besson, J. (Director). (1997). *The fifth element* [Film: DVD with director's commentary]. Twentieth Century Fox.

Coogler, R. (Director). (2018). *Black panther* [Film]. Marvel Studios.

H19 Online videos, e.g. YouTube, TED talks

Use the person or group that uploaded the video as the author. If they are not the presenter, note this person in your text. Use a timestamp in the in-text citation to highlight a specific place in the recording.

Citation order:

♦ Author (surname followed by initials) and/or [screen name]
♦ Year, month day (in round brackets)
♦ Title of video (in italics)
♦ [Video]
♦ Name of website
♦ https://doi.org/ or URL

Example

In-text citation

Professor González described 'Gravity's symphony' (Cambridge Cosmology, 2021, 27:45).

Reference list

Cambridge Cosmology (2021, January 12) *Professor Gabriella González: Black holes and gravitational waves* [Video]. YouTube. https://www.youtube.com/watch?v=Txuq1sO8fkY

H20 Podcasts

Citation order:

♦ Name of host
♦ Host (in round brackets)
♦ Date the podcast was published/last updated (in round brackets)
♦ Title of podcast (in italics)
♦ [Audio podcast] or [Video podcast]
♦ Production company
♦ https://doi.org/ or URL

Example

In-text citation

Dr. Williams (2021) offered advice.

Reference list

Williams, C. (Host). (2021, March 2) *Audio: Unhelpful thinking* [Audio podcast]. NHS Choices Wellbeing podcasts. https://www.nhs.uk/mental-health/self-help/guides-tools-and-activities/mental-wellbeing-audio-guides/#confidence

H21 Sound/music recordings

H21.1 Song/track on an album

You do not need to include how you heard the recording (such as CD, Spotify, iTunes). For classical works, include the date of the original composition at the end of the reference and alongside the date of the recording you have heard for the in-text citation.

Citation order:

- Artist or group
- Year of recording (in round brackets)
- Title of song/recording
- [Description]
- On
- Title of album (in italics)
- Label

Examples

In-text citations

Iconic music by Elgar (1899/2016) and Journey (1981) …

Reference list

Elgar, E. (2016). Op. 36: IX. Nimrod [Song recorded by Royal Philharmonic Orchestra]. On *Elgar: Enigma variations.* Decca. (Original work published 1899).

Journey (1981). Don't stop believin' [Song]. On *Escape.* Columbia.

H21.2 Whole album

Citation order:

- Artist/songwriter (surname followed by initials)
- Year (in round brackets)
- Title of album (in italics)
- [Album]
- Label
- Date of recording (if different from copyright date)

Example

In-text citation

The second EP from Girl in Red (2019) …

Reference list

Girl in Red. (2019). *Beginnings* [Album]. AWAL.

H22 Works of art: photographic prints, paintings, sculptures and installations

Citation order:

- Artist (surname followed by initials)
- Year of production (in round brackets)
- Title of work (in italics)
- [Medium]
- Location of the work

Examples

In-text citations

Her favourite pieces were by Cartier-Bresson (1938), Gormley (1998), Rodin (1882) and Martin (1817).

Reference list

Cartier-Bresson, H. (1938). *Juvisy, France* [Photograph]. Museum of Modern Art, New York City.

Gormley, A. (1998). *Angel of the North* [Sculpture]. Low Fell, Gateshead.

Martin, J. (1817). *The bard* [Painting]. Laing Art Gallery, Newcastle upon Tyne.

Rodin, A. (1882). *The kiss* [Sculpture]. Musee Rodin, Paris, France.

H23 Online images, including infographics

Citation order:

♦ Creator
♦ Year of production (in round brackets)
♦ Title of work (in italics)
♦ [Medium]
♦ Publisher/company/website name
♦ Location or URL

Examples

In-text citations

I've looked at images by The Health Foundation (2021) and Reed (2009).

Reference list

The Health Foundation (2021, February 18). *What does the pandemic mean for health and health inequalities?* [Infographic]. The Health Foundation. https://www.health.org.uk/sites/default/files/2021-02/hf_covid_infographic_blue.png

Reed, E. (2009). *Brazil. Sao Paolo. Ibirapuera park* [Photograph]. ArtStor. https://library-artstor-org.ezphost.dur.ac.uk/asset/AWSS35953_35953_37875434

NB: For images on Facebook, Twitter, Instagram, Tumblr and Reddit, see Section H15.

H24 Maps

Citation order:

♦ Cartographer
♦ Year of publication (in round brackets)
♦ Title of map section

♦ [Map]
♦ Sheet number or tile, scale (if available)
♦ Publication information (for print)
♦ https://doi.org/ *or* URL

If citing a dynamic map with no title, provide a description in square brackets, as in the Google example below.

Examples

In-text citations

The leisure centre is close to Tiddenfoot Lake (Ordnance Survey, 2020), whilst the access road can be located on Google Maps (Google, 2021).

Reference list

Google. (n.d.). [Google Maps directions for driving from Reading to Tiddenfoot Lake]. Retrieved May 6, 2021 from https://goo.gl/maps/hC5pUfsYCiW1Yuyw5

Ordnance Survey. (2020). Tiddenfoot Lake [Map]. Tile sp92sw, 1:10,000. http://edina.ac.uk/digimap

H25 Images in publications: graphs, tables, figures, plates, equations

The general principle of referencing is to cite what you have seen. Use the citation order for that source (e.g. a book or a journal article), ending with the page number or the figure/illustration number after the in-text reference number.

Examples

In-text citations

Trestman's table of laser power ratings (2017, p. 98, table 4.2) and the schematic of an LD driver (2017, p. 58, figure 7.1) …

Reference list

Trestman, G. A. (2017). *Powering laser diode systems*. SPIE Press.

H26 Course materials

H26.1 Published online lecture notes and presentation slides

If referencing lecture slides or notes that are publicly available, that is, they do not require a login or invitation via Zoom, Teams or Panopto, use this format.

Citation order:

- Author (surname followed by initials)
- Date (in round brackets)
- Title of work (in italics)
- [Medium]
- Name of site or department and URL

Example

In-text citation

The excellent presentation by Singh and Kumar (2015) …

Reference list

Singh, R. V., & Kumar, A. (2015). *Biodiversity and its types* [PowerPoint slides]. Slideshare. https://www.slideshare.net/ravivikram121/biodiversity-45077737

H26.2 Unpublished lecture notes, presentation slides and recorded lectures

If the lecture recording, notes and slides are not publicly available, as the reader would require a login or invitation via Zoom, Teams or Panopto, use the login page URL.

Example

In-text citation

The techniques, outlined by Peto (2021) …

Reference list

Peto, G. (2021). Psychometric tests [PowerPoint slides]. Durham University Online. https://duo.dur.ac.uk/webapps/login

H26.3 Recorded lectures

If the lecture was recorded and is publicly available, cite the medium in which you viewed it (see H19 for online videos; for audio podcasts see H20).

If the recorded lecture is not publicly available, cite this as a personal communication (see H28).

H27 Interviews

H27.1 Published interviews

Cite published interviews according to the format in which they appeared. For example, cite an interview in a newspaper like a newspaper article.

Example

In-text citation

Riley (Jones, 2018) related her concerns …

Reference list

Jones, J. (2018, July 5). The life of Riley. An interview with Bridget Riley. *The Guardian*, 33.

H27.2 Unpublished interviews

Quote from unpublished interviews in your text (with the interviewee's permission). No date is required.

Example

In-text citation

Professor Wang discussed her research into dementia and highlighted the importance of sleep. She believes that "People over fifty who get less than six hours sleep per night are more susceptible".

H28 Personal communications

If the information is in a format that cannot be obtained by a reader, including live speeches or lectures, emails, Snapchat, WhatsApp and text messages, telephone calls and letters, cite these in your text as personal communications. No reference list entry is required for these sources.

Examples

In-text citations

T. Jones (personal communication, May 5, 2021) emailed her support.

In his lecture Dr Gupta analysed FTSE 100 share prices (personal communication, April 14, 2021).

Comments via WhatsApp were positive (R. Fosshage, J.-L. Farmer, & K. Huber, personal communications, May 9, 2021).

Sample text

The following sample text illustrates how various sources are cited in the text of your work.

Technology has been used to enhance student learning for decades, but the concept of the "flipped classroom" or "flipped learning" emerged in the last 30 years (AdvanceHE, 2020). King (1993) called for face-to-face teaching to be based on students' understanding and use of knowledge, rather than the transmission of information from the teacher into students' "empty brains" (p. 30). Students read information before the lesson, so that contact time is used for problem solving with the teacher and together in groups. The idea was developed by Lage, Platt and Treglia (2000). Extensive application of the model led to books (including Carbaugh & Doubet, 2016), scholarly journals (such as Erbil, 2020) and bloggers (Trach, 2020) providing guidance. There are concerns about students' varied access to technology at home (Stöhr, C., Demazière, C., & Adawi, T., 2020). Today, international organisations, such as the Flipped Learning Global Initiative (2021), advocate for flipped learning.

Sample reference list

List sources alphabetically by author, or by title if there isn't an author. Use hanging indents so that the authors are easily identifiable.

AdvanceHE. (2020). *Flipped learning*. https://www.advance-he.ac.uk/knowledge-hub/flipped-learning

Carbaugh, E. M., & Doubet, K. (2016). *The differentiated flipped classroom: A practical guide to digital learning*. Corwin.

Erbil, D. G. (2020). A review of flipped classroom and cooperative learning method within the context of Vygotsky theory. *Frontiers in Psychology*, *11*, Article 1157. https://www.frontiersin.org/article/10.3389/fpsyg.2020.01157

Flipped Learning Global Initiative. (2021). *About FLGI*. https://www.flglobal.org/about/

King, A. (1993). From sage on the stage to guide on the side. *College Teaching*, *41*(1), 30–35. https://doi.org/10.1080/87567555.1993.9926781

Lage, M. L., Platt, G. J., & Treglia, M. (2000). Inverting the classroom: A gateway to creating an inclusive learning environment. *Journal of Economic Education*, *31*(1), 30–43.

Stöhr, C., Demazière, C., & Adawi, T. (2020). The polarizing effect of the online flipped classroom. *Computers & Education, 147*, Article 103789. https://doi.org/10.1016/j.compedu.2019.103789

Trach, E. (2020, January 1). *A beginner's guide to the flipped classroom*. Schoology exchange. https://www.schoology.com/blog/flipped-classroom

There are two formats within Chicago referencing style: Notes and Bibliography (NB) and Author-Date. The Chicago NB format is used in the humanities, and this guide mainly focuses on this NB format. The Author-Date format is used in social sciences (briefly described on pp. 172–173). For more information on using the Chicago referencing style, see *Chicago Manual of Style*. 17th ed. Chicago: University of Chicago Press, 2017; and University of Chicago Press. *Chicago Manual of Style Online*. Accessed: 25 June 2021. https://www.chicagomanualofstyle.org/home.html.

Chicago Notes and Bibliography (NB) format

This format uses **footnotes** below your text and a **bibliography** at the end of your text.

Instead of naming authors in the text, which can be distracting for the reader, numbers are used to denote **citations**. These numbers in the text are linked to a full **reference** in **footnotes** or **endnotes** and in your **bibliography**. Word-processing software such as Microsoft Word can create this link between citation number and full reference.

Cited publications are numbered in the order in which they are first referred to in the text. They are usually identified by a **superscript number**, for example, 'Thomas corrected this error'.[1]

Conventions when using the Chicago (NB) referencing style

Footnotes or endnotes

♦ Check whether footnotes or endnotes are preferred for the work you are producing
♦ Comma then page number in the footnotes
♦ All notes end with a full stop

Author names

♦ In the footnotes, author names should be forename followed by surname/family name, for example Francis Wheen. In the bibliography, author names should be surname followed by forename, for example Wheen, Francis
♦ If there are two or three authors list all of them in the footnotes and bibliography. If there are four or more authors list only the first followed by **et al**. in the footnotes, but list all authors in the bibliography. The first author's name is given in the bibliography as surname, first name, but other authors are written as first name surname

Titles

♦ Italicise the titles of books, journals and websites. Titles of articles, chapters, unpublished sources such as PhDs, and web pages within a website are placed within double quotation marks

Bibliography

♦ List all the authors of a source in the bibliography
♦ List works in alphabetical order by surname of the first author
♦ Names are given as surname, forename for the first author, but subsequent authors and editors are given as forename surname. For example: Williams, Edith, Jane Thompson, and Claire Hopper
♦ Sources without an author are listed by title in the alphabetical list
♦ References in your bibliography end with a full stop
♦ List all your sources, including those you have read but not cited in footnotes or endnotes, in the bibliography

First citation and subsequent short citations

The first time you cite a source, give full details in the footnote or endnote. Subsequent entries of the same source can be abbreviated to author's surname and the first few words of the title, plus a page number if you are citing a specific part of the text, giving you a **short citation**, for example:

Worsley, *Classical Architecture*, 5.

The sample text at the end of this section shows examples of a first citation and subsequent short citation of this book by Worsley.

Ibid.

Ibid. (from Latin, *ibidem*) means 'in the same place'. If two (or more) consecutive references are from the same source, then the second (or others) is cited ibid. Capitalise ibid. if used at the beginning of a note, for example:

1. Paulina Grainger, *Imagery in Prose*, London: Dale Press, 2009, 133–81.
2. Ibid., 155.
3. Ibid., 170.

Capitalisation

♦ Capitalise the first letter of the first word of the title and subtitle and subsequent main words (but not articles such as the, of, and). Capitalise articles if they are the first words of a subtitle after a colon, for example *Cite Them Right: The Essential Referencing Guide*

Dates

♦ For serials such as journals and newspapers, dates should be written as month day, year

Place of publication: publisher, year of publication

♦ All in round brackets in footnotes but not in bibliography

Internet addresses (URLs), Digital Object Identifiers (DOIs) and databases

♦ Whenever possible, use a DOI rather than an URL.
♦ The URL is given in full
♦ If you have obtained the source from a database that requires the reader to log in, give the name of the database and omit the URL

- If the source does not include a published date or date of last revision, include an accessed date before the URL

Page numbers

- Omit p. or pp. but give page numbers for references to information cited, paraphrasing or quotations taken from the original source
- In the footnote, give the specific page number of information you have used in a source after the publication details
- In the bibliography, give the span of pages of the whole chapter or section you have used in an edited book before the publication details

Formatting and punctuation

- Chicago referencing style has regulations for formatting your footnotes and references. The first line of footnotes should be indented by ½ inch (1.3cm) and subsequent lines are not indented. For the bibliography, the first line of references is not indented, but the second and subsequent lines have a hanging indent of ½ inch (1.3cm)
- Chicago style has different punctuation for entries in your footnotes and in your bibliography. Use commas to separate elements of the reference in the footnote, but use commas or full stops to separate the elements of the reference in the bibliography. In your footnote, the place of publication, publisher and year are enclosed in round brackets, but are unenclosed in the bibliography entry. Editors are referred to as 'ed.' in the footnote, but the phrase 'edited by' is used in the bibliography

Example

Footnote

1. Jane Dickson, "Female Managers in Industry," in *Corporate Leadership*, ed. Janesh Singh (Oxford: Oxford University Press, 2014), 49.

Bibliography

Dickson, Jane. "Female Managers in Industry." In *Corporate Leadership*, edited by Janesh Singh, 48–56. Oxford: Oxford University Press, 2014.

Secondary referencing

Whenever possible, you should read a source yourself, but if it is unavailable you can provide a secondary reference in a footnote by giving the original source and then where it was quoted in the source you read.

Example

Footnote

1. Donald Keane, ed. *Anthology of Japanese Literature*, 3rd ed. (London: Grove, 1955), 49, quoted in Sue Curl, *Japanese Poetry* (New York: Scholars Press, 2019), 209.

How to reference common sources in footnotes and bibliography

I1 Books

Citation order:

♦ Author
♦ Title (in italics)
♦ Edition (only include the edition number if it is not the first edition)
♦ Place of publication: publisher, year of publication (all in round brackets in footnote, but not in bibliography)
♦ Comma then page reference in footnote

Examples

Footnotes

1. Giles Worsley, *Classical Architecture in Britain: The Heroic Age* (London: Published for the Paul Mellon Centre for Studies in British Art by Yale University Press, 1995), 47.

2. Robert Chitham, *The Classical Orders of Architecture*, 2nd ed. (Amsterdam: Elsevier, 2005), 22.

Bibliography

Chitham, Robert. *The Classical Orders of Architecture*. 2nd ed. Amsterdam: Elsevier, 2005.
Worsley, Giles. *Classical Architecture in Britain: The Heroic Age*. London: Published for the Paul Mellon Centre for Studies in British Art by Yale University Press, 1995.

I2 Ebooks

Cite ebooks in the same format as print books, but add the DOI, URL or name of the online collection or database. If you have read the ebook on a personal device, state the format, for example Kindle. If you are unable to give page numbers for an ebook, give the most accurate information you can, such as chapter.

Citation order:

♦ Author/editor
♦ Title (in italics)
♦ Edition (only include the edition number if it is not the first edition)
♦ Place of publication: publisher, year of publication (all in round brackets in footnote, but not in bibliography)
♦ Page reference in footnote
♦ https://doi.org/, URL, name of database or media

Examples

Footnotes

1. Anne Cleeve, *White Nights* (London: Pan Books, 2008), chap. 30, Kindle.

2. Robert Adam, *Ruins of the Palace of the Emperor Diocletian at Spalatro in Dalmatia* (London: Printed for the author, 1764), plate 14, Eighteenth Century Collections Online.

3. Michael Shapland, *Anglo-Saxon Towers of Lordship* (Oxford: Oxford University Press, 2019), 47, https://doi.org/10.1093/oso/9780198809463.001.0001.

Bibliography

Adam, Robert. *Ruins of the Palace of the Emperor Diocletian at Spalatro in Dalmatia.* London: Printed for the author, 1764. Eighteenth Century Collections Online.

Cleeve, Anne. *White Nights.* London: Pan Books, 2008. Kindle.

Shapland, Michael. *Anglo-Saxon Towers of Lordship*. Oxford: Oxford University Press, 2019. https://doi.org/10.1093/oso/9780198809463.001.0001.

I3 Translated books

Citation order:

♦ Author
♦ Title (in italics)
♦ Edition (only include the edition number if it is not the first edition)
♦ Translated by
♦ Forename surname of translator
♦ Place of publication: publisher, year of publication (all in round brackets in footnote, but not in bibliography)
♦ Comma then page reference in footnote

Example

Footnote

1. Miguel Delibes, *The Path*, trans. John Haycraft and Rita Haycraft (London: Dolphin Books, 2013), 13.

Bibliography

Delibes, Miguel. *The Path*. Translated by John Haycraft and Rita Haycraft. London: Dolphin Books, 2013.

I4 Ancient texts

Citation order:

♦ Author
♦ Title (in italics)
♦ Edition (only include the edition number if it is not the first edition)
♦ Edited by editor (if applicable)
♦ Translated by
♦ Forename surname of translator
♦ Name of collection (if required)
♦ Place of publication: publisher, year of publication (all in round brackets in footnote, but not in bibliography)
♦ Comma and page number in footnote

Example

Footnote

1. Pliny the Younger, *Letters, Volume II: Books 8–10. Panegyricus*, trans. Betty Radice, Loeb Classical Library (Cambridge, MA: Harvard University Press, 1969), 12.

Bibliography

Pliny the Younger. *Letters, Volume II: Books 8–10. Panegyricus*. Translated by Betty Radice. Loeb Classical Library. Cambridge, MA: Harvard University Press, 1969.

I5 Sacred texts

I5.1 Bible

The Chicago Manual of Style (596–600) has a list of abbreviations for books of the Bible and published versions. You should provide references in footnotes; no entry is required in your bibliography.

Citation order:

♦ Book abbreviation
♦ Chapter: verse(s)
♦ Version (written out in first footnote, abbreviated in subsequent notes)

Example

Footnote

1. Eph. 6:10–17 (Revised Standard Version).

I5.2 Qur'an

Citation order:

♦ Qur'an
♦ Surah: verse(s)

Example

Footnote

1. Qur'an, 19: 10–11.

I5.3 The Torah

Citation order:

♦ Book title
♦ Chapter: verse(s)
♦ Torah

Example

Footnote

1. Shemot 3:14, Torah.

I6 Edited books, encyclopedias and anthologies

I6.1 Whole books

Citation order:

♦ Author/editor
♦ Title (in italics)
♦ Edition (only include the edition number if it is not the first edition)
♦ Number of volumes
♦ Place of publication: publisher, year of publication (all in round brackets in footnote, but not in bibliography)
♦ Comma then page reference in footnote

Example

Footnote

1. Donald Keane, ed., *Anthology of Japanese Literature*, 3rd ed. (London: Grove, 1955), 42–49.

Bibliography

Keane, Donald, ed. *Anthology of Japanese Literature*. 3rd ed. London: Grove, 1955.

I6.2 Chapters of edited books, poems in anthologies, encyclopedia entries

Citation order:

♦ Author of the chapter
♦ Title of chapter (in double quotation marks)
♦ in (when used in footnote), In (when used in bibliography)
♦ Title of book (in italics)
♦ ed. or edited by

- Name of editor of book (first name surname)
- Page span of chapter or section (only in bibliography)
- Place of publication: publisher, year of publication (all in round brackets in footnote, but not in bibliography)
- Comma then page reference in footnote

If online:

- online ed., year of update (if different from print details, include in round brackets)
- URL *or* https://doi.org/

Examples

Footnotes

1. Alexandrina Buchanan, "Interpretations of Medieval Architecture," in *Gothic Architecture and Its Meanings 1550–1830*, ed. Michael Hall (Reading: Spire Books, 2002), 32.

2. Peter Conradi, "Murdoch, Dame (Jean) Iris (1919–1999)," in *Oxford Dictionary of National Biography* (Oxford University Press, 2004; online ed., 2015), https://doi.org/10.1093/ref:odnb/71228.

3. William Wordsworth, "Written in Very Early Youth," in *Poetical Works of William Wordsworth*, vol. 1, eds. Ernest De Selincourt and Helen Darbishire (Oxford: Oxford University Press, 2015), 3.

Bibliography

Buchanan, Alexandrina. "Interpretations of Medieval Architecture." In *Gothic Architecture and Its Meanings 1550–1830*, edited by Michael Hall, 27–52. Reading: Spire Books, 2002.

Conradi, Peter. "Murdoch, Dame (Jean) Iris (1919–1999)." In *Oxford Dictionary of National Biography*. Oxford: Oxford University Press, 2004; online ed., 2015. https://doi.org/10.1093/ref:odnb/71228.

Wordsworth, William. "Written in Very Early Youth." In *Poetical Works of William Wordsworth*. Vol. 1, edited by Ernest De Selincourt and Helen Darbishire, 3. Oxford: Oxford University Press, 2015.

I7 Multi-volume works

Citation order:

- Author/editor
- Title (in italics)
- Edition (only include the edition number if it is not the first edition)
- Number of volumes
- Place of publication: publisher, year of publication (all in round brackets in footnote, but not in bibliography)

Example

Footnote

1. Damie Stillman, *English Neo-classical Architecture,* 2 vols. (London: Zwemmer, 1988).

Bibliography

Stillman, Damie. *English Neo-classical Architecture*. 2 vols. London: Zwemmer, 1988.

I8 Plays

Citation order:

- ♦ Author
- ♦ Title (in italics)
- ♦ Edited by forename/surname
- ♦ Place of publication: publisher, year of publication (all in round brackets in footnote, but not in bibliography)
- ♦ Reference to cited Act. Scene. Line number, or page number (only in footnote)

Example

Footnote

1. William Shakespeare, *Hamlet*, ed. T.J.B. Spencer (London: Penguin, 1980), I. 2. 177.

Bibliography

Shakespeare, William. *Hamlet*. Edited by T.J.B. Spencer. London: Penguin, 1980.

I9 Journal articles

Citation order:

- ♦ Author
- ♦ Title of article (in double quotation marks)
- ♦ Title of journal (in italics)
- ♦ Volume number, issue number
- ♦ Year of publication (in round brackets)
- ♦ Colon then page reference in footnote or page span in bibliography

If online, add:

- ♦ https://doi.org/ *or* URL *or* name of database

Footnotes

Example of print article

1. Peter Leach, "James Paine's Design for the South Front of Kedleston Hall: Dating and Sources," *Architectural History* 40 (1997): 160.

Example of article with DOI

2. Edwina Thomas Washington, "An Overview of Cyberbullying in Higher Education," *Adult Learning* 26 (2015): 21–27, https://doi.org/10.1177/1045159514558412.

Example article in database

3. Robert T. Teske, "Fifty Years in Folklore," *Journal of American Folklore* 131, no. 531 (Summer 2018): 303, Project MUSE.

Bibliography

Leach, Peter. "James Paine's Design for the South Front of Kedleston Hall: Dating and Sources." *Architectural History* 40 (1997): 159–70.

Teske, Robert T. "Fifty Years in Folklore." *Journal of American Folklore* 131, no. 531 (Summer 2018): 301–17. Project Muse.

Washington, Edwina Thomas. "An Overview of Cyberbullying in Higher Education." *Adult Learning* 26 (2015): 21–27. https://doi.org/10.1177/1045159514558412.

I10 Newspaper and magazine articles

Citation order:

- Author
- Title of article (in double quotation marks)
- Title of newspaper (in italics)
- Date
- Section (if applicable)
- Page number (in footnote, but not in bibliography)

If online, add:

- https://doi.org/ *or* URL *or* name of database

Omit *The from* newspaper titles, unless there is only one word after *The*, for example write *New York Times*, not *The New York Times*, but use *The Guardian*, not *Guardian*.

Example

Footnotes

    1. Soo Kim, "Child COVID cases are highest in these states," *Newsweek*, May 5, 2021, https://www.newsweek.com/coronavirus-states-highest-child-covid-cases-children-1588815.

    2. Mark Bentham, "Homelessness rises to a record high," *Evening Standard*, June 19, 2019, 8.

    3. Benjamin Haas, "Tears flow as separated South and North Korean Families Reunite," *Guardian*, August 20, 2018, Factiva.

Bibliography

Bentham, Mark. "Homelessness rises to a record high." *Evening Standard*, June 19, 2019.

Haas, Benjamin. "Tears flow as separated South and North Korean Families Reunite." *Guardian*, August 20, 2018. Factiva.

Kim, Soo. "Child COVID cases are highest in these states." *Newsweek*, May 5, 2021. https://www.newsweek.com/coronavirus-states-highest-child-covid-cases-children-1588815.

I11 Book reviews

Citation order:

- Author of review
- Title of review article (in double quotation marks, if available)
- Review of
- Title of work being reviewed (in italics)
- By
- Name of author of work being reviewed
- Title of publication where review published (in italics)
- Date
- Page number reference (if available)

If online, add:

- https://doi.org/ *or* URL

Example

Footnote

1. Willy Maley, "Where No Man Has Gone Before," review of *Samuel Johnson and the Journey into Words*, by Lynda Mugglestone, *Times Higher Education*, September 24, 2015, https://www.timeshighereducation.com/books/review-samuel-johnson-and-the-journey-into-words-lynda-mugglestone-oxford-university-press.

Bibliography

Maley, Willy. "Where No Man Has Gone Before." Review of *Samuel Johnson and the Journey into Words*, by Lynda Mugglestone. *Times Higher Education*. September 24, 2015. https://www.timeshighereducation.com/books/review-samuel-johnson-and-the-journey-into-words-lynda-mugglestone-oxford-university-press.

I12 Conference proceedings

I12.1 Whole conference proceedings

If the conference proceedings are published as an edited book, use the citation order in I6.1.

Citation order:

♦ Author/editor
♦ Title (in italics)

♦ Edition (only include the edition number if it is not the first edition)
♦ Number of volumes
♦ Place of publication: publisher, year of publication (all in round brackets in footnote, but not in bibliography)

Example

Footnote

1. Hilary Jones, ed., *Proceedings of the 10th Conference in Romance Studies, 18 May 2014* (Derby: University of Derby Press, 2014).

Bibliography

Jones, Hilary, ed. *Proceedings of the 10th Conference in Romance Studies, 18 May 2014*. Derby: University of Derby Press, 2014.

I12.2 Conference papers or poster presentations

Citation order:

♦ Author
♦ Title of paper (in double quotation marks)
♦ Paper presented at
♦ Name of conference, location and date
♦ Publication details

If online, add:

♦ https://doi.org/ *or* URL

Example

Footnote

1. Balakrishna Hosangadi, "Folktales, Myths and Legends on Sculptors of South India," (presentation, Asian Conference on Literature 2017, Kobe, Japan, March 2017), http://papers.iafor.org/submission34635.

Bibliography

Hosangadi, Balakrishna. "Folktales, Myths and Legends on Sculptors of South India." Paper presented at the Asian Conference on Literature 2017, Kobe, Japan, March 2017. http://papers.iafor.org/submission34635.

If the paper was published in conference proceedings, cite it as a chapter in a book (I6.2), or if it was published in a journal, cite it as an article (I9).

I13 Theses and dissertations

Chicago style follows the American terminology for Master's thesis and PhD dissertation (rather than Master's dissertation and PhD thesis as in the UK).

Citation order:

♦ Author
♦ Title of thesis (in double quotation marks)
♦ Degree level, university, year (all in round brackets in footnote, but not in bibliography)
♦ Page number (in footnote, but not in bibliography)
♦ If online, add URL *or* name of database and thesis/dissertation number

Examples

Footnotes

1. Brian Wragg, "The Life and Works of John Carr of York: Palladian Architect" (PhD diss., University of Sheffield, 1976), 47.

2. Michael Johnson, "Architectural Taste and Patronage in Newcastle upon Tyne, 1870–1914" (PhD diss., Northumbria University, 2009), http://nrl.northumbria.ac.uk/id/eprint/2867.

3. Andrew Stewart Cunningham, "Sympathy in Man and Nature" (PhD diss., University of Toronto, 1999), ProQuest Dissertations Publishing (NQ41132).

Examples in bibliography

Cunningham, Andrew Stewart. "Sympathy in Man and Nature." PhD diss., University of Toronto, 1999. ProQuest Dissertations Publishing (NQ41132).

Johnson, Michael. "Architectural Taste and Patronage in Newcastle upon Tyne, 1870–1914." PhD diss., Northumbria University, 2009. http://nrl.northumbria.ac.uk/id/eprint/2867.

Wragg, Brian. "The Life and Works of John Carr of York: Palladian Architect." PhD diss., University of Sheffield, 1976.

I14 Pamphlets, reports and command papers

Citation order:

- ♦ Author (person or organisation)
- ♦ Title (in italics)
- ♦ Volume details and command number if available
- ♦ Place of publication: publisher, year
- ♦ Comma, then page reference in footnote
- ♦ URL (if online)

Example

Footnotes

1. Department for Energy & Climate Change, *Community Energy Strategy*, URN 14D/019 (London: The Stationery Office, 2014), 4, https://www.gov.uk/government/publications/community-energy-strategy.

Bibliography

Department for Energy & Climate Change. *Community Energy Strategy*, URN 14D/019. London: The Stationery Office, 2014. https://www.gov.uk/government/publications/community-energy-strategy.

I15 Legal sources

I15.1 Legislation

Citation order:

- ♦ Title of legislation, year, chapter number

Examples

Footnotes

1. Human Rights Act, 1998, c. 42.

2. Banking Act, 2009, c. 1.

Bibliography

Banking Act, 2009, c. 1.
Human Rights Act, 1998, c. 42.

I15.2 Cases

Citation order:

- ♦ Party names (A v B)
- ♦ Year
- ♦ Citation

Example

Footnote

1. R. v Antoine, 2000, UKHL 20; [2000] 2 All ER 208.

Bibliography

R. v Antoine. 2000. UKHL 20; [2000] 2 All ER 208.

I16 Organisation or personal websites and web pages

If the details of the website can be given in your text, you do not need to add a footnote and bibliography entry; for example: "The text was published on the Auden Society website on August 4, 2019." If you are providing footnote and bibliography entries, use the following.

Citation order in footnote:

♦ Title of web page (in double quotation marks)
♦ Author/organisation
♦ Accessed date *or* date last modified and URL

Citation order in bibliography:

♦ Author/organisation
♦ Title of webpage (in double quotation marks)
♦ Accessed date *or* date last modified and URL

Examples

Footnotes

1. "Quote Library," Trollope Society, accessed May 21, 2021, https://trollopesociety.org/works/quotes/.

2. "Dynamics of Anion Formation," J. R. R. Verlet, accessed May 14, 2021, http://www.verlet.net/edc.html.

Bibliography

Trollope Society. "Quote Library." Accessed May 21, 2021. https://trollopesociety.org/works/quotes/.

Verlet, J. R. R. "Dynamics of Anion Formation." Accessed May 14, 2021. http://www.verlet.net/edc.html.

I17 Blogs

Citation order:

♦ Author
♦ Title of post (in double quotation marks)
♦ Title of blog (in italics)
♦ (blog)
♦ Date and URL

Example

Footnote

1. Claire Davies, "Inspiring Thursday: Greta Thunberg," *Wave Blog* (blog), October 24, 2019, https://blog.wave-network.org/inspiring-thursday-greta-thunberg.

Bibliography

Davies, Claire. "Inspiring Thursday: Greta Thunberg." *Wave Blog* (blog). October 24, 2019. https://blog.wave-network.org/inspiring-thursday-greta-thunberg.

I18 Social media

I18.1 Facebook and Instagram

Citation order:

♦ Author
♦ Title of post (in double quotation marks)
♦ Site name
♦ Date of post and URL

Example

Footnotes

1. natgeotv, "Orca in the waters off of the North Island in New Zealand," Instagram photo, April 20, 2021, https://www.instagram.com/p/CN5aU_QrkpA/.

2. Durham University Library, "Durham Priory Library Recreated," Facebook, July 29, 2015, https://www.facebook.com/dulib/videos/10153270708178099.

Bibliography

Durham University Library. "Durham Priory Library Recreated." Facebook, July 29, 2015. https://www.facebook.com/dulib/videos/10153270708178099.

natgeotv. "Orca in the waters off of the North Island in New Zealand." Instagram photo, April 20, 2021. https://www.instagram.com/p/CN5aU_QrkpA/.

I18.2 Twitter

Citation order:

♦ Author or organisation (real name)
♦ Screen name (in round brackets)
♦ Text of post (in double quotation marks)
♦ Twitter
♦ Date and time
♦ URL

Example

Footnote

1. Jane March (@JMarch), "University entry grades rose by an average of four points in 2018," Twitter, November 14, 2018, 1.20 p.m., http://twitter.com/JMarch/status/151509635204723087.

Bibliography

Jane March (@JMarch). "University entry grades rose by an average of four points in 2018." Twitter, November 14, 2018, 1.20 p.m. http://twitter.com/JMarch/status/151509635204723087.

I19 Films

Citation order:

♦ Film title (in italics)
♦ Directed by First name Last name
♦ Year released (if different from medium you have used);
♦ Place: distributor, year released in this medium
♦ Medium

Examples

Footnotes

1. *Brief Encounter*, directed by David Lean (1945; London: ITV Studios Home Entertainment, 2009), DVD.

2. *Chasing Coral*, directed by Jeff Orlowski (Los Gatos, CA: Netflix, 2017), https://www.netflix.com/gb/title/80168188.

Bibliography

In the bibliography, place the director first.

Lean, David, dir. *Brief Encounter*. 1945; London: ITV Studios Home Entertainment, 2009. DVD.

Orlowski, Jeff, dir. *Chasing Coral*. Los Gatos, CA: Netflix, 2017. https://www.netflix.com/gb/title/80168188.

I20 Television or radio broadcasts

Citation order:

♦ Episode title (if applicable, in double quotation marks)
♦ Programme/series title (in italics)
♦ Name of broadcaster/channel
♦ Month day, year

Examples

Footnotes

1. "Scarlet Macaw," *Tweet of the Day*, BBC Radio 4, February 2, 2018.

2. "Perfume," *The Apprentice*, BBC One, December 4, 2019.

Bibliography

"Perfume." *The Apprentice*. BBC One. December 4, 2019.

"Scarlet Macaw." *Tweet of the Day*. BBC Radio 4. February 2, 2018.

I21 Podcasts/online videos

Citation order:

♦ Creator
♦ Title (in double quotation marks)
♦ Date of posting
♦ Format
♦ Length of recording
♦ URL

Example

Footnote

1. Gabriella González, "Black Holes and Gravitational Waves," January 12, 2021, video, 39:13, https://www.youtube.com/watch?v=Txuq1sO8fkY.

Bibliography

González, Gabriella. "Black Holes and Gravitational Waves." January 12, 2021. Video, 39:13. https://www.youtube.com/watch?v=Txuq1sO8fkY.

I22 Audio recordings

Citation order:

♦ Name of composer or artist
♦ Title of track (in double quotation marks)
♦ Track number (if citing one item on an album)
♦ on
♦ Title (in italics)
♦ Other contributors
♦ Date of publication
♦ Publication details
♦ Medium

Examples

Footnotes

1. Gustav Mahler, *Symphony no. 10*, performed by Berliner Philharmoniker, conductor Sir Simon Rattle, recorded September 24–25, 1999, Warner Classics UPC 724355697226, 2000, compact disc.

2. Girl in Red, "Apartment 402," track 8 on *If I Could Make it Go Quiet*, AWAL, 2019, https://open.spotify.com/album/10nQ1u8Y1zlOb61zwZavDk.

Bibliography

Girl in Red. "Apartment 402." Track 8 on *If I Could Make it Go Quiet*. AWAL, 2019. https://open.spotify.com/album/10nQ1u8Y1zlOb61zwZavDk.

Mahler, Gustav. *Symphony no. 10*. Performed by Berliner Philharmoniker, conductor Sir Simon Rattle. Recorded September 24–25, 1999. Warner Classics UPC 724355697226, compact disc.

I23 Works of art: photographs, paintings, sculptures and installations

References to works of art can be made in your text, but if you wish to include a footnote and bibliography entry, use this citation order. For works of art viewed online, add an URL at the end of the reference. For images of works of art published in books, articles, catalogues, etc., cite as a page reference within that source.

Citation order:

♦ Artist
♦ Title of work (in italics)
♦ Date
♦ Medium
♦ Dimensions
♦ Location or URL

Examples

Footnotes

1. Auguste Rodin, *The Kiss*, 1882, marble, Musee Rodin, Paris, France.

2. John Martin, *The Bard*, 1817, oil on canvas 215cm × 157cm, Laing Art Gallery, Newcastle upon Tyne.

3. Cartier-Bresson, Henri. *Juvisy, France*, 1938, photograph, Museum of Modern Art, New York City.

4. Anthony Gormley, *Angel of the North*, 1998, sculpture, Low Fell, Gateshead.

5. Eli Reed, *BRAZIL. Sao Paolo. 2009. Ibirapuera park*, 2009, photograph, https://library-artstor-org.ezphost.dur.ac.uk/asset/AWSS35953_35953_37875434.

Bibliography

Cartier-Bresson, Henri. *Juvisy, France*. 1938. Photograph. Museum of Modern Art, New York City.
Gormley, Anthony. *Angel of the North*. 1998. Sculpture. Low Fell, Gateshead.
Martin, John. *The Bard*, 1817, oil on canvas 215cm × 157cm. Laing Art Gallery, Newcastle upon Tyne.
Reed, Eli. *BRAZIL. Sao Paolo. 2009. Ibirapuera park*. 2009. Photograph. https://library-artstor-org.ezphost.dur.ac.uk/asset/AWSS35953_35953_37875434.
Rodin, Auguste. *The Kiss*. 1882. Marble. Musee Rodin, Paris, France.

I24 Music scores

Citation order:

♦ Composer
♦ Title of work (in italics)
♦ Place of publication: publisher, year (all in round brackets in footnotes, but not in bibliography)

Example

Footnote

1. Peter Maxwell Davies, *An Orkney Wedding, with Sunrise* (London: Boosey & Hawkes, 1985).

Bibliography

Davies, Peter Maxwell. *An Orkney Wedding, with Sunrise*. London: Boosey & Hawkes, 1985.

I25 Manuscripts in archives

In the footnote, begin with the item you are citing. In the bibliography, list the collection rather than specific items.

Citation order for single item:

♦ Description of document
♦ Reference number
♦ Name of archive
♦ Location

Example

Footnote

1. Gian Tommaso Scala, View of Newcastle upon Tyne, c.1545. Cotton Augustus Mss I.ii, item no. f.4. British Library, London.

Bibliography

Cotton Augustus Mss. British Library, London.

I26 Course materials

I26.1 Lectures

A live lecture should be mentioned in your text or a footnote, but not the bibliography. If the lecture is recorded but not publicly available (for example in a VLE), use the example below. For publicly accessible lectures, see I21.

Citation order:

♦ Author
♦ Title of lecture (in double quotation marks)
♦ Lecture to/at
♦ Name of event, location and date.
♦ Publication details

Examples

Footnotes

1. Jane Stanton, "Wordsworth's Imagination" (lecture at Durham Book Festival, Gala Theatre, Durham, September 18, 2018).

2. Clare Willard, "Wordsworth in Context" (lecture to MA Literature course, Durham University, February 2, 2020), http://duo.dur.ac.uk.

Bibliography

Stanton, Jane. "Wordsworth's Imagination." Lecture to Durham Book Festival. Gala Theatre, Durham. September 18, 2018.
Willard, Clare. "Wordsworth in Context." Lecture to MA Literature course. Durham University. February 2, 2020. http://duo.dur. ac.uk.

I26.2 Lecture notes

Citation order:

♦ Tutor
♦ Title of item (in double quotation marks)
♦ Module code: module title (in italics)
♦ Year of publication (in round brackets in footnote, but not in bibliography)
♦ URL of VLE

Example

Footnote

1. Steve Hadley, "Biomechanics: Introductory Readings," *BM289: Sport Biomechanics* (2018), https://mylearning.cumbria.ac.uk.

Bibliography

Hadley, Steve. "Biomechanics: Introductory Readings." *BM289: Sport Biomechanics*. 2018. https://mylearning.cumbria.ac.uk.

I27 Interviews

I27.1 Personal interviews

If you want to cite an interview you have conducted but not published, use the following.

Citation order:

♦ Name of interviewee
♦ Interview by
♦ Date of interview

Example

Footnote

1. Claire Johnson, "Performing Shakespeare," interview by Danielle Roberts, August 14, 2021.

Bibliography

Johnson, Claire. Interviewed by Danielle Roberts. August 14, 2021.

I27.2 Published interviews: print or online

Citation order:

♦ Name of interviewee
♦ Title of interview (in double quotation marks, if available)
♦ Interview by
♦ Name of interviewer (forename, surname)
♦ Publication details

Example

Footnotes

1. Jessica Staton, "Sometimes I Feel Like a Jack of All Trades," interview by Giverny Masso, *Stage*, September 25, 2018, https://www.thestage.co.uk/features/interviews.

Bibliography

Staton, Jessica. "Sometimes I Feel Like a Jack of All Trades." Interview by Giverny Masso. *Stage*, September 25, 2018. https://www.thestage.co.uk/features/interviews.

I28 Personal communications: emails, text messages and telephone calls

Personal communications can be cited in your text rather than in a footnote or bibliography. For example: "In her email to the author on December 1, 2020 Amanda Hollis listed … ". If you wish to cite a personal communication, do so in a footnote.

> **Example**
>
> **Footnote**
>
> 1. Amanda Hollis, email message to the author, December 1, 2020.

Sample text

This sample piece of text shows how various sources would be included as in-text citations.

Worsley's *Classical Architecture* highlighted the variety of styles that eighteenth-century architects employed in their buildings.[1] Rich patrons wanted designs in the latest fashion and among those to profit from this demand was Robert Adam, who published his studies of Roman buildings.[2] With this first-hand knowledge he designed many country houses and public buildings, and was even able to take over projects begun by other architects, as at Kedleston in Derbyshire.[3] His work was not always as revolutionary as he claimed,[4] but it certainly impressed clients and was copied by other architects including John Carr.[5] Although most patrons favoured classical styles, Horace Walpole suggested that the Gothic style was 'our architec-ture', the national style of England.[6] Later authors have suggested that Gothic style signified ancient lineage and the British Constitution.[7]

Sample footnotes

The first line of each footnote is indented by 1.3cm (½ inch). Text should be double line spaced.

1. Giles Worsley, *Classical Architecture in Britain: The Heroic Age* (London: Published for the Paul Mellon Centre for Studies in British Art by Yale University Press, 1995), 47.

2. Robert Adam, *Ruins of the Palace of the Emperor Diocletian at Spalatro in Dalmatia* (London: Printed for the author, 1764), Eighteenth Century Collections Online.

3. Peter Leach, "James Paine's Design for the South Front of Kedleston Hall: Dating and Sources," *Architectural History* 40 (1997): 160.

4. Worsley, *Classical Architecture*, 265.

5. Brian Wragg, "The Life and Works of John Carr of York: Palladian Architect" (PhD diss., University of Sheffield, 1976).

6. Horace Walpole, cited in S. Lang, "The Principles of the Gothic Revival in England," *Journal of the Society of Architectural Historians* 25, no. 4 (1966): 244, http://www.jstor.org/stable/988353.

7. Alexandrina Buchanan, "Interpretations of Medieval Architecture," in *Gothic Architecture and Its Meanings 1550–1830*, ed. Michael Hall (Reading: Spire Books, 2002): 27–52.

NB: Footnote 4 is an example of a **short citation** and footnote 6 is a **secondary reference**.

Sample bibliography

Sources listed in your bibliography should have a hanging indent of 1.3cm (½ inch) and text should be double line spaced.

Adam, Robert. *Ruins of the Palace of the Emperor Diocletian at Spalatro in Dalmatia.* London: Printed for the author, 1764. Eighteenth Century Collections Online.

Buchanan, Alexandrina. "Interpretations of Medieval Architecture." In *Gothic Architecture and Its Meanings 1550–1830*, edited by Michael Hall, 27–52. Reading: Spire Books, 2002.

Lang, S. "The Principles of the Gothic Revival in England." *Journal of the Society of Architectural Historians* 25, no. 4 (1966): 240–67. http://www.jstor.org/stable/988353.

Leach, Peter. "James Paine's Design for the South Front of Kedleston Hall: Dating and Sources." *Architectural History* 40 (1997): 159–70.

Worsley, Giles. *Classical Architecture in Britain: The Heroic Age.* London: Published for the Paul Mellon Centre for Studies in British Art by Yale University Press, 1995.

Wragg, Brian. "The Life and Works of John Carr of York: Palladian Architect." PhD diss., University of Sheffield, 1976.

Chicago Author-Date format

As with APA and Harvard styles, the Chicago Author-Date format uses in-text citations comprising the author's name and year of publication (and specific page reference if required).

Examples of in-text citations

Washington (2018, 27) concurred with an earlier assessment (Dickson 2016) …

A reference list (rather than a bibliography) at the end of the work provides full bibliographical details for sources used. These sources are listed in alphabetical order by authors' names.

The major difference in the form of the references is the position of the year of publication. In the Notes and Bibliography format, the year comes towards the end of the reference, but in Author-Date format, it is moved to second place in the reference, after the author's name, or if this is unavailable, the title of the source.

Examples

Bibliography in NB format

Dickson, Jane. "Female Managers in Industry." In *Corporate Leadership*, edited by Javid Singh, 48–56. Oxford: Oxford University Press, 2014.

Washington, Edwina Thomas. "An Overview of Cyberbullying in Higher Education." *Adult Learning* 26 (2015): 21–27. https://doi.org/10.1177/1045159514558412.

Dickson, Jane. 2014. "Female Managers in Industry." In *Corporate Leadership*, edited by Javid Singh, 48–56. Oxford: Oxford University Press.

Washington, Edwina Thomas. 2015. "An Overview of Cyberbullying in Higher Education." *Adult Learning* 26: 21–27. https://doi.org/10.1177/1045159514558412.

Note how the date now comes after the author's name and the date is also without round brackets in Author-Date format. Other details and punctuation in Author-Date format match the examples for Notes and Bibliography format.

Footnotes in Author-Date format

Unlike Harvard, Chicago Author-Date format allows the use of footnotes to elaborate on something you have mentioned in the text. Footnotes are *not* used to give full bibliographic details, as these are given in the reference list.

Example: in-text citation with footnote

Washington (2018, 27) concurred with an earlier assessment.[1]

Footnote

1. Dickson (2016, 50) had examined bullying in male-dominated occupations.

Sample reference list in Chicago Author-Date format

Adam, Robert. 1764. *Ruins of the Palace of the Emperor Diocletian at Spalatro in Dalmatia.* London: Printed for the author, 1764. Eighteenth Century Collections Online.

Buchanan, Alexandrina. 2002. "Interpretations of Medieval Architecture." In *Gothic Architecture and Its Meanings 1550–1830*, edited by Michael Hall, 27–52. Reading: Spire Books.

Lang, S. 1966. "The Principles of the Gothic Revival in England." *Journal of the Society of Architectural Historians* 25, no. 4: 240–67. http://www.jstor.org/stable/988353.

Leach, Peter. 1997. "James Paine's Design for the South Front of Kedleston Hall: Dating and Sources." *Architectural History* 40: 159–70.

Worsley, Giles. 1995. *Classical Architecture in Britain: The Heroic Age*. London: Published for the Paul Mellon Centre for Studies in British Art by Yale University Press.

Wragg, Brian. 1976. "The Life and Works of John Carr of York: Palladian Architect." PhD diss., University of Sheffield.

Section J
IEEE referencing style

The Institute of Electrical and Electronics Engineers was founded in 1963. Today it uses the name IEEE as it represents technical professionals from many industries. The IEEE referencing style is a numeric citation system used in engineering, electronics, computer science and information technology publications. This section is based on IEEE. *IEEE Reference Guide.* (2021). Accessed: Jun. 24, 2021. [Online]. Available: http://journals. ieeeauthorcenter.ieee.org/wp-content/uploads/sites/7/IEEE-Reference-Guide-Online-v.04-20-2021.pdf. Please note that there are contradictions within this document, particularly in the documentation of online sources (see examples for online monographs on p. 4). Our examples below have applied the principles of IEEE style to a fuller range of sources than are covered by the *IEEE Reference Guide*.

Conventions when using the IEEE referencing style

♦ IEEE uses numeric references in the text, with numbers in square brackets [1]
♦ Each source has its own in-text number
♦ The same citation number is used whenever a source is cited in your text
♦ These in-text numbers are matched to full, numbered **references** for each publication in a list of References

♦ Sources are listed in References in the order they appear in the text, not alphabetically
♦ In the References, the reference numbers in square brackets are aligned flush left as if in a separate column, while the source information is indented
♦ Dates are given as abbreviated month day, year
♦ Months with more than four letters are abbreviated: Jan. Feb. Mar. Apr. Aug. Sep. Oct. Nov. Dec., but May, June and July are written in full
♦ There are well-established abbreviations for titles of journals and conference proceedings
♦ Places of publication include US state abbreviation and country
♦ Finish with a full stop (period) after a DOI, but not after a URL
♦ No access date is needed with a DOI. If there isn't a DOI, add Accessed: date, if the format for that source requires this

Author names

♦ You do not need to include an author name in your in-text citation, unless you wish to do so

Examples

Collins [4] tested the theory …

A recent test of the theory [4] …

♦ Authors should be cited in the References by initial(s) of their given name, then surname (family name).

Example

[4] G. S. Collins

Multiple authors

♦ Many publications are the result of collaborative work, resulting in multiple authors. If there are two to five authors, list each in the order they appear in the source, with 'and' between the fourth and fifth authors' names

Example

[5] K. Leonis, F. Johnson, M. Willis, P. Chakraborty and S. Asturias.

♦ If there are six or more authors, use *et al.* after the first author. *Et al.* should be in italics

Example

[6] D. Bourne, P. Davis, E. Fuller, A. J. Hanson, K. N. Price, P. Singh, C. A. Thompson, S. Kim and J. T. Vaughan

would appear in the References as

[6] D. Bourne *et al.*

Organisations as authors

♦ Names of organisations are spelt out, not abbreviated

Example

Microsoft Corporation

No authors identified

♦ If no authors or editors are listed, use the title of the source

Example

3D Printing Manual. Birmingham, UK: Innovations Ltd, 2018.

Multiple citations

♦ If you have written a section of text based on several references, these are indicated by listing each source in its own square brackets

Example

Implementations of the new software [2], [3], [5] revealed …

♦ If you are citing consecutive sources, you can link these with a dash

Example

Foster's bridge designs [6]–[9] …

Quoting or paraphrasing

If you quote or paraphrase from a source, or wish to highlight part of it, include the page, paragraph or section numbers after the reference number.

Example

Wind power contributes around 4% of UK energy supply [4, p. 21] …

Secondary referencing

If you want to cite work by an author quoted in another publication, but you have not read the original author's own work, you must indicate that you read it in the second publication. This is because you are relying on the second author who you have read to give an accurate representation of the first author's work and to have used the first author's work in the correct context. You should not give a reference to the first author unless you have read their work yourself.

Examples

In-text citation

Data mining analysis by Chen [1, p. 45] …

Or

Data mining analysis by Chen, cited in Thompson [1, p. 45] …

References

[1] R. Thompson, *Advanced Data Analysis*. London, UK: IT Publ. Ltd, 2020.

NB: In the References, there is no mention of Chen, because you are relying on Thompson to represent her work correctly.

How to reference common sources in the reference list

J1 Books

Citation order:

♦ Author's given names initial(s) then surname
♦ Title (capitalise all major words; title in italics)
♦ Edition, abbreviated to ed. (only include the edition number if it is not the first edition)

♦ Place of publication: abbreviated name of publisher
♦ Year of publication

Example: single author

References

[1] A. R. Hambley, *Electrical Engineering: Principles and Applications*, 7th ed. Upper Saddle River, NJ, USA: Pearson, 2018.

Example: less than six authors

References

[2] N. Mohan, T. M. Undeland, and W. P. Robbins, *Power Electronics: Converters, Applications, and Design*, 3rd ed. New York, NY, USA: Wiley, 2003.

Example: six or more authors

References

[3] D. Bourne *et al.*, *AI Futures*, Piscataway, NJ, USA: IEEE Publ., 2018.

NB: Publishing is abbreviated to Publ.

J2 Ebooks

Citation order:

♦ Author's given names initial(s) then surname
♦ Title (capitalise all major words; title in italics)
♦ Edition, abbreviated to ed. (only include the edition number if it is not the first edition)

- Place of publication: publisher, year
- DOI *or* [Online]. Available: URL

Examples

References

[4] J. F. Manwell, J. G. McGowan, and A. Rogers, *Wind Energy Explained: Theory, Design and Application*, 2nd ed. Chichester, UK: Wiley, 2009. [Online]. Available: http://library.dur.ac.uk/record=b2722155~S1

[5] G. Szekely, *Sustainable Process Engineering*. Berlin, Germany: De Gruyter, 2021, doi: 10.1515/9783110717136.

NB: There is a full stop after the DOI, but not after the URL.

J3 Chapters/sections of edited books

Citation order:

- Author's given names initial(s) then surname
- Title of chapter in book (in double quotation marks)
- in
- Title of book (capitalise all major words; title in italics)
- Series and number (if given, in round brackets)
- Editor's initial(s) then surname
- Ed. or Eds.
- Place of publication: publisher, year
- Page numbers (preceded by pp.)
- DOI *or* [Online]. Available: URL

Example

References

[6] M. Akrich, "The de-scription of technical objects," in *Shaping Technology/Building Society: Studies in Sociotechnical Change* (Inside Technology), W. E. Bijker and J. Law, Eds., Cambridge, MA, USA: MIT Press, 1994, pp. 205–224.

J4 Handbooks/manuals

Citation order:

- Author's given names initial(s) then surname
- Title of handbook/manual (in italics)
- Edition
- Initial and surname of editors followed by eds. *or* name of company
- Location of organisation/company
- Year

If viewed online, add:

- DOI or [Online]. Available: URL

Examples

References

[7] *Electric Power Engineering Handbook*, 2nd ed., L. L. Grigsby and J. H. Harlow, Eds., Boca Raton, FL, USA: CRC Press, 2007.

[8] *Raspberry Pi: The Complete Manual*, Bournemouth, UK, 2016. [Online]. Available: https://archive.org/stream/Raspberry_Pi_The_Complete_Manual_7th_Edition#page/n3/mode/2up

J5 Journal articles

J5.1 Published journal articles

Citation order:

♦ Author's given names initial(s) then surname
♦ Title of article (in double quotation marks)
♦ Abbreviated title of journal (in italics)
♦ Volume, issue number
♦ Pages (preceded by pp.) *or* Art. no.
♦ Abbreviated month and year of publication

If viewed online, add:

♦ DOI *or* [Online]. Available: URL

Notes for the examples below

The full titles of the journals are *IEEE Transactions on Communications Systems* and *IEEE Transactions on Information Forensics and Security*; they have been abbreviated using the titles listed in *IEEE Reference Guide* (2021) Available at: http://journals.ieeeauthorcenter.ieee.org/wp-content/uploads/sites/7/IEEE-Reference-Guide-Online-v.04-20-2021.pdf (Accessed: 15 June 2021). Note that *Proceedings of the IEEE* is not abbreviated.

The article by Majumdar has seven authors, but following the IEEE guidance only the first named author of the article is given followed by *et al*.

The article by Strogatz does not have volume number, issue number or page numbers, so these are omitted.

The article by Iacobellis has an article number (Art. no.) instead of page numbers.

Example for print journal article

References

[9] J. Hopson, "Harmonic structure of modulated light beams," *IEEE Trans. Commun. Syst.*, vol. 11, no. 4, pp. 464–469, Dec. 1963.

Example for electronic journal article with DOI

References

[10] S. Majumdar *et al.*, "User-level runtime security auditing for the Cloud," *IEEE Trans. Inf. Forensics Security*, vol. 13, no. 5, pp. 1185–1199, May 2018, doi: 10.1109/TIFS.2017.2779444.

Example for electronic journal article with URL but no DOI

References

[11] S. Strogatz, "Explaining why the Millennium Bridge wobbled," *ScienceDaily*, Nov. 2005. Accessed: July 14, 2021. [Online]. Available: http://www.sciencedaily.com/releases/2005/11/051103080801.htm

Example for electronic journal article with Article number instead of page numbers

References

[12] G. Iacobellis, "COVID-19 and diabetes: Can DPP4 inhibition play a role?," *Diabetes Res. Clinical Pract.*, vol. 162, Apr. 2020, Art. no. 108125, doi: 10.1016/j.diabres.2020.108125.

J5.2 Advance online publication journal articles

Citation order:

♦ Author's given names initial(s) then surname
♦ Title of article (in double quotation marks)
♦ Abbreviated title of journal in which article will be published (in italics)
♦ To be published

If viewed online, add:

♦ DOI *or* Accessed: date. [Online]. Available: URL

Example

References

[13] G. Zhong, A. Dubey, T. Cheng, and T. Mitra, "Synergy: A HW/SW framework for high throughput CNNs on embedded heterogeneous SoC," *ACM Trans. Embedded Comput. Syst.*, to be published. Accessed: Dec. 1, 2020. [Online]. Available: https://arxiv.org/abs/1804.00706

J5.3 Magazine articles

Citation order:

♦ Author's given names initial(s) then surname
♦ Title of article (in double quotation marks)
♦ Abbreviated title of journal (in italics)
♦ Volume, issue number
♦ Pages (preceded by pp.)
♦ Abbreviated month and year of publication

If viewed online, add:

♦ DOI *or* Accessed: date. [Online]. Available: URL

Examples

References

[14] "The Undervalued Wasp," *The Week*, p. 23, Sep. 29, 2018.
[15] T. Bajarin, "Is Silicon Valley Over? Not by a Long Shot," *PC Magazine*, Apr. 16, 2018. Accessed: Nov. 21, 2020. [Online]. Available: http://uk.pcmag.com/opinion/94387/is-silicon-valley-over-not-by-a-long-shot

NB: If no author is identified, use the title of the article as the first part of the reference.

J6 Newspaper articles

Citation order:

♦ Author's given names initial(s) then surname
♦ Title of article (in double quotation marks)

- Title of newspaper (in italics)
- Pages (preceded by p. or pp.)
- Abbreviated month day, year of publication

If online, add:

- Accessed: date. [Online]. Available: URL

Example: print newspaper article

References

[16] D. Murray, "Thousands facing chaos in DLR strike," *Evening Standard*, p. 6, Mar. 27, 2018.

Example: article in online subscription newspaper database

References

[17] "Guidelines issued to boost 'big science,'" *Shenzen Daily*, Apr. 3, 2018. Accessed: Apr. 4, 2021. [Online]. *Nexis UK*, https://library.dur.ac.uk/record=b2045034~S1

Example: online news website article

References

[18] R. Cellan-Jones, "Microsoft gambles on a quantum leap in computing," *BBC News*, Mar. 31, 2018. Accessed: Apr. 4, 2021. [Online]. Available: http://www.bbc.co.uk/news/technology-43580972

Example: article in mobile news app

References

[19] M. Gurman, "Apple is said to work on touchless control, curved iPhones screen," *Bloomberg*, Apr. 4, 2021. Accessed: Apr. 7, 2021. [Online]. Mobile news app.

J7 Reports and working papers

Citation order:

- Author's given names initial(s) then surname
- Title of report (in double quotation marks)
- Name of organisation/company
- Location of organisation/company
- Series and report number
- Date

If viewed online, add:

- DOI *or* Accessed: date. [Online]. Available: URL

Example

References

[20] K. Serkh, "A note of the use of the spectra of multiplication operators as a numerical tool," Dep. Comp. Sci., Yale Univ., New Haven, CT, USA, Tech. Rep. YALEU/DCS/TR1541, Mar. 2018. Accessed: Apr. 24, 2021. [Online]. Available: https://cpsc.yale.edu/sites/default/files/files/tr1541.pdf

J8 Conferences

J8.1 Unpublished papers or posters presented at a conference

Citation order:

♦ Author's given names initial(s) then surname
♦ Title of paper (in double quotation marks)
♦ presented at
♦ Name of the conference (in italics and use abbreviations for words but not initials)
♦ City of conference, US state abbreviation, *or* country if not USA
♦ Year when conference was held if not included in conference title

Example

References

[21] B. Leigh, "Google analytics applications for websites," presented at *9th Int. Blackboard Conf.*, York, UK, Nov. 1–2, 2017.

J8.2 Papers published in conference proceedings

Citation order:

♦ Author's given names initial(s) then surname
♦ Title of paper (in double quotation marks)
♦ in
♦ Name of conference (in italics and use abbreviations for words but not initials)
♦ City of conference, US state abbreviation, *or* country if not USA
♦ Year
♦ Page numbers

If viewed online, add:

♦ DOI *or* [Online]. Available: URL

Example

References

[22] C. Wen and Q. Liu, "Mobile remote medical monitoring system," in *Proc. of the 2016 IEEE Int. Conf. on Consumer Electronics China*, Guangzhou, China, 2016, pp. 1–6, doi: 10.1109/ICCE-China.2016.7849727.

J8.3 Full conference proceedings

Citation order:

♦ Editor's given names initial(s) then surname
♦ Name of conference (in italics and use abbreviations for words but not initials)
♦ City of conference, US state abbreviation, *or* country if not USA
♦ Month, day(s), year
♦ Place of publication: publisher, year

If viewed online, add:

♦ DOI *or* [Online]. Available: URL

Example

References

[23] A. Bilgin, M. W. Marcellin, J. Serra-Sagrista, and J. A. Storer, Eds., *Data Compression Conf.*, Snowbird, UT, April 4–7, 2017. [Online]. Available: https://ieeexplore.ieee.org/xpl/conhome/7921793/proceeding

J9 Theses/dissertations

Citation order:

- ♦ Author's given names initial(s) then surname
- ♦ Title of thesis (in double quotation marks)
- ♦ Degree level
- ♦ Abbreviated names of university department, university
- ♦ City and US state abbreviation (if relevant)
- ♦ Year

If viewed online, add:

- ♦ DOI *or* [Online]. Available: URL

Example

References

[24] C. M. Wastell, "Communication patterns for randomized algorithms," Ph.D thesis, Dept. Eng. Comp. Sci., Durham Univ., Durham, UK, 2017. [Online]. Available: http://etheses.dur.ac.uk/12525/

J10 Research datasets

Citation order:

- ♦ Author's given names initial(s) then surname
- ♦ Date
- ♦ Title of dataset (in double quotation marks)
- ♦ Version or edition
- ♦ Title of repository/collection (in italics)
- ♦ Year

If viewed online, add:

- ♦ DOI *or* [Online]. Available: URL

Examples

References

[25] C. Bambra *et al.*, 2015, "Brownfield land dataset," *Durham Research Online DATAsets Archive*, doi: 10.15128/ba0f9472-7587-4393-989a-8f729ef20103.

[26] T. Le, R. Poplin, F. Bertsch, A. S. Toor, and M. L. Oh, 2021, "SyntheticFur dataset for neural rendering," *Arxiv.org*. [Online]. Available: https://arxiv.org/abs/2105.06409

J11 Technical standards

Citation order:

- ♦ Title of standard (in italics)
- ♦ Standard number
- ♦ Date

If viewed online, add:

- ♦ DOI *or* [Online]. Available: URL

Example

References

[27] *Environmental testing. Tests. Test M: Low air pressure*, BS EN IEC 60068-2-13:2021, 2021. [Online]. Available: https://bsol-bsigroup-com

J12 Patents

J12.1 Printed patents

Citation order:

- ♦ Author's given names initial(s) then surname

◆ Title of patent (in double quotation marks)
◆ Country abbreviation
◆ Patent followed by number
◆ Abbreviated month day, year

Example

References

[28] A. J. Ciniglio, "Soldering nozzle," UK Patent GB2483265, Feb. 27, 2018.

J12.2 Patents online

Citation order:

◆ Name of invention
◆ By inventor's name (initial(s) then surname)
◆ Date (in round brackets)
◆ Country abbreviation
◆ Patent followed by number
◆ DOI *or* [Online]. Available: URL

Example

References

[29] Radiator isolating valve, by S. Padley. (2015, Nov. 21). UK Patent GB 2463069 [Online]. Available: https://worldwide. espacenet.com/

J13 Software, computer programs, computer codes and computer games

Citation order:

◆ Creator's name or organisation (if available)
◆ Title of software (in italics)

◆ Version or year (in round brackets)
◆ Publisher
◆ Accessed: date. [Online]. Available: URL

Examples

References

[30] *Windows 10.* (Oct. 2020). Microsoft.
[31] *Camtasia 2020.* (Version 2021.0.0). TechSmith. Accessed: Jul. 3, 2021 [Online]. Available: https://www.techsmith.com/ video-editor.html
[32] *Halo: The Master Chief Collection.* (2020). 343 Industries. Accessed: Dec. 20, 2020. [Online]. Available: https://www.xbox.com/en-GB/ games/halo-the-master-chief- collection

J14 Mobile apps

Citation order:

◆ Creator's name or organisation (if available)
◆ Title of app (in italics)
◆ Version or year (in round brackets)
◆ Publisher
◆ Accessed: date. [Mobile app]. Available: URL

Example

References

[33] NHS Digital. *NHS COVID-19 app.* (Version 4.9 (185)). NHSX. Accessed: Jan. 3, 2021. [Mobile app]. Available: https://play. google.com/store/apps/ details?id=uk.nhs.covid19. production

J15 Government documents

Citation order:

♦ Author's given names initial(s) then surname, *or* Country. Government department
♦ Title (in italics)
♦ Document number (if available)
♦ Place of publication: publisher, year

If online, add:

♦ DOI *or* [Online]. Available: URL

Examples

References

[34] United Kingdom. Department for Education and Skills, *21st Century Skills: Realising our Potential*. Cm5810. London: Stationery Office, 2003.
[35] Australia. Department of Industry, Science, Energy and Resources, *Australia's Emissions Projections 2020*. Canberra: Australian Government, 2020. [Online]. Available: https://www.industry. gov.au/sites/default/files/2020-12/ australias-emissions-projections-2020.pdf

J16 Legal sources

J16.1 Legislation

Citation order:

♦ Legislative body
♦ Title of legislation and year (in italics)
♦ Number
♦ [Online]. Available: URL

Examples

References

[36] United Kingdom Parliament, *Fire Safety Act 2021*, c.24 [Online]. Available: https://www.legislation. gov.uk/ukpga/2021/24/contents/ enacted
[37] Singapore, *Vulnerable Adults Act 2018* [Online]. Available: https:// sso.agc.gov.sg/Act/VAA2018

J16.2 Legal cases

The case name is in italics when cited in the text, but not in the reference list. Publication details can include a legal database such as BAILII, LexisLibrary or Westlaw.

Citation order:

♦ Case name
♦ Publication details (in italics)
♦ Court reference (in round brackets)

Examples

In-text citation

Lessons from the case of *Humphreys v. Revenue and Customs Commissioners* [ ] …

References

[38] Humphreys v. Revenue and Customs Commissioners, *Weekly Law Reports*, vol. 1, 2012, p. 1545 (U.K. Supreme Court, 2012/18).
[39] Humphreys v. Revenue and Customs Commissioners. [Online]. LexisLibrary (U.K. Supreme Court, 2012/18).

J17 Maps

Citation order:

♦ Creator's name or organisation
♦ Title (in italics) or description (in double quotation marks)

If print, add:

♦ [Map]
♦ Place of publication: publisher; year
♦ Description, including size in cms
♦ colour/black and white
♦ Series; and number

If online, add:

♦ Accessed: date. [Online]. Available: URL

Examples

References

[40] Ordnance Survey. *Kendal to Morecambe* [Map]. Southampton, U.K.: Ordnance Survey; 1982. 1 sheet: 80x80cm; colour. Landranger 1:50,000 series; 97.
[41] Google Maps. "Directions for driving from Reading to Tiddenfoot Lake." Accessed: May 17, 2021. [Online]. Available: https://goo.gl/maps/hC5pUfsYCiW1Yuyw5

J18 Images

J18.1 Photographic prints or slides, drawings, paintings

Citation order:

♦ Creator's name or organisation
♦ Title of image (in italics)
♦ Year of production
♦ Medium (in square brackets)
♦ Collection reference, if available
♦ Location

Examples

References

[42] H. N. King, *London Bridge, seen from Southwark*, 1872. [Photographic print]. Ref. RIBA7357, RIBA Library, London, UK.
[43] G. Arnald, *Menai Bridge*, 1828. [Painting]. Plas Newydd, Anglesey, UK.
[44] J. Green and B. Green, *High Level Tyne Bridge: Plan and section*, 1839. [Architectural drawing]. Ref. D.NCP/4/36, Tyne and Wear Archives, Newcastle upon Tyne, UK.

J18.2 Images in publications: graphs, tables, figures, plates, equations

Use the citation order for the source (e.g. a book or a journal article) in which the image appeared, ending with the page number or the figure/illustration number after the in-text reference number. You may mention the artist of the image in your text, but cite the publication in which it appeared.

Examples

In-text citations

Trestman's table of laser power ratings [50, p. 98, table 4.2] and the schematic of an LD driver [50, p. 58, figure 7.1] ...

Leonardo's designs for flying machines [36, p. 211] ...

References

[45] G. A. Trestman, *Powering Laser Diode Systems*. Washington, DC, USA: SPIE Press, 2017.

[46] C. Nichol, *Leonardo Da Vinci: The Flights of the Mind*. London, UK: Penguin, 2007, p. 211.

J18.3 Images available online, including infographics

Citation order:

♦ Creator's name or organisation
♦ Title of image (in italics)
♦ Accessed: date. [Online]. Available: URL

Examples

References

[47] Gettyimages, *AWACS aircraft midair refuelling*. Accessed: Apr. 23, 2021. [Online]. Available: https://www.gettyimages.co.uk/detail/photo/aircraft-midair-refueling-royalty-free-image/506217256/

[48] The Health Foundation. *What does the pandemic mean for health and health inequalities?* Feb. 18, 2021. Accessed: Aug. 11, 2021. [Online]. Available: https://www.health.org.uk/news-and-comment/charts-and-infographics/what-does-the-pandemic-mean-for-health-and-health-inequaliti

J19 Radio or television programmes

Citation order:

♦ Presenter's given names initial(s) then surname
♦ Episode of television programme if relevant (in double quotations)
♦ Name of television programme (in italics)
♦ Abbreviated month day, year of broadcast
♦ [Television broadcast]
♦ Place of broadcast: broadcaster

Example

References

[49] K. McCloud, "Herefordshire," *Grand Designs*. Jun. 8, 2020. [Television broadcast]. London: Channel Four Television Corporation.

J20 Podcasts

Citation order:

♦ Creator's name or organisation
♦ Title of podcast (in italics)
♦ Date released (in round brackets)
♦ Accessed: date. [Podcast]. Available: URL

Example

References

[50] M. M. Hussain, *IEEE EDS Podcasts with Luminaries: Episode 2: Prof. Jayant Baliga*. (Jan. 25, 2021). Accessed: Apr. 18, 2021. [Podcast]. Available: https://www.podbean.com/media/share/pb-vu8en-f88e6e

J21 Online videos: YouTube, Vimeo, Kanopy, Amazon, Netflix

If the broadcast or video is publicly available, use this format. If you have to be invited or log in to view it, see J26.2.

Citation order:

♦ Creator's name or organisation
♦ Title of video (in italics)
♦ Date released (in round brackets)
♦ Accessed: date. [Online Video]. Available: URL

Example

References

[51] K. J. Hardrict, *Why Should You Choose Engineering?* (Aug. 16, 2019). Accessed: Feb. 4, 2021. [Online Video]. Available: https://www.youtube.com/watch?v=iHqh45mDktY

J22 DVDs

Citation order:

♦ Director's given names initial(s) then surname, if available
♦ Director
♦ Title of DVD (in italics)
♦ [DVD]
♦ Place of distribution: distributor, year

Example

References

[52] M. Akdogan, S. Everett, and M. Ibeji, Directors, *Engineering the Impossible*. [DVD]. Burbank, CA, USA: Warner Home Video for National Geographic Channel, 2007.

J23 Organisation or personal websites

Citation order:

♦ Author's given names initial(s) then surname, or organisation, if available
♦ Title of webpage (in double quotation marks)
♦ Title of website (in italics)
♦ Abbreviated month day, year of web page or last update
♦ Accessed: date. [Online]. Available: URL

Example

References

[53] "Canadian Honeynet Chapter," *Canadian Institute of Cybersecurity*, Feb. 17, 2018. Accessed: Jul. 9, 2021. [Online]. Available: http://www.unb.ca/cic/research/honeynet.html

J24 Blogs

Citation order:

♦ Author's given names initial(s) then surname, if available
♦ Title of blog post (in double quotation marks)
♦ Title of website
♦ URL (accessed date)

Example

References

[54] C. Davies. "Inspiring Thursday: Greta Thunberg." Wave Blog. https://blog.wave-network.org/inspiring-thursday-greta-thunberg (accessed May 23, 2021).

J25 Social media: Facebook, Twitter, Instagram

Citation order:

- Author's given names initial(s) then surname, *or* username *or* organisation
- Title of post (in double quotation marks)
- Title of site
- Date
- URL (accessed date)

Examples

References

[55] STEM Technology, "The effectiveness and possible risks from the use of ozone are at the center of medical discussions." Facebook. Apr. 2, 2021. https://www.facebook.com/stemtechnology/photos/a.686804701421911/3191612557607767/ (accessed Apr. 23, 2021).

[56] kat_echz, "Women in STEM: We are strong. We are resilient. We are accomplished. We won't let 'no' stop us." Instagram. Feb. 2, 2021. https://www.instagram.com/p/CHoFUd2D3gO/ (accessed Feb. 16, 2021).

[57] @IEEEorg, "#3Dprinting and #AugmentedReality technologies may be making more frequent appearances in operating rooms in the near future." Twitter. Apr. 2, 2021. https://twitter.com/IEEEAwards/status/1392926051538456576 (accessed Apr. 19, 2021).

J26 Course materials

J26.1 Lecture notes

Citation order:

- Author's given names initial(s) then surname
- Year (in round brackets)
- Title of lecture
- [Medium]
- Available: URL

Example

References

[58] A. M. Chan. (2021). Forces on structures [PowerPoint slides]. Available: https://www.my.bham.ac.uk/

J26.2 Online lectures: Zoom, Teams, Collaborate, Panopto, etc.

Use this format if the lecture if you need to log in or be invited to view the lecture. If it is publicly available, use J21.

Citation order:

- Institution name
- Year (in round brackets)
- Title of course/module
- [Online]. Available: URL

Example

References

[59] Durham University. (2021). ENGI2231 Mathematics for engineers: lecture 2. [Online]. Available: https://duo.dur.ac.uk

J27 Interviews

If the interview is published, cite it according to the format (journal article, broadcast or website). If the interview is unpublished, cite it as a personal communication.

Citation order for interview published on a website:

♦ Name of interviewer
♦ Title of interview (in double quotation marks)
♦ Title of publication (in italics)
♦ Publication details

Example of interview on a website

References

[60] J. Perlow, "Interview with Masato Endo, OpenChain Project Japan," *TheLinuxFoundation*, Mar. 21, 2018. Accessed: July 2, 2021. [Online]. Available: https://www.linuxfoundation.org/blog/good-compliance-practices-good-engineering/

J28 Unpublished sources, including personal communications: email, WhatsApp, social media private messages, conversation, unrecorded interview, telephone, letter

The *IEEE Reference Guide* (2021) provides two options for unpublished sources. These are sources that are unavailable to your readers.

Citation order 1:

♦ Author's forename initial(s) then surname
♦ Title (if available, in double quotation marks)
♦ unpublished
♦ *or*

Citation order 2:

♦ Author's forename initial(s) then surname
♦ Private communication
♦ Abbreviated month day, year

Examples

References

[61] S. James, "Interview with J. Ionides", unpublished.
[62] M. Greatbatch, private communication, Apr. 6, 2021.

Sample text

The decade 2011–2020 is the hottest on record, and since 1900, the Global Mean Surface Temperature (GMST) has risen by 1.2 ± 0.1 °C [1]. Around the world, governments and the private sector are seeking alternatives to fossil fuels to combat greenhouse gas emissions. This switch to cleaner fuels is essential as global temperatures continue to rise [2]. In the UK, the COVID19 pandemic reduced energy consumption 2019–2020, whilst strong winds throughout 2019 increased wind-powered output and renewable sources "contributed a 42.9 per cent share of generation, outpacing for the first time annual fossil fuel generation" [3, p. 1].

New technology is increasing wind power output, but public opposition to the installation of wind turbines continues [4]–[6]. This may make the sustained achievement of renewable energy use difficult [3]. More optimistically, there is community support for green initiatives [7].

References for sample text

[1] World Meteorological Organization, "State of the global climate 2020." Accessed: May 17, 2021. [Online]. Available: https://storymaps.arcgis.com/stories/6942683c7ed54e51b433bbc0c50fbdea

[2] IPCC, *Global Warming of 1.5°C*, V. Masson-Delmotte *et al.*, Eds., World Meteorological Organization, Geneva, Switzerland. Accessed: May 17, 2021. [Online]. Available: https://www.ipcc.ch/sr15/

[3] UK Dept. for Business, Energy & Industrial Strategy, "Energy trends: UK October to December 2020", Mar. 25, 2021. Accessed: May 17, 2021. [Online]. Available: https://assets. publishing.service.gov.uk/government/uploads/system/uploads/attachment_data/file/972790/Energy_Trends_March_2021.pdf

[4] F. Blaabjerg and K. Ma, "Wind energy systems," *Proceedings of the IEEE*, vol. 105, no.11, Nov. 2017, pp. 2116–2131, doi: 10.1109/JPROC.2017.2695485.

[5] J. F. Manwell, J. G. McGowan, and A. Rogers, *Wind Energy Explained: Theory, Design and Application*, 2nd ed. Chichester: Wiley, 2009. Accessed: May 17, 2021. [Online]. Available: http://library.dur.ac.uk/record=b2722155~S1

[6] M. Hyland and V. Bertsch, "The role of community involvement mechanisms in reducing resistance to energy infrastructure development," *Ecol. Econ*, vol. 146, Apr. 2018, pp. 447–474, doi: 10.1016/j.ecolecon.2017.11.016.

[7] F. B. Slimane and A. Rousseau, "Crowdlending campaigns for renewable energy: Success factors," *J. Cleaner Product.*, vol. 249, Mar. 2020, Art. no. 119330, doi: 10.1016/j.jclepro.2019.119330.

Section K
Modern Humanities Research Association (MHRA) referencing style

The MHRA referencing style is used in some arts and humanities publications. For more information on using the MHRA referencing style, see Richardson, Brian, and others, eds, *MHRA Style Guide*, 3rd edn (London: Modern Humanities Research Association, 2013) <http://www.mhra.org.uk/style/> [accessed: 26 June 2021].

Conventions when using the MHRA referencing style

Citing sources in your text

♦ Instead of naming authors in the text, which can be distracting for the reader, numbers are used to denote **citations**. These numbers in the text are linked to a full **reference** in **footnotes** or **endnotes**
♦ Cited publications are numbered in the order in which they are first referred to in the text. They are usually identified by a **superscript number**, for example 'Thomas corrected this error.[1]'
♦ Superscript numbers can be created in Microsoft Word by selecting 'References' from the Menu bar, then 'Insert Footnote'

Footnotes and endnotes

♦ Check whether footnotes or endnotes are preferred for the work you are producing
♦ In the footnotes, author names should be forename followed by surname, for example: Francis Wheen
♦ Footnotes/endnotes end with a full stop, except for online sources with DOIs or URL [accessed date]

First citation and subsequent short citations

♦ The first time you cite a source, give full details in the footnote or endnote
♦ Subsequent entries to the same source can be abbreviated to author's surname and the first few words of the title, plus a page number if you are citing a specific part of the text, giving you a **short citation**, for example: Worsley, *Classical Architecture*, p. 25.
♦ The sample text at the end of this section shows examples of a first citation and subsequent short citation of this book by Worsley
♦ Use short citations, which are more precise, not op. cit.

Ibid

♦ **Ibid**. (from Latin, *ibidem*) means 'in the same place'. If two (or more) consecutive references are from the same source, then the second (or others) is cited ibid. Capitalise ibid. if used at the beginning of a note, for example:

1. Paulina Grainger, *Imagery in Prose* (London: Dale Press, 2009), pp. 133–81.

2. Ibid., p. 155.

3. Ibid., p. 170.

Bibliography

♦ Check with your department how the bibliography should be arranged. Generally, all primary sources, such as archive manuscripts and unpublished documents, are listed separately from secondary or published sources

♦ List all secondary or published works in alphabetical order by surname of the first author

♦ In the bibliography, author names should be surname followed by forename, for example Wheen, Francis

♦ Names are given as surname, forename for the first author, but subsequent authors and editors are given as forename, surname. For example: Williams, Edith, Jane Thompson and Claire Hopper

♦ List multiple works by the same author in order of the first title word, and after the first source replace the author's name with a 2-em dash —, for example:

    Khan, Ahmad, *Literary Criticism* …

    —, *Poetry for a New Decade* …

♦ Sources without an author are listed by title in the alphabetical list

♦ If there are up to three authors of a source, give their names in your bibliography, in the order they are shown in the source. If there are four or more authors, give the name of the first author, followed by 'and others'

♦ References in your bibliography do not end with a full stop

♦ Indent the second and subsequent lines of each reference in the bibliography but not in footnotes

♦ Any sources you read but did not cite in footnotes/endnotes should be listed in the bibliography

Capitalisation

♦ Capitalise the first letter of the first word, all nouns, verbs and adjectives. Also capitalise articles if they are the first words of a subtitle after a colon, for example *Cite Them Right: The Essential Referencing Guide*

URLs and Digital Object Identifiers (DOIs)

♦ Use DOI or <URL> or ebook supplier/ collection

♦ DOIs should be used if they are available as these are a permanent locator

♦ If using a DOI, an ebook read on a device, for example Kindle, or the name of a freely available collection, such as Google Books, Internet Archive or HathiTrust, you do not need to give the accessed date

♦ If the source is in an online database that you need to log in to use, give the name of the database, the URL to access the database and the accessed date, for example *Literature Online* <https://www.proquest.com/lion/> [accessed 23 June 2001]

♦ The internet address is given in full, but with < in front and > after the address, for example <http://news.bbc.co.uk> then [accessed date]

Commas

♦ Use commas to separate the elements of the reference

Page numbers

♦ Use p. or pp. for books but not for journal articles

How to reference common sources in footnotes and bibliography

K1 Books

Citation order:

♦ Author
♦ Title (in italics)
♦ Edition (only include the edition number if it is not the first edition)
♦ Place of publication: publisher, year of publication (all in round brackets)

Example

Footnote

1. David Olusoga, *Black and British: A Forgotten History* (London: Macmillan, 2016), p. 339.

Bibliography

Olusoga, David, *Black and British: A Forgotten History* (London: Macmillan, 2016)

K2 Ebooks

Citation order:

♦ Author
♦ Title (in italics)

♦ Edition (only include the edition number if it is not the first edition)
♦ Place of publication: publisher, year of publication (all in round brackets)
♦ DOI *or* ebook supplier/collection *or* <URL> [accessed date]

Examples

Footnotes

1. Rush Rehme, *Understanding Greek Tragic Theatre*, 2nd edn (London: Routledge, 2017), p. 23. Taylor & Francis ebook.
2. Anne Cleeve, *White Nights* (London: Pan Books, 2008), chap. 30, Kindle ebook.
3. Michael Shapland, *Anglo-Saxon Towers of Lordship* (Oxford: Oxford University Press, 2019), 47, <https://doi.org/10.1093/oso/9780198809463.001.0001>

Bibliography

Cleeve, Anne, *White Nights* (London: Pan Books, 2008). Kindle ebook.
Rehme, Rush, *Understanding Greek Tragic Theatre*, 2nd edn (London: Routledge, 2017). Taylor & Francis ebook
Shapland, Michael, *Anglo-Saxon Towers of Lordship* (Oxford: Oxford University Press, 2019) <https://doi.org/10.1093/oso/9780198809463.001.0001>

K3 Translated works

Citation order:

♦ Author of original work
♦ Title (in italics)
♦ Trans. by name of translator (forename surname)
♦ Place of publication: publisher, year of publication (all in round brackets)
♦ DOI *or* ebook supplier/collection *or* <URL> [accessed date]

Example

Footnote

1. Ignazio Silone, *Fontamara*, trans. by Gwenda David and Eric Mosbacher (London: Redwords, 1994).

Bibliography

Silone, Ignazio, *Fontamara*, trans. by Gwenda David and Eric Mosbacher (London: Redwords, 1994)

K4 Ancient texts

If citing an ancient text that existed before the invention of printing, reference the published (and translated) edition you have read using the citation order for K3.

Examples

Footnotes

1. Pliny the Younger, *Letters, Volume II: Books 8–10. Panegyricus*, trans. by Betty Radice (Cambridge, MA: Harvard University Press, 1969) in *Loeb Classical Library* <https://www.loebclassics.com> [accessed 21 May 2021]
2. Homer, *The Iliad*, trans. by Robert Fagles. Introduction and notes by Bernard Knox (London: Penguin Books, 1991).

Bibliography

Homer, *The Iliad*, trans. by Robert Fagles. Introduction and notes by Bernard Knox (London: Penguin Books, 1991)

Pliny the Younger, *Letters, Volume II: Books 8–10. Panegyricus*, trans. by Betty Radice (Cambridge, MA: Harvard University Press, 1969) in *Loeb Classical Library* <https://www.loebclassics.com> [accessed 21 May 2021]

K5 Sacred texts

K5.1 Bible

Citation order:

♦ Book abbreviation
♦ Chapter: verse(s)
♦ Version (written out in first footnote, abbreviated in subsequent notes)

Example

Footnote

1. Eph 6:10–17, King James Bible. (New York: National Council of Churches, 1989).

Bibliography

King James Bible. (New York: National Council of Churches, 1989)

K5.2 Qur'an

Citation order:

♦ The Qur'an
♦ Surah: verse(s)
♦ Trans. by name of translator
♦ Publication details

Example

Footnote

1. The Qur'an, 19: 10–11, trans. by Mustafa Khattab <https://quran.com/20> [accessed 21 May 2021].

Bibliography

The Qur'an, trans. by Mustafa Khattab <https://quran.com/20> [accessed 21 May 2021]

K5.3 The Torah

Citation order:

♦ Book
♦ Chapter: verse
♦ The Torah (not in italics)
♦ Version (written out in first footnote, abbreviated in subsequent notes)

Example

Footnote

1. Shemot 3: 14, The Torah: The Five Books of Moses (Philadelphia, PA: Jewish Publication Society of America, 1962).

Bibliography

The Torah: The Five Books of Moses (Philadelphia, PA: Jewish Publication Society of America, 1962)

K6 Edited books, encyclopedias and anthologies

K6.1 Whole book with editor(s)

Citation order for footnote:

♦ Title of book (in italics)
♦ ed. by
♦ Name(s) of editor(s)
♦ Place of publication: publisher, year of publication (all in round brackets)
♦ DOI *or* <URL> *or* ebook supplier/collection

Example

Footnote

1. *The Oxford History of the Classical World*, ed. by John Boardman, Jasper Griffin and Oswyn Murray (Oxford: Oxford University Press, 1991).

Citation order for bibliography:

♦ Name(s) of editor(s)
♦ ed. *or* eds
♦ Title of book (in italics)
♦ Place of publication: publisher, year of publication (all in round brackets)
♦ DOI *or* ebook supplier/collection *or* <URL> [accessed date]

Example

Bibliography

Boardman, John, Jasper Griffin and Oswyn Murray, eds, *The Oxford History of the Classical World* (Oxford: Oxford University Press, 1986)

K6.2 Chapters in edited books, encyclopedia entries, poems in anthologies

Citation order:

♦ Author of the chapter/section/poem
♦ Title of chapter/section/poem (in single quotation marks)
♦ in
♦ Title of book (in italics)
♦ ed. by
♦ Name of editor of book
♦ Place of publication: publisher, year of publication (all in round brackets)
♦ Page numbers of chapter/section (preceded by pp.)
♦ DOI *or* ebook supplier/collection *or* <URL> [accessed date]

NB: Footnote reference has (p.).

Examples

Footnotes

1. Martin West, 'Early Greek Philosophy', in *The Oxford History of the Classical World*, ed. by John Boardman, Jasper Griffin and Oswyn Murray (Oxford: Oxford University Press, 1991), pp. 113–23 (p. 120).
2. John Masefield, 'Sea-Fever', in *Poetry Please*, ed. by Charles Causley (London: J.M. Dent, 1996), pp. 74–5.
3. Edward Ayers, 'Portraying Power', in *Jumpin' Jim Crow: Southern Politics from Civil War to Civil Rights*, ed. by Jane Dailey, Glenda Elizabeth Gilmore and Bryant Simon (Princeton, NJ : Princeton University Press, 2000), pp. 301–04 (p. 303). De Gruyter ebooks.
4. Peter Conradi, 'Murdoch, Dame (Jean) Iris (1919–1999)', in *Oxford Dictionary of National Biography* (Oxford University Press, 2004; online ed., 2015) <https://doi.org/10.1093/ref:odnb/71228>

Bibliography

Ayers, Edward, 'Portraying Power', in *Jumpin' Jim Crow: Southern Politics from Civil War to Civil Rights*, ed. by Jane Dailey, Glenda Elizabeth Gilmore and Bryant Simon (Princeton, NJ : Princeton University Press, 2000), pp. 301–04. De Gruyter ebooks
Conradi, Peter, 'Murdoch, Dame (Jean) Iris (1919–1999)', in *Oxford Dictionary of National Biography*

(Oxford University Press, 2004; online ed., 2015) <https://doi.org/10.1093/ref:odnb/71228>

Masefield, John, 'Sea-Fever', in *Poetry Please*, ed. by Charles Causley (London: J.M. Dent, 1996), pp. 74–5

West, Martin, 'Early Greek Philosophy', in *The Oxford History of the Classical World*, ed. by John Boardman, Jasper Griffin and Oswyn Murray (Oxford: Oxford University Press, 1991), pp. 113–23

K7 Multi-volume works

Citation order:

♦ Author
♦ Title (in italics)
♦ Number of volumes
♦ Place of publication: publisher, year of publication (all in round brackets)
♦ DOI *or* ebook supplier/collection *or* <URL> [accessed date]

Example

Footnote

1. Roger Butcher, *New Illustrated British Flora*, 2 vols (London: Leonard Hill, 1961).

Bibliography

Butcher, Roger, *New Illustrated British Flora*, 2 vols (London: Leonard Hill, 1961)

If citing *part of a volume*, include the volume number (in capital Roman numerals) and the page number(s).

Example

Footnote

1. Roger Butcher, *New Illustrated British Flora*, 2 vols (London: Leonard Hill, 1961), II, 96–8.

Bibliography

Butcher, Roger, *New Illustrated British Flora*, 2 vols (London: Leonard Hill, 1961)

K8 Plays

Citation order:

♦ Author
♦ Title
♦ ed. by forename surname
♦ Place of publication: publisher, year (in round brackets)
♦ Reference to cited Act. Scene. Line number, or page number
♦ DOI *or* ebook supplier/collection *or* <URL> [accessed date]

Example

Footnote

1. William Shakespeare, *Hamlet*, ed. by T.J.B. Spencer (London: Penguin, 1980), I. 2. 177.

Bibliography

Shakespeare, William, *Hamlet*, ed. by T.J.B. Spencer (London: Penguin, 1980)

K9 Journal articles

Citation order:

♦ Author
♦ Title of article (in single quotation marks)
♦ Title of journal (in italics and capitalise first letter of each word in title, except for linking words such as and, of, the, for)
♦ Volume number. Issue number (if available)
♦ Year of publication (in round brackets)
♦ Page numbers of article (not preceded by pp.)
♦ *or* <URL> [accessed date]

NB: Footnote reference has (p.).

Example

Footnotes

1. Peter Leach, 'James Paine's Design for the South Front of Kedleston Hall: Dating and Sources', *Architectural History*, 40 (1997), 159–70 (p. 160).
2. Sarah Lang, 'The Principles of the Gothic Revival in England', *Journal of the Society of Architectural Historians*, 25.4 (1966), 240–67 (p. 244) <http://www.jstor.org/stable/988353> [accessed 20 May 2021]
3. Edwina Thomas Washington, 'An Overview of Cyberbullying in Higher Education', *Adult Learning*, 26 (2015), 21–7 (p. 26) <https://doi.org/10.1177%2F1045159514558412>

Bibliography

Lang, Sarah, 'The Principles of the Gothic Revival in England', *Journal of the Society of Architectural Historians*, 25.4 (1966), 240–67 <http://www.jstor.org/stable/988353> [accessed 20 May 2021]
Leach, Peter, 'James Paine's Design for the South Front of Kedleston Hall: Dating and Sources', *Architectural History*, 40 (1997), 159–70
Washington, Edwina Thomas, 'An Overview of Cyberbullying in Higher Education', *Adult Learning*, 26 (2015), 21–7 <https://doi.org/10.1177%2F1045159514558412>

K10 Newspaper and magazine articles

Citation order:

♦ Author
♦ Title of article (in single quotation marks)
♦ Title of newspaper (in italics and capitalise first letter of each word in title, except for linking words such as and, of, the, for)
♦ Date
♦ Section (if applicable)
♦ Page number, preceded by p.
♦ *or* <URL> [accessed date]

Examples

Footnotes

1. Dan Hyde, 'Parents Funding Adult Offspring's Holidays', *Daily Telegraph*, 14 September 2015, p. 2.
2. Chen Nan, 'Musicals Find Their Voice Again', *China Daily European Edition*, 14 May 2021 <https://www.nexis.com> [accessed 21 May 2021]

Bibliography

Hyde, Dan, 'Parents Funding Adult Offspring's Holidays', *Daily Telegraph*, 14 September 2015, p. 2
Nan, Chen, 'Musicals Find Their Voice Again', *China Daily European Edition*, 14 May 2021 <https://www.nexis.com> [accessed 21 May 2021]

K11 Book reviews

Citation order:

♦ Author
♦ Review of
♦ Author, title (in italics) and publication year of work being reviewed
♦ Publication information for work in which review is published

Example

Footnote

1. Rachel Haworth, review of David Looseley, *Édith Piaf: A Cultural History* (2015), *Journal of European Studies*, 47.2 (2017), 228–29.

Bibliography

Haworth, Rachel, review of David Looseley, *Édith Piaf: A Cultural History* (2015), *Journal of European Studies*, 47.2 (2017), 228–29

K12 Conference sources

K12.1 Published proceedings of a conference

Citation order:

♦ Title of conference proceedings publication (in italics)
♦ ed. by
♦ Name of editor
♦ (Place of publication: publisher, year)

Example

Footnote

1. *Proceedings of the Tenth Conference in Romance Studies, 18 May 2014*, ed. by Hilary Jones (Derby: University of Derby Press, 2014), pp. 27–39.

Bibliography

Proceedings of the Tenth Conference in Romance Studies, 18 May 2014, ed. by Hilary Jones (Derby: University of Derby Press, 2014), pp. 27–39

K12.2 Lecture or poster presentations

Citation order:

♦ Author
♦ Title of lecture/poster presentation (in single quotation marks)
♦ Lecture at/poster presentation at
♦ Title of conference (in italics)
♦ (City: venue, date)

Example

Footnote

1. Frances MacIntosh, 'Wordsworth's Inspiration', poster presentation at *Tenth Conference in Romance Studies* (Derby: University of Derby, 18 May 2014).

Bibliography

MacIntosh, Frances, 'Wordsworth's Inspiration', poster presentation at *Tenth Conference in Romance Studies* (Derby: University of Derby, 18 May 2014)

If the lecture or poster presentation was published in conference proceedings, cite it as a chapter in an edited book (K6.2), or if it was published in a journal, cite it as an article (K10).

K13 Manuscripts in archives

Citation order:

♦ Place
♦ Name of archive
♦ Reference number
♦ Description of document

Example

Footnote

1. London, The National Archives, Public Record Office, PROB 3/42/93 Inventory of Elizabeth Bennett of Deptford, 10 November 1743.

Bibliography

London, The National Archives, Public Record Office, PROB 3/42/93 Inventory of Elizabeth Bennett of Deptford, 10 November 1743

K14 Theses and dissertations

Citation order:

♦ Author
♦ Title of thesis (in single quotation marks)
♦ Degree level, university, year (in round brackets)
♦ DOI *or* <URL> [accessed date] *or* database name [accessed date]

Example

1. Josephine Rosa Perry, 'Whose News: Who is the Political Gatekeeper in the Early 21st Century' (unpublished doctoral thesis, London School of Economics and Political Science, 2007) in Proquest Dissertations & Theses Global database [accessed 21 May 2021]

Perry, Josephine Rosa. 'Whose News: Who is the Political Gatekeeper in the Early 21st Century' (unpublished doctoral thesis, London School of Economics and Political Science, 2007) in Proquest Dissertations & Theses Global database [accessed 21 May 2021]

K15 Organisation or personal internet sites

Citation order:

♦ Author
♦ Title of internet site (in italics)
♦ Year the site was published/last updated (in round brackets)
♦ <URL> [accessed date]

Example

1. Salvatore Ciro Nappo, *Pompeii: Its Discovery and Preservation* (2012) <http://www.bbc.co.uk/history/ancient/romans/pompeii_rediscovery_01.shtml> [accessed 21 May 2021]

Nappo, Salvatore Ciro, *Pompeii: Its Discovery and Preservation* (2012) <http://www.bbc.co.uk/history/ancient/romans/pompeii_rediscovery_01.shtml> [accessed 21 May 2021]

For *web pages where no author can be identified*, you should use the web page's title.

Example

1. *Palladio's Italian Villas* (2005) <http://www.boglewood.com/palladio/> [accessed 21 May 2021]

Palladio's Italian Villas (2005) <http://www.boglewood.com/palladio/> [accessed 21 May 2021]

K16 Blogs

Citation order:

♦ Author
♦ Title of post (in single quotation marks)
♦ Title of blog (in italics)
♦ <URL> [accessed date]

Example

Footnote

1. Claire Davies, 'Inspiring Thursday: Greta Thunberg', *Wave Blog* <https://blog.wave-network.org/inspiring-thursday-greta-thunberg> [accessed 24 May 2021]

Bibliography

Davies, Claire, 'Inspiring Thursday: Greta Thunberg', *Wave Blog* <https://blog.wave-network.org/inspiring-thursday-greta-thunberg> [accessed 24 May 2021]

K17 Social media

K17.1 Facebook and Instagram

Give the full text of the Facebook post in your footnote and bibliography.

Citation order:

♦ Author
♦ Title of post (in single quotation marks)
♦ Medium (in square brackets)
♦ <URL> Date of post [accessed date]

Examples

Footnotes

1. Durham University Library, 'Check out our blog post highlighting our #DULibWellbeing guide' [Facebook] <https://www.facebook.com/dulib/posts/10158393581818099> 25 May 2021 [accessed 26 May 2021]
2. harrypottercast, 'Lego Quidditch pitch' [Instagram photo] <https://www.instagram.com/p/BnHOn1rn-hg4/?taken-by=harrypottercast> 30 August 2018 [accessed 2 February 2021]

Bibliography

Durham University Library, 'Check out our blog post highlighting our #DULibWellbeing guide' [Facebook] <https://www.facebook.com/dulib/posts/10158393581818099> 25 May 2021 [accessed 26 May 2021]
harrypottercast, 'Lego Quidditch pitch' [Instagram photo] <https://www.instagram.com/p/BnHOn1rnhg4/?taken-by=harrypottercast> 30 August 2018 [accessed 2 February 2021]

K17.2 Twitter

The full text of tweets should be given, either in your text or in a footnote, retaining hashtags # and @handles.

Citation order:

♦ Author
♦ Text of post (in single quotation marks)
♦ Medium, hashtags # and @handle, date (in round brackets)

Example

Footnote

1. Laura Kuenssberg, 'And, not quite white smoke on what was actually decided, but a flavour, govt source says, "Liz left the room happier than Eustice"' (tweet @bbclaurak, 20 May 2021).

Bibliography

Kuenssberg, Laura, 'And, not quite white smoke on what was actually decided, but a flavour, govt source says, "Liz left the room happier than Eustice"' (tweet @bbclaurak, 20 May 2021)

K18 Television or radio broadcasts

Citation order:

♦ Episode title (if applicable, in single quotation marks)
♦ Broadcast/programme/series title (in italics)
♦ Channel name
♦ Day month year
♦ Time of broadcast

Examples

Footnotes

1. 'Scarlet Macaw', *Tweet of the Day*, BBC Radio 4, 2 February 2018, 5.58am.
2. 'Perfume', *The Apprentice*, BBC One, 4 December 2019, 9.00pm.

Bibliography

'Perfume', *The Apprentice*, BBC One, 4 December 2019, 9.00pm.
'Scarlet Macaw', *Tweet of the Day*, BBC Radio 4, 2 February 2018, 5.58am.

If you are citing a recording of a broadcast, use the citation order for that format, see K19 and K20.

K19 Films and programmes on DVD, streaming services or in databases, including Netflix, Amazon Prime, Disney+, Kanopy, Box of Broadcasts

Citation order:

♦ Film title (in italics)
♦ dir. by forename surname
♦ Distributor, date (in round brackets)
♦ [on DVD] *or* <URL> [accessed date]

Examples

Footnotes

1. *Brief Encounter*, dir. by David Lean (Eagle-Lion Distributors Ltd, 1945) [on DVD].
2. *Chasing Coral*, dir. by Jeff Orlowski (Netflix, 2017). <https://www.netflix.com/gb/title/80168188> [accessed 1 August 2021]
3. *A South American Journey with Jonathan Dimbleby*, dir. by Chris Boulding (BBC2, 4 October 2011, 11.50pm) <https://learningon-screen.ac.uk/ondemand/index.php/prog/0205A987?bcast=71582484> [accessed 26 May 2021]

Bibliography

A South American Journey with Jonathan Dimbleby, dir. by Chris Boulding (BBC2, 4 October 2011, 11.50pm) <https://learningonscreen.ac.uk/ondemand/index.php/prog/0205A987?bcast=71582484> [accessed 26 May 2021]

Brief Encounter, dir. by David Lean (Eagle-Lion Distributors Ltd, 1945) [on DVD]

Chasing Coral, dir. by Jeff Orlowski (Netflix, 2017) <https://www.netflix.com/gb/title/80168188> [accessed 1 August 2021]

K20 Podcasts and online videos, including YouTube, Vimeo, IGTV, Dailymotion, TED

Citation order:

- ◆ Author
- ◆ Title (in italics)
- ◆ Type of source
- ◆ Title of the website (not in italics)
- ◆ Date of publication
- ◆ <URL> [accessed date]

Example

Footnote

1. Cambridge Cosmology, *Professor Gabriella González: Black holes and gravitational waves*, online video recording, YouTube, 12 January 2021, <https://www.youtube.com/watch?v=Txuq1sO8fkY> [accessed 23 June 2021]

Bibliography

Cambridge Cosmology, *Professor Gabriella González: Black holes and gravitational waves*, online video recording, YouTube, 12 January 2021, <https://www.youtube.com/watch?v=Txuq1sO8fkY> [accessed 23 June 2021]

K21 Sound recordings

Citation order:

- ♦ Composer
- ♦ Title (in italics)
- ♦ Artist, orchestra or conductor (as relevant)
- ♦ Recording company, CD reference, date (in round brackets)
- ♦ [on DVD] *or* URL [accessed date]

Examples

Footnotes

1. Gustav Mahler, *Symphony no. 10*, BBC National Orchestra of Wales, cond. by Mark Wigglesworth (BBC, MM124, 1994) [on CD].
2. Johannes Brahms, *Piano Quintet in F Minor, op.34*. Ives Quartet and Delores Stevens (AIX Records, 2018) <www.naxosmusiclibrary.com/catalogue/item.asp?cid=5099921662256> [accessed 12 June 2021]

Bibliography

Brahms, Johannes. *Piano Quintet in F Minor, op.34*. Ives Quartet and Delores Stevens (AIX Records, 2018) <www.naxosmusiclibrary.com/catalogue/item.asp?cid=5099921662256> [accessed 12 June 2021]

Mahler, Gustav, *Symphony no. 10*, BBC National Orchestra of Wales, conducted by Mark Wigglesworth (BBC, MM124, 1994) [on CD]

K22 Music scores

Citation order:

- ♦ Composer
- ♦ Title of work (in italics)
- ♦ Place of publication: publisher, year (in round brackets)

Example

Footnote

1. Wolfgang A. Mozart, *Don Giovanni: Overture to the Opera*, K 527 (New York: Dover, 1964).

Bibliography

Mozart, Wolfgang A., *Don Giovanni: Overture to the Opera*, K 527 (New York: Dover, 1964)

K23 Works of art, including photographs

Citation order:

- ♦ Artist
- ♦ Title of work (in italics)
- ♦ Date
- ♦ Medium
- ♦ Location *or* publication details *or* <URL> [accessed date]

Examples

1. John Martin, *The Bard*, 1817, oil on canvas, Laing Art Gallery, Newcastle upon Tyne.
2. Auguste Rodin, *The Kiss*, 1886, marble, Musée Rodin, Paris, France.
3. Angela Vane, *Boxers*, 2016, photograph, from *Sporting Lives* (Cardiff: Virtue Press, 2017), Figure 14.
4. Will Pryce, *Interior of Theatre Royal, Bury St Edmunds*, 2008, photograph, *Country Life Picture Library*, image no. 553952 <http://www.countrylifeimages.co.uk> [accessed 25 May 2021]

Bibliography

Martin, John, *The Bard*, 1817, oil on canvas, Laing Art Gallery, Newcastle upon Tyne

Pryce, Will, *Interior of Theatre Royal, Bury St Edmunds*, 2008, photograph, *Country Life Picture Library*, image no. 553952 <http://www.countrylifeimages.co.uk> [accessed 25 May 2021]

Rodin, Auguste, *The Kiss*, 1886, marble, Musée Rodin, Paris, France

Vane, Angela, *Boxers*, 2016, photograph, from *Sporting Lives* (Cardiff: Virtue Press, 2017)

K24 Course materials: lectures

If the lecture is recorded but not publicly available (for example in a VLE), use the example below. For publicly accessible lectures, see K20.

Citation order:

- ♦ Author/speaker
- ♦ Title
- ♦ lecture to
- ♦ Course details and date (in round brackets)
- ♦ <URL> [accessed date]

Example

Footnote

1. Clare Willard, 'Wordsworth in Context', lecture to MA Literature module (Durham University, 19 October 2021) <http://duo.dur.ac.uk> [accessed 25 October 2021]

Bibliography

Willard, Clare, 'Wordsworth in Context', lecture to MA Literature module (Durham University, 19 October 2021) <http://duo.dur.ac.uk> [accessed 25 October 2021]

K25 Interviews

If the interview is unpublished, cite it as a personal communication. If the interview is published, cite it using the following.

Citation order:

- ♦ Name of interviewee
- ♦ Title of article (in single quotation marks)
- ♦ interviewed by
- ♦ Name of interviewer
- ♦ Publication details *and/or* <URL> [accessed date]

Example

Footnote

1. Jessica Staton, 'Sometimes I Feel Like a Jack of All Trades', interviewed by Giverny Masso, *Stage*, 25 September 2018 <https://www.thestage.co.uk/features/interviews> [accessed 21 May 2021]

Bibliography

Staton, Jessica, 'Sometimes I Feel Like a Jack of All Trades', interviewed by Giverny Masso. *Stage*, 25 September 2018 <https://www.thestage.co.uk/features/interviews> [accessed 21 May 2021]

K26 Personal communications: emails, text messages and telephone calls

Personal communications can be cited in your text rather than in a footnote or bibliography. For example: "In her email of December 1, 2020 Amanda Hollis listed … " or 'When interviewed on 26 May 2021, Maria Guevara stated … '.

Sample text

This sample piece of text shows how various sources would be included as in-text citations.

Worsley's *Classical Architecture* highlighted the variety of styles that eighteenth-century architects employed in their buildings.[1] Initially British architects relied on the designs of Andrea Palladio, a sixteenth-century Italian architect, who was believed to have studied ancient Roman buildings.[2] As the century progressed, however, more authentic Roman examples were studied, particularly after the discovery of Pompeii.[3] Rich patrons wanted designs in the latest fashion and among those to profit from this demand was Robert Adam, who published his studies of Roman architecture.[4] With this first-hand knowledge he designed many country houses and public buildings.[5] His work was not always as revolutionary as he claimed,[6] but it impressed clients. Adam was even able to take over projects begun by other architects, as at Kedleston in Derbyshire.[7]

Although most patrons favoured classical styles, Horace Walpole suggested that the Gothic style was 'our architecture', the national style of England.[8] Later authors have suggested that Gothic style signified ancient lineage and the British Constitution.[9]

Sample footnotes

1. Giles Worsley, *Classical Architecture in Britain: The Heroic Age* (London: Published for the Paul Mellon Centre for Studies in British Art by Yale University Press, 1995).
2. *Palladio's Italian Villas* (2005) <http://www.boglewood.com/palladio/> [accessed 21 May 2021]
3. Salvatore Ciro Nappo, *Pompeii: Its Discovery and Preservation* (2012) <http://www.bbc.co.uk/history/ancient/romans/pompeii_rediscovery_01.shtml> [accessed 21 May 2021]
4. Robert Adam, *Ruins of the Palace of the Emperor Diocletian at Spalatro in Dalmatia* (London: Printed for the author,

1764), in *Eighteenth Century Collections Online* <https://library.dur.ac.uk/record=b2274207~S1> [accessed 21 May 2021]

5. *Treasures of Britain and Treasures of Ireland* (London: Reader's Digest Association Ltd, 1990).
6. Worsley, *Classical Architecture*, p. 265.
7. Peter Leach, 'James Paine's Design for the South Front of Kedleston Hall: Dating and Sources', *Architectural History,* 40 (1997), 159–70.
8. Horace Walpole, cited in S. Lang, 'The Principles of the Gothic Revival in England', *Journal of the Society of Architectural Historians*, 25.4 (1966), 240–67 <http://www.jstor.org/stable/988353> [accessed 21 May 2021]
9. Alexandrina Buchanan, 'Interpretations of Medieval Architecture', in *Gothic Architecture and Its Meanings 1550–1830*, ed. by Michael Hall (Reading: Spire Books, 2002), pp. 27–52.

NB: Footnote 6 is an example of a **short citation**, and footnote 8 is a **secondary reference**.

Sample bibliography

Adam, Robert, *Ruins of the Palace of the Emperor Diocletian at Spalatro in Dalmatia* (London: Printed for the author, 1764), in *Eighteenth Century Collections Online* <https://library.dur.ac.uk/record=b2274207~S1> [accessed 21 May 2021]

Buchanan, Alexandrina, 'Interpretations of Medieval Architecture', in *Gothic Architecture and Its Meanings 1550–1830*, ed. by Michael Hall (Reading: Spire Books, 2002), pp. 27–52

Lang, S., 'The Principles of the Gothic Revival in England', *Journal of the Society of Architectural Historians*, 25.4 (1966), 240–67 <http://www.jstor.org/stable/988353> [accessed 21 May 2021]

Leach, Peter, 'James Paine's Design for the South Front of Kedleston Hall: Dating and Sources', *Architectural History*, 40 (1997), 159–70

Nappo, Salvatore Ciro, *Pompeii: Its Discovery and Preservation* (2012) <http://www.bbc.co.uk/history/ancient/romans/pompeii_rediscovery_01.shtml> [accessed 21 May 2021]

Palladio's Italian Villas (2005) <http://www.boglewood.com/palladio/> [accessed 21 May 2021]

Treasures of Britain and Treasures of Ireland (London: Reader's Digest Association Ltd, 1990)

Worsley, Giles, *Classical Architecture in Britain: The Heroic Age* (London: Published for the Paul Mellon Centre for Studies in British Art by Yale University Press, 1995)

Section L
Modern Language Association (MLA) referencing style

The MLA referencing style is used in humanities subjects, including languages and literature. It is an **author-page style**: sources are identified in your text by the author's surname (or, if not available, the title of the source), and a page number if you are quoting or paraphrasing a specific part of the author's work. These **in-text citations** using author names are related to a list of **Works Cited** at the end of your work. To find the full details of the source being cited, the reader must refer to the list of Works Cited.

Conventions when using the MLA referencing style

This section is based on Modern Language Association, *MLA Handbook*. 9th edn. Modern Language Association of America, 2021. Updates on citations for sources are available online at *MLA Style Center*. 2021. https://style.mla.org/.

The MLA style uses a template of core principles for documenting sources. When citing a source, look for the following elements in this order:

1. Author or creator
2. Title of the source
3. Title of the container if the source is part of a greater collection; for example, a chapter in a book, an article in a journal, a page or post within a website, or an online journal in a collection such as JSTOR
4. Other contributors; for example, editors, translators, illustrators
5. The version or edition of the source you have used
6. Any numbers that denote the source; for example, volume, issue and page numbers of a journal article, or document reference
7. Publisher
8. Publication date
9. Location

If any of these elements are missing from your source (for example, a book is a stand-alone work so does not have a container, and may not have editors or translators), these are omitted in your Works Cited reference. If a source does not have an author, use the next available element in the list above for your in-text citation.

> **Example: in-text citation with an author**
>
> According to Jones (51) …
>
> **Example: in-text citation without an author, using title of source**
>
> The *Oxford Dictionary of Abbreviations* (42) …

Containers

The MLA style uses the concept of a 'container', where a source may be accessed. This can be a journal containing articles, a book containing chapters by different authors, a website containing different pages, or a social media site containing different posts. The title of the container should be in italics.

It is possible for a source to have more than one container, for example an article in a journal accessed within a database such as *JSTOR*. In the example below, the titles of both containers are italicised.

Example

Gapinski, James H. "The Economics of Performing Shakespeare." *The American Economic Review*, vol. 74, no. 3, 1984, pp. 458–466. *JSTOR*, www.jstor.org/stable/1804020.

Compiling your list of Works Cited

♦ Sources are listed in alphabetical order by author (or source title if there is no author)
♦ Second and subsequent lines of the reference should be indented by ½ inch (1.3cm)
♦ Each element of your reference in the Works Cited should end with the punctuation shown at the end of each point above, for example a full stop after the title of the source
♦ MLA uses abbreviations in the Works Cited for time periods, organisation names, countries, counties and US states. A full list of abbreviations is given in Appendix 1 of the 9th edition of the *MLA Handbook*

Author's name

♦ The author's full name, as written on the title pages, should be used. If the forename is not given, use the initial(s), for example S. Lang. End the author's name with a full stop
♦ If the source has more than one author, see 'Multiple authors' below
♦ For in-text citations and footnotes, give the author's name as forename(s) or initials followed by surname, for example Martin Roberts. For the Works Cited, give surname, then forename(s) or initials, for example Roberts, Martin, or Lang, S.
♦ If you have two authors with the same surname, use their forename in your prose citations to distinguish them, for example Audrey Jones (21), or their forename initials in parenthetical citations, for example (C. Jones 94)

Several sources by the same author

If you are citing more than one publication by the same author, include a short version of the title of each work in the in-text citation. In the Works Cited, give the author's name for the first entry only, and for subsequent references use three hyphens and a full stop ---. to replace the author's name.

Example

Thornberry's research (*Labour Pains* and "Political spin") …

Thornberry, Jane. *Labour Pains: Politics in the Blair Era*. New Vantage, 2017.

---. "Political Spin in the 21st Century," *New Political Thought*, vol. 14, no. 1, 2015, pp. 45–48.

Multiple authors

For a source with two authors, refer to them by their surnames in your in-text citation. In the Works Cited, the first author is written as surname then forename, but the subsequent authors are written as forename then surname.

Example

A new review (Willis and Singh 14) …

Willis, Anne, and Avjeet Singh. *Digital Music*. SoundMachine, 2019.

If there are three or more authors of a single work, write the name of the first author then use **et al**. instead of the names of the other authors in a parenthetical citation and the Works Cited, but use 'and others' for a narrative citation. Note that et al. is not italicised.

Examples

This new monograph (Lefevre et al.) …

Lefevre and others showed (35) …

Lefevre, Michelle, et al. *Contemporary Dance*. Springer, 2018.

Multiple citations in your text

If referring to more than one source to reinforce a point in your text, include them in round brackets in your in-text citation separated by a semicolon.

Example

This point has been made by several authors (Bowey 12; Liu 32; Singh 4) …

Books with no authors

Use the title as the first part of the reference.

Example

As defined in the *Oxford Dictionary of Abbreviations* …

Oxford Dictionary of Abbreviations. Clarendon P, 1992.

Titles of sources

♦ Capitalise the first word, all nouns, verbs and adjectives. Capitalise articles if they are the first words of a subtitle after a colon, for example *Cite Them Right: The Essential Referencing Guide*

♦ The title of the source should be in italics if it is a stand-alone item (such as a book), or in double quotation marks if it is within a container, such as an article in a journal or newspaper, or a song on an album

♦ Some sources may not have a title, for example tweets, advertisements or graffiti. In these instances, provide a description in normal font as the first element of the citation

♦ For non-English titles, give the title in the original language (unless you are using a translation), but you may include a short translated title after the original in square brackets, for example *I Quattro Libri Dell'Archittetura* [*The Four Books of Architecture*]

Other contributors

The exact nature of work by other contributors is indicated by phrases before their names; for example: edited by, translated by, illustrated by, directed by.

Examples

Buchanan, Alexandrina. "Interpretations of Medieval Architecture." *Gothic Architecture and Its Meanings 1550–1830*, edited by Michael Hall, Spire, 2002, pp. 27–52.

Silone, Ignazio. *Fontamara*. Translated by Gwenda David and Eric Mosbacher. Redwords, 1994.

Version

State which version you have used. Use abbreviated words to indicate edition (ed.), volume (vol.) and number (no.), but do not abbreviate the word version.

Publisher

In the Works Cited list, omit business words (Limited, Corporation, Incorporated) from the name of the company, for example instead of Pergamon Ltd use Pergamon. If the publisher is a university press, abbreviate this to UP, for example Cambridge UP.

Date

Spell out the names of months and days in your text, but abbreviate them in the list of Works Cited; for example: Jan., Feb., Mar., Apr., May, Jun., Jul., Aug., Sept., Oct., Nov. and Dec. and Mon., Tues., Wed., Thu., Fri., Sat. and Sun.

Location

The location may be the page numbers of a journal article or book chapter, or the specific pages that you are quoting. For online sources, the location will be the **URL** or **DOI**. For a physical object, such as a work of art, the location will be the museum or gallery in which you viewed it.

Page numbers

Provide a page number in your in-text citation if you are quoting or paraphrasing. The in-text citation does not include p. before the page number, but in the Works Cited page references for book chapters or journal articles include pp. Do not elide page ranges.

Example

The costs of the theatre production (Gapinski 461) …

Gapinski, James H. "The Economics of Performing Shakespeare." *The American Economic Review*, vol. 74, no. 3, 1984, pp. 458–466. *JSTOR*, www.jstor.org/stable/1804020.

Include page numbers (in round brackets) in your in-text citation, after the author's name, if referring to the source indirectly, or put the page number in round brackets at the end of the sentence if this is more convenient for the flow of your text.

Example

The performance divided critics' opinions: one thought it was 'moving' (Ali 12) and Blanche (34) called it 'captivating'. However, Williams was unimpressed by the leading actor's delivery (41).

URLs and DOIs

If the source has a DOI or a stable URL (sometimes called a 'permalink'), this should be used in preference to URLs.

When using an URL, copy it from the browser but omit the http:// or https://. Do not use shortened URLs such as bit.ly.

Accessed date

Only include an accessed date if the source does not have a publication or last updated date.

Place of publication

With most sources, you do not need to list a place of publication. However, if a work was published before 1900, works were associated with the city of publication or may have been produced by a printer. For more recent works, it may be useful to include a place of publication if a publisher has produced editions with different spellings and vocabulary (for example a British and an American edition of a book).

Date of original publication

If an older source has been republished, you may give the original date of publication immediately after the title to help your reader distinguish between the original and the new versions. The new version may have additional information, such as an editor's introduction.

Footnotes or endnotes

Footnotes or endnotes can be used for supplementary information or where a digression might otherwise disturb the flow of your main text. Use a superscript number for the footnote or endnote.

Example

Schultz has disputed the traditional method (67).[1]

1. As have Weike 42–53 and Thomas 12–17.

Sources cited in footnotes or endnotes should also be included in the Works Cited.

Secondary references

Only provide references to sources you have read. If you read a summary of other works, you are relying on the author of the summary to accurately represent the words and meaning of the other works. You should cite the source information for the summary in your in-text citations and Works Cited.

How to reference common sources

The following are given as examples of frequently used sources in academic work. If the source you wish to cite is not included, use the core principles and list of elements at the beginning of this chapter to produce your reference.

L1 Books and ebooks

Citation order:

♦ Author (surname, forenames)
♦ Title (in italics)
♦ Edition
♦ Publisher, year of publication
♦ Series, if relevant

For ebooks with URLs or DOIs, add:

♦ Title of container (in italics)
♦ DOI *or* URL

For ebooks without URLs or DOIs (read on personal device, e.g. Kindle), use the following.

Citation order:

♦ Author (surname, forenames)
♦ Title (in italics)
♦ Edition and/or ebook ed.
♦ Publisher, year of publication
♦ Series, if relevant

Examples

In-text citations

Using the workbook by Banno and others …

She cited books by Hadfield, Bredehoft and McInnis.

In Olusoga's retelling (23) …

Works Cited

Banno, Eri et al. *Genki. An Integrated Course in Elementary Japanese II*. 3rd ed., ebook ed., Japan Times Publ. 2020.

Bredehoft, Thomas A. *Early English Metre*. U of Toronto P, 2005. Toronto Old English Series.

Hadfield, Andrew. *Shakespeare and Republicanism*. Cambridge UP, 2005. *ACLS Humanities Ebook*, hdl. handle.net/2027/heb.32852.

McInnis, David. *Shakespeare and Lost Plays: Reimagining Drama in Early Modern England*. Cambridge UP, 2021. *Cambridge Core*, https://doi. org/10.1017/9781108915250.

Olusoga, David. *Black and British: A Forgotten History*. Macmillan, 2016.

L2 Translated books, including ancient texts

Citation order:

♦ Author (surname, forenames)
♦ Title (in italics)
♦ Edition
♦ Translated by forename surname
♦ Publisher, year of publication

Examples

In-text citation

Homer's description of the fall of Troy (22–27) …

With the publication of *Fontamara* (Silone) …

Works Cited

Homer. *The Iliad*. Translated by David Green, U of California P, 2015.
Silone, Ignazio. *Fontamara*. Translated by Gwenda David and Eric Mosbacher, Redwords, 1994.

To highlight the role of the translator of a source, for example to discuss differences between editions of the source, place their name and their role as the first element of your reference. The original author may not be known, or, if they are, they can be identified after the title of the source.

Example

In-text citation

Green's translation differs from that of Fagles and emphasises …

Works Cited

Fagles, Robert, translator. *The Iliad*. By Homer. Introduction and notes by Bernard Knox, Penguin Books, 1991.
Green, David, translator. *The Iliad*. By Homer, U of California P, 2015.

L3 Sacred texts

When referring generally to sacred texts, they are not italicised, but when citing specific editions, these should be italicised. Include information about the specific edition or translation you have used in the Works Cited.

Citation order:

- ◆ Title (in italics)
- ◆ Version (if required)
- ◆ Editor (if available)
- ◆ Publisher, year of publication

Example

In-text citation

The Bible, Talmud and Qu'ran are read by millions of people. Reading *The New Jerusalem Bible* …

Works Cited

The Bible. King James Version, Collins, 2011.
The Qur'an. Translated by Mustafa Khattab, quran.com.
The Torah: The Five Books of Moses. Jewish Publication Society of America, 1962.

L4 Edited books, encyclopedias and anthologies

L4.1 Whole books

Citation order:

- ◆ Editor's surname, followed by forename
- ◆ editor
- ◆ Title (in italics)

- Edition (only include the edition number if it is not the first edition)
- Publisher, year of publication
- Series title, if available

Examples

In-text citation

Keene's skilful editing of the anthology …

A collection of essays (Rollason) …

Works Cited

Keane, Donald, editor. *Anthology of Japanese Literature*. 3rd ed. Grove, 1955.

Rollason, David, editor. *Princes of the Church: Bishops and their Palaces*. Routledge, 2017. Society for Medieval Archaeology Monograph 39.

L4.2 Chapter in an edited book/ poem in an anthology/ encyclopedia entry

Citation order:

- Author of the chapter/section (surname, forename)
- Title of chapter/section (in double quotation marks)
- Title of book (in italics)
- edited by forename surname of editor
- Publisher, year of publication
- Page numbers of chapter/section

Examples

In-text citations

Agbabi's poem critiqued the English country house.

As argued by Falco (30) …

Conradi's assessment of Murdoch's career …

Works Cited

Agbabi, Patience. "The Doll's House." *The Forward Book of Poetry 2014*. Forward Worldwide in association with Faber, 2013.

Conradi, Peter. "Murdoch, Dame (Jean) Iris (1919–1999)." *Oxford Dictionary of National Biography*, Oxford UP, 2004; online ed., 2015), https://doi.org/10.1093/ref:odnb/71228.

Falco, Raphael. "Tudor Transformations." *Shakespeare and the Soliloquy in Early Modern English Drama*, edited by A. D. Cousins and Daniel Derrin, Cambridge UP, 2018, pp. 29–42. https://doi.org/10.1017/9781316779118.

L5 Multi-volume works

Citation order:

- Author/editor (surname, forename)
- Title (in italics)
- Edition (only include the edition number if it is not the first edition)
- Publisher, year of publication
- Number of volumes

Example

In-text citation

Stillman's comprehensive work …

Works Cited

Stillman, Damie. *English Neo-classical Architecture*. Zwemmer, 1988. 2 vols.

If citing from only one volume, specify the volume in the Works Cited entry.

Example

In-text citation

Classical details on public buildings (Stillman 290) …

Works cited

Stillman, Damie. *English Neo-classical Architecture*. Vol. 2, Zwemmer, 1988.

If citing from several volumes, include the volume number and page number in the in-text citation.

Example

In-text citation

Exterior details on public buildings (Stillman 2: 47) were more restrained than those in private houses (1: 27–93).

Works cited

Stillman, Damie. *English Neo-classical Architecture*. Zwemmer, 1988. 2 vols.

L6 Plays

L6.1 Script

Citation order:

♦ Author (surname, forename)
♦ Title of play (in italics)
♦ Publisher, year of publication

Example

In-text citation

The imagery of the fairies (Shakespeare 46) …

Works Cited

Shakespeare, William. *A Midsummer Night's Dream*. Routledge, 1988.

L6.2 Performance

Citation order:

♦ Author (surname, forename)
♦ Title of play (in italics)
♦ Directed by name of director (forename surname)
♦ Company, date, location

Example

In-text citation

The portrayal of the fairy realm (*A Midsummer Night's Dream*) …

Works Cited

Shakespeare, William. *A Midsummer Night's Dream*. Directed by Ian Judge, Royal Shakespeare Company, 1 Mar. 1995, Theatre Royal, Newcastle upon Tyne.

L7 Journal articles

Citation order:

- Author (surname, forename)
- Title of article (in double quotation marks)
- Title of journal (in italics)
- volume number, issue number (if available)
- Year of publication
- Page numbers

If online, add:

- Name of collection (in italics)
- DOI *or* URL

Example

In-text citation

Leach and Lang have published articles on Georgian architecture.

Works Cited

Lang, S. "The Principles of the Gothic Revival in England." *Journal of the Society of Architectural Historians*, vol. 25, no. 4, 1966, pp. 240–267. *JSTOR*, www.jstor.org/stable/988353.

Leach, Peter. "James Paine's Design for the South Front of Kedleston Hall: Dating and Sources." *Architectural History*, vol. 40, 1997, pp. 159–170.

L8 Newspaper and magazine articles

Citation order:

- Author (surname, forename)
- Title of article (in double quotation marks)
- Title of publication (in italics)
- Date
- Page numbers of printed magazine article

If online, add:

- Name of collection (in italics, if available)
- DOI *or* URL

Examples

In-text citations

There was positive news from Korea (Haas).

MD (9) summed up the government's failings.

Reisz took a central European view.

Works Cited

Haas, Benjamin. "Tears flow as separated South and North Korean families reunite." *The Guardian*, 20 Aug. 2018. *Factiva*, professional.dowjones.com/factiva/.

MD. "Pandemic Update." *Private Eye*, Apr 30–May 13 2021, pp. 8–9.

Reisz, Matthew. "History: From a Different Perspective." *Times Higher Education*, 16 Aug. 2018, www.timeshighereducation.com/features/history-different-perspective.

L9 Book reviews

Citation order:

- Reviewer (surname, forename)
- Review of
- Title of book being reviewed (in italics)
- by

- Author of book being reviewed (forename, surname)
- Publication title (in italics)
- volume and issue numbers (if available)
- Date
- Page numbers
- Name of collection (in italics)
- DOI *or* URL

Example

In-text citation

Howarth wrote a favourable review of *Édith Piaf*.

Works Cited

Haworth, Rachel. Review of *Édith Piaf: A Cultural History*, by David Looseley. *Journal of European Studies*, vol. 47, no. 2, 2017, pp. 228–229. *Sage Journals*, https://doi-org/10.1177/0047244117705930h.

L10 Conference sources

L10.1 Full published proceedings

Citation order:

- Name of editor (surname, forename)
- editor
- Conference title (in italics), date and location (in italics if part of title)
- Conference date and location (if not part of the conference title)
- Publisher, year of publication

Example

In-text citation

The conference papers covered a range of research (Jones).

Works Cited

Jones, Hilary, editor. *Proceedings of the Tenth Conference in Romance Studies, Derby 18 May 2014*. U of Derby P, 2014.

L10.2 Papers in published proceedings of a conference

Citation order:

- Author (surname, forename)
- Title of paper (in double quotation marks)
- Conference title (in italics)
- Conference date and location (if not part of the conference title)
- Edited by
- Name of editor(s)
- Publisher, year of publication
- If online, add DOI *or* URL

Example

In-text citation

Hosangadi gave a paper on Indian folklore.

Works Cited

Hosangadi, Balakrishna B.M. "Folktales, Myths and Legends on Sculptors of South India." *Asian Conference on Literature 2017 Official Conference Proceedings*, 30 Mar.–2 Apr. 2017, Kobe, Japan. *IAFOR*, 2020, papers.iafor.org/submission34635.

L11 Manuscripts in archives

Citation order:

♦ Author (surname, forename) (if available)
♦ Title of item (in italics)
♦ Date
♦ Name of archive, city
♦ Manuscript reference

Examples

In-text citations

Building accounts by Newton and Smirke …

Works Cited

Newton, William. *Letter to William Ord.* 23 June 1785, Northumberland Archives, Woodhorn, MS. Ord 324 E11/4.
Smirke, Sydney. *Report to the Board of Customs.* 16 May 1829, National Archives, Kew, CUST 33/6.

L12 Theses and dissertations

Citation order:

♦ Author (surname, forename)
♦ Title of thesis or dissertation (in italics)
♦ Year of award
♦ Awarding institution
♦ Level of qualification

If accessed online, add:

♦ Repository name (in italics)
♦ URL

Examples

In-text citations

Theses can be available in hardcopy (Baines) and online (Thobakgale).

Works Cited

Baines, John. *Musical Composition.* 2007. Durham U, PhD dissertation.
Thobakgale, Raphehli M. *The Influence of O. K. Matsepe in Sepedi Literature.* 2006. U of Pretoria (South Africa), PhD dissertation. *ProQuest*, search. proquest.com/docview/304907700.

L13 Organisation or personal internet sites

Citation order:

♦ Organisation, author or editor (if available)
♦ Title of page (in double quotation marks)
♦ Title of the website (in italics)
♦ Date last updated (if no date, add date accessed after DOI *or* URL)
♦ DOI *or* URL

Examples

In-text citations

FAQs on the *MLA Style Center* …

Italy has much to offer, from Roman Pompeii (Nappo) to Renaissance villas (*Vicenza and the Palladian Villas*).

Works Cited

MLA Style Center. 2021, https://style.mla.org/.

Nappo, Salvatore Ciro. "Pompeii: Its Discovery and Preservation." *BBC History*, 17 Feb. 2011, www.bbc.co.uk/history/ancient/romans/pompeii_rediscovery_01.shtml.

"Vicenza and the Palladian Villas." *Italia Agenzia Nationale Turismo*. www.italia.it/en/travel-ideas/unesco-world-heritage-sites/vicenza-and-the-palladian-villas.html. Accessed 16 Jun. 2021.

L14 Blogs

Citation order:

- Author (surname, forename)
- Title of article (in double quotation marks)
- Title of website (in italics)
- Date of post
- URL

Example

In-text citation

Davies comments on Greta's impact …

Works Cited

Davies, Claire. "Inspiring Thursday: Greta Thunberg." *Wave Blog*, 24 Oct. 2019, blog.wave-network.org/inspiring-thursday-greta-thunberg.

L15 Social media

Citation order:

- Author (surname, forename) or organisation
- Title of post (in double quotation marks) *or* description (in normal font)
- Title of website (in italics), date of post, timestamp (if relevant), URL

Examples

In-text citations

The event was promoted on social media (Jones), while Smith had other holiday hopes and Australia News Today enticed us too.

Works Cited

Australia News Today. Photo of surfer in turquoise sea. *Instagram*, 5 Apr. 2021, https://www.instagram.com/p/CNQyOB-FqoG/.

Jones, Mark. "Guided Walk." *Facebook*, 31 Jul., 2021. www.facebook.com/whickhamhistory/.

Smith, Jane [js24notts]. "Hoping to visit Paris." *Twitter*, 22 Jan. 2021, 9:06 a.m., twitter.com/js24notts/status/230954569.

L16 Film or video recordings

Citation order:

♦ Title (in italics)
♦ Directed by
♦ Name of director (forename, surname)
♦ Distributor, year

If viewed online:

♦ Title of streaming service (in italics)
♦ Location (URL)

Examples

In-text citations

Alien was a truly terrifying film, but *War of the Worlds* relied heavily on CGI effects.

Works Cited

Alien. Directed by Ridley Scott, MGM, 1979.
War of the Worlds. Directed by Steven Speilberg, Dreamworks Pictures, 2005. *Amazon Prime*, https://www.amazon.co.uk/gp/video/detail/B00FZ2ZSXC/.

To highlight the work of a specific director or performer, begin the citation with their name (surname, first name), followed by a description of their role.

Example

In-text citation

With *Alien*, Scott combined sci-fi and horror genres.

Works Cited

Scott, Ridley, director. *Alien*. MGM, 1979.

L17 Online videos, including YouTube, Vimeo, IGTV, Dailymotion, TED

Citation order:

♦ Author's name (if not the uploader)
♦ Title of video (in double quotation marks)
♦ Name of website (in italics)
♦ uploaded by name of person/ organisation
♦ Date posted, URL

Example

In-text citation

Professor González amazed her audience with her lecture (Cambridge Cosmology).

Works Cited

"Professor Gabriella González: Black holes and gravitational waves." *YouTube*, uploaded by Cambridge Cosmology, 12 Jan. 2021, www.youtube.com/watch?v=Txuq1sO8fkY.

L18 Radio and television programmes

L18.1 Television or radio programme episode

Citation order:

♦ Title of episode (in double quotation marks)
♦ Title of programme (in italics)
♦ created by (if applicable)
♦ Broadcaster, broadcast date

If viewed online:

♦ Title of streaming service (in italics), URL

Examples

In-text citations

The confrontation with the Daleks ("Asylum of the Daleks") …

Princess Margaret's love life was exposed in "Gloriana".

Works Cited

"Asylum of the Daleks." *Doctor Who*, created by Steven Moffat, series 33, episode 1, BBC One Television, 1 Sept. 2012.

"Gloriana." *The Crown*, season 1, episode 10, Left Bank Pictures/ Sony Pictures Television Production UK, 4 Nov. 2016. *Netflix*, www. netflix.com/gb/title/80025678.

L18.2 Television or radio series

Citation order:

♦ Title of programme (in italics)
♦ created by (if applicable)
♦ Broadcaster, years of broadcasts

If viewed online:

♦ Title of streaming service (in italics), URL

Example

In-text citation

In *The Crown,* Morgan recreated the early years of the Queen's reign.

Works Cited

The Crown, created by Peter Morgan. Left Bank Pictures and Sony Pictures Television, 2016. *Netflix*, www.netflix.com.

L19 Sound recordings

Sound recordings can be cited in several ways, depending on the containers you used to hear them, e.g. CDs, radio, internet sites such as YouTube or Spotify. You may also cite a recording by the composer or the performer.

L19.1 Complete works

Citation order:

♦ Artist/composer (surname, forename)
♦ Title of work (in italics)
♦ Distributor, year
♦ Optional format (such as CD, DVD, audio cassette, vinyl)

Example

In-text citation

The haunting violin accompaniment to Brahms's work …

Works Cited

Brahms, Johannes. *Piano Quintet in F Minor, op.34*. BBC Music, 2015. CD.

or

Brahms, Johannes. *Piano Quintet in F Minor, op.34*. Performed by Ives Quartet and Delores Stevens, AIX Records, 2018. *Naxos*, www.naxosmusiclibrary.com/catalogue/item.asp?cid=5099921662256.

L19.2 Song on an album

Citation order:

♦ Artist (surname, forename)
♦ Title of item (in double quotation marks)
♦ Title of full recording (in italics)
♦ Distributor, year
♦ Optional format

If viewed online, add:

♦ Title of container, URL

Examples

In-text citations

She chose "Domino" (Jessie J) and "Don't Stop Believin'" by Journey.

Works Cited

Jessie J. "Domino." *Who You Are*, Universal Republic Records, 2011. *Spotify* app.
Journey. "Don't Stop Believin'." *Escape*, Columbia, 1981, *YouTube*, www.youtube.com/watch?v=VcjzHMhBtf0.

L19.3 Podcasts

Citation order:

♦ Surname, forename of host/presenter
♦ Host/presenter
♦ Title of episode (in double quotation marks)
♦ Title of programme (in italics)
♦ Broadcaster, broadcast date
♦ Title of website (in italics), URL

Example

In-text citation

The discussion focused on Ovid's influence (Bragg).

Works Cited

Bragg, Melvyn, host. "Ovid." *In Our Time*, BBC Radio 4, 29 Apr. 2021. *BBC*, www.bbc.co.uk/programmes/m000vhk5.

L20 Music scores

The citation order for recordings can also be used for music scores.

Example

In-text citation

His beautiful music (Mozart) …

Works Cited

Mozart, Wolfgang A. *Don Giovanni: Overture to the Opera, K 527*. Dover Music, 1964.

L21 Works of art

When citing an original work of art you have seen (not an image or reproduction of the original), such as a sculpture, painting, photograph or other illustration, start with the name of the artist or creator of the work and include the location.

Citation order:

♦ Artist (surname, forename)
♦ Title of work (in italics)
♦ Year
♦ Location

Examples

In-text citations

Her favourite pieces were by Gormley, Rodin and Martin.

Works Cited

Gormley, Anthony. *Angel of the North*. 1998, Low Fell, Gateshead.
Martin, John. *The Bard*. 1817, Laing Art Gallery, Newcastle upon Tyne.
Rodin, Auguste. *The Kiss*. 1886, Musée Rodin, Paris, France.

If you are citing an image of a work of art in a publication, use the citation order for that format.

Example

In-text citation

Rodin's fine modelling of the figures …

Works Cited

Rodin, Auguste. *The Kiss*. 1886. *Bridgeman Images*, www. bridgemaneducation.com/en/asset/848255.

L22 Exhibitions

Citation order:

♦ Title of exhibition (in italics)
♦ Opening and closing dates
♦ Location

Example

In-text citation

Bodies of Evidence revealed what lay beneath the library garden.

Works Cited

Bodies of Evidence: How Science Unearthed Durham's Dark Secret, 9 Jun.–7 Oct. 2018, Palace Green Library, Durham.

L23 Course materials

Citation order:

♦ Surname, forename of speaker
♦ Title of speech or lecture (in double quotation marks)

- ◆ Title of meeting
- ◆ Date
- ◆ Location

Examples

In-text citations

After attending Stanton's talk on Wordsworth, students on the literature module attended a lecture by their tutor (Willard).

Works Cited

Stanton, Jane. "Wordsworth's Imagination." Lecture to Durham Book Festival, 18 Sept. 2018, Gala Theatre, Durham.

Willard, Clare. "Wordsworth in Context." Lecture to MA Literature module, 19 Sept. 2018, Durham University.

L24 Interviews

L24.1 Unpublished interviews

Citation order:

- ◆ Surname, forename of interviewee
- ◆ Interview
- ◆ Conducted by forename surname of interviewer
- ◆ Date of interview

Example

Works Cited

Palanza, Luis. Interview. Conducted by Karen Jones, 26 Apr. 2021.

L24.2 Published interviews: print or online

Citation order:

- ◆ Surname, forename of interviewee
- ◆ Title of interview (in double quotation marks, if available)
- ◆ Interview by
- ◆ Name of interviewer (forename, surname)
- ◆ Title of container (in italics)
- ◆ Publication details *or* URL

Example

In-text citation

President Obama stated …

Works Cited

Obama, Barack. Interview by Jon Sopel. *BBC News*, 24 Jul. 2015, www.bbc.co.uk/news/world-uscanada-33646543.

L25 Emails and text messages

Citation order:

- ◆ Author of the email (surname, forename)
- ◆ Email/text message to
- ◆ Name of recipient (forename surname)
- ◆ Date

Example

In-text citation

Schultz's email to the student …

Works Cited

Schultz, Julia. Email to Helena Braun, 17 Aug. 2021.

Sample text

The course "Un-English" featured a range of sources that looked beyond English literature. The Classical tradition was well represented with analysis of Homer and Ovid (Bragg), and more recent European literature such as *Fontamara* (Silone). Art from Pompeii (Nappo) and a study of Rodin's work were contrasted (Hosangadi) with Indian sculpture. Examples of South African (Thobakgale) and Japanese literature (Keane) were also studied.

Works Cited for sample text

Bragg, Melvyn, host. "Ovid." *In Our Time*, BBC Radio 4, 29 Apr. 2021. *BBC*, www.bbc.co.uk/programmes/m000vhk5.

Homer. *The Iliad*. Translated by David Green, U of California P, 2015.

Hosangadi, Balakrishna B.M. "Folktales, Myths and Legends on Sculptors of South India." *Asian Conference on Literature 2017 Official Conference Proceedings,* 30 Mar.– 2 Apr. 2017, Kobe, Japan. *IAFOR*, 2020, papers.iafor.org/submission34635.

Keane, Donald, editor. *Anthology of Japanese Literature*. 3rd ed. Grove, 1955.

Nappo, Salvatore Ciro. "Pompeii: Its Discovery and Preservation." *BBC History*, 2011. www.bbc.co.uk/history/ancient/romans/pompeii_rediscovery_01.shtml.

Rodin, Auguste. *The Kiss*. 1886. *Bridgeman Images*, www.bridgemaneducation.com/en/asset/848255.

Silone, Ignazio. *Fontamara*. Translated by Gwenda David and Eric Mosbacher. Redwords, 1994.

Thobakgale, Raphehli M. *The Influence of O. K. Matsepe in Sepedi Literature.* 2006. U of Pretoria (South Africa), PhD dissertation. *ProQuest*, search.proquest.com/docview/304907700.

Section M
Oxford University Standard for Citation of Legal Authorities (OSCOLA)

OSCOLA is used in many UK law schools and legal publications. For more information, see S. Meredith and D. Nolan, *The Oxford University Standard for Citation of Legal Authorities* (4th edn, 2012); OSCOLA, *Citing International Law Sources Section* (2006) and *OSCOLA FAQs* (2021) <https://www.law.ox.ac.uk/oscola-faqs> accessed 16 June 2021.

Conventions when using the OSCOLA referencing style

♦ OSCOLA uses numeric **references** in the text linked to full **citations** in **footnotes**
♦ Very little punctuation is used. Remove punctuation such as full stops in publication abbreviations. If you use more than one citation in a footnote, separate them with a semicolon
♦ Well-established abbreviations are used for the titles of legal sources such as law reports and parliamentary publications; for example the journal title *Modern Law Review* is abbreviated to MLR. For details of the accepted abbreviations for legal publications, see the Cardiff University *Cardiff Index to Legal Abbreviations* <http://www.legalabbrevs.cardiff.ac.uk/> accessed 16 June 2021
♦ OSCOLA assumes that you are referencing UK legal sources. If you are writing about legal material in several countries, use abbreviations of the nations to denote different jurisdictions, for example Deregulation Act 2015 (UK); Homeland Security Act 2001 (USA)

Tables of primary sources and bibliographies

♦ In addition to references to all sources in footnotes, some law schools require students to include tables of cases, legislation and treaties (primary legal sources) and a bibliography listing secondary sources (books, articles, reports, etc.). If so, we suggest that you provide the tables of cases, legislation and treaties after your text and any appendices and before the bibliography of secondary sources
♦ In the table of cases, list cases in alphabetical order by name. In the table of cases, the case names should be in normal font, not italics
♦ List all legislation in alphabetical order by name
♦ In the bibliography, authors' names should have surname, then initials of given names (not full given names). This should be in alphabetical order by authors' names

Authors

♦ In the footnotes, give the author's name as written in the source, with the first name or initial(s) followed by surname, for example Joan Bell. In the bibliography, reverse this and give the author's surname, followed by the initials (not the full first name), for example Bell, J
♦ If there are two or three authors, list these in the order given in the source,

not alphabetically, with 'and' between the second and third authors If there are four or more authors, give the name of the first author followed by 'and others'

♦ An organisation can be cited as the author if there are no individual authors

♦ If the source does not have an author, use two em dashes instead (— —), but if it is an editorial without a named author, use Editorial instead of the author's name

♦ List sources without authors at the beginning of the bibliography in alphabetical order by the first major word of the title after the em dashes (— —)

Examples in footnotes

One author

1. Jane Sendall, *Family Law* (OUP 2018).

Two authors

2. Alan Dignam and John Lowry, *Company Law* (11th edn, OUP 2020).

Three authors

3. Alan Dignam, Andrew Hicks and SH Goo, *Hicks & Goo's Cases and Materials on Company Law* (7th edn, OUP 2011).

Four or more authors

4. FE Forrest and others, *Political Theory* (Ashfield 1999).

Organisation as author

5. European Parliament, 'Cross-border Mergers and Divisions, Transfers of Seat: Is There a Need to Legislate?' (2016) PE 556.960.

No author

6. — —, 'Brexit Referendum: Local Results' (*Durham Voice* July 2016).

Examples in bibliography

— —, 'Brexit Referendum: Local Results' (*Durham Voice* July 2016)

Dignam A, Hicks A and Goo SH, *Hicks & Goo's Cases and Materials on Company Law* (7th edn, OUP 2011)

Dignam A and Lowry J, *Company Law* (11th edn, OUP 2020)

European Parliament, 'Cross-border Mergers and Divisions, Transfers of Seat: Is There a Need to Legislate?' (2016) PE 556.960

Forrest FE and others, *Political Theory* (Ashfield 1999)

Sendall J, *Family Law* (OUP 2018)

General principles

Although OSCOLA provides examples of many sources, it is not comprehensive. If the type of source is not listed in the OSCOLA guidelines, general principles should be followed.

If the source has an ISBN, cite it like a book and have the title in *italics*. Although older books did not have ISBNs, they had author, title, place of publication and publisher, so would be cited with the title in *italics*.

If the source is recent and does not have an ISBN, use the general principles for secondary sources (OSCOLA 2012, p. 33) for the citation order:

♦ Author
♦ Title (in single quotation marks)
♦ Additional information such as report number, publisher, date of publication (all in round brackets)
♦ If online, add <URL> and accessed date.

These can be applied to a wide range of sources.

Examples in footnotes

1. Competition & Markets Authority, 'Decision of the Competition and Markets Authority: Online resale price maintenance in the bathroom fittings sector' (Case CE/9857-14, 2016) <https://assets.publishing.service.gov.uk/media/573b150740f0b-6155b00000a/bathroom-fittings-sector-non-conf-decision.pdf> accessed 26 May 2021.
2. Roberta Panizza, 'The Principle of Subsidiarity' (Factsheets on European Union, May 2018) <http://www.europarl.europa.eu/ftu/pdf/en/FTU_1.2.2.pdf > accessed 26 May 2021.

Online sources

It may be difficult to establish the type of publication online, especially if you have located PDFs of reports, articles or book chapters. Look for authors, publishing organisations, details of any series or larger work that the source may be part of, identification number, ISBNs, DOIs or titles. If in doubt, apply the general principles on page 33 of the OSCOLA 4th edition, as in the above examples, giving as much information as you can to help your reader locate the source.

Pinpointing

If you wish to cite a specific page within a source, include this page number at the end of the reference. For example, if you wished to pinpoint something on page 1357 of a report running from pages 1354 to 1372, you would write:

R v Dunlop [2006] EWCA Crim 1354, 1357.

If your source uses paragraph numbers rather than page numbers (for example neutral citations) give the citation followed by the number of the paragraph in square brackets:

Humphreys v Revenue and Customs [2012] UKSC 18 [8].

If you are citing a range of pages or paragraphs:

R v Dunlop [2006] EWCA Crim 1354, 1357–1360

Humphreys v Revenue and Customs [2012] UKSC 18 [8]–[12].

Repeated references and cross-referencing

If you are referencing in your text a source you have already cited in the footnotes, you do not need to give the full reference again. If you are referring again to the previous source, you can use **ibid** (note that this is not italicised). If you are referencing a source earlier than the previous one, use the footnote number of the original reference and a short title or author surname. If you are referencing a different page than the earlier footnote, give the new page number at the end of the new footnote.

Examples in footnotes

1. *R v Edwards (John)* (1991) 93 Cr App R 48.
2. Ibid 50.
3. CMV Clarkson, *Criminal Law: Text and Materials* (7th edn, Sweet & Maxwell 2010).
4. *R v Edwards* (n1) 53.

NB: Footnote 2 uses ibid as it follows immediately after the same source, but directs the reader to a different page. Footnote 4 refers the reader back to footnote 1 (n1) where the full reference is given, but directs attention to what is written on page 53.

Referencing several works by the same author

If you have two publications by Smith, give full details of each source the first time you cite it, and subsequently use their name and a short form of the title of the source.

Examples in footnotes

1. Smith, *Corporate Liability*.
2. Smith, 'Shareholder responsibilities'.

How to reference common sources

M1 Books

Citation order:

- ◆ Author
- ◆ Book title (in italics and capitalise first letter of each word in title, except for linking words such as and, or, the, for)
- ◆ Edition, publisher year (in round brackets)

Example in footnotes

1. Alan Dignam and John Lowry, *Company Law* (11th edn, OUP 2020).

M2 Ebooks

The guidance in *OSCOLA FAQs* (https://www.law.ox.ac.uk/oscola-faqs) is that if an ebook has the same page numbers and appearance as the printed books (as is often the case with library ebooks), cite the ebook as if it was a printed book. You can use pinpoints to page numbers as you would in the printed book.

Example in footnotes: ebook with same pagination as a printed book

1. Keith N Hylton, *Tort Law: A Modern Perspective* (CUP 2016) 47.

If the ebook does not have page numbers, for example if you are reading it on an ebook reader such as a Kindle, cite the book as if it was a printed book but include the type of ebook or format before the publisher in your reference. If there are no page numbers, use volume, part, chapter or section numbers, and if necessary a descriptive location.

Examples in footnotes: ebooks with different pagination to printed books

1. Alex McBride, *Defending the Guilty: Truth and Lies in the Criminal Courtroom* (Kindle edn, Penguin 2011), ch 1, text above n 4.
2. *Redgrave's Health and Safety* (9th edn, Lexis Library edn, Lexis Nexis 2016) Part 6 2(3) definition of 'Load'.

M3 Chapters in edited books

Citation order:

♦ Author
♦ Chapter title (in single quotation marks)
♦ in editor (ed)
♦ Book title (in italics)
♦ Edition, publisher year (in round brackets)

Example in footnotes

1. Paul Matthews, 'The Legal and Moral Limits of Common Law Tracing' in Peter Birks (ed), *Laundering and Tracing* (Clarendon Press 1995).

M4 Translated works

Citation order:

♦ Author
♦ Title (in italics)
♦ Name of translator tr, publisher year (all in round brackets)

Example in footnotes

1. Antonio Padoa-Schioppa, *A History of Law in Europe* (Caterina Fitzgerald tr, CUP 2017).

M5 Encyclopedias

Citation order:

♦ Title of encyclopedia (in italics)
♦ Edition, year of issue (in round brackets)
♦ If pinpointing, add volume and page or paragraph number

Example in footnotes

1. *Halsbury's Laws* (5th edn, 2018) vol 6, para 363.

M5.1 Authored entry within an encyclopedia

Citation order:

♦ Author
♦ Title of entry (in single quotation marks)
♦ Title of encyclopedia (in italics)
♦ Edition, year of issue (in round brackets)
♦ If online, add <URL> accessed date

Example in footnotes

1. Maria Schmeeckle, 'Foster Care', *The Wiley Blackwell Encyclopedia of Family Studies* (2016) <https://library.dur.ac.uk/record=b2898148~S1> accessed 26 May 2021.

M6 Works of authority

Older texts that are accepted as definitive guides to the law at the time of their publication use abbreviations, see p. 36 of the OSCOLA guide.

Example

A reference to a quotation on page 329 in the fourth volume of William Blackstone, *Commentaries on the Laws of England* (4 vols Oxford 1765–69)

is abbreviated in footnotes to

1. 4 Bl Comm 329.

M7 Looseleaf services

Citation order:

♦ Title of the source (in italics)

NB: You do not need to include publication details.

Example in footnotes

1. *Blackstone's Criminal Practice.*

If pinpointing in a footnote, include the volume and paragraph number.

Example in footnotes

2. *Blackstone's Criminal Practice*, part B4, para 100.

M8 Pamphlets

Citation order:

♦ Author
♦ Title (in italics)
♦ Pamphlet series title, number, abbreviation of publisher and year of publication (all in round brackets)

Example in footnotes

1. John W Jones, *The Nazi Conception of Law* (Oxford Pamphlets on World Affairs no 21, OUP 1939).

M9 Theses and dissertations

Citation order:

♦ Author
♦ Title (in single quotation marks)
♦ Level, university year of award (in round brackets)
♦ If online, add <URL> accessed date

Example in footnotes

1. Sarah Emily Morley, 'Takeover Litigation: the US Does It More Than the UK, But Why and Does It Matter?' (PhD thesis, Durham University 2017) <http://etheses.dur.ac.uk/12228/> accessed 26 May 2021.

M10 Working and discussion papers

Citation order:

♦ Author
♦ Title of working paper (in single quotation marks)
♦ Year (in round brackets)
♦ Working paper series title
♦ Number
♦ <URL> accessed date

Examples in footnotes

1. City of London Law Society, 'Wayleave Agreement' (2018) CLLS Precedent Documents <https://www.citysolicitors.org.uk/clls/clls-precedent-documents/wayleave-agreement/> accessed 26 May 2021.
2. Sonia Livingstone, John Carr and Jasmina Byrne, 'One in Three: Internet Governance and Children's Rights' (2016) UNICEF Office of Research – Innocenti Discussion Paper 2016-1 <https://www.unicef-irc.org/publications/pdf/idp_2016_01.pdf> accessed 26 May 2021.

M11 Journal and ejournal articles

Citation order:

♦ Author
♦ Article title (in single quotation marks)
♦ Year (use square brackets if it identifies the volume; use round brackets if there is a separate volume number)
♦ Volume number
♦ Abbreviated journal title
♦ First page number
♦ If online, add <URL> accessed date

Example in footnotes: with volume number

1. Andrew J Roberts, 'Evidence: Bad Character – Pre-Criminal Justice Act 2003 Law' (2008) 4 Crim LR 303.

Example in footnotes: with no volume number

2. Po-Jen Yap, 'Defending Dialogue' [2012] PL 527.

Example in footnotes: ejournal article

3. Cormac Behan and Ian O'Donnell, 'Prisoners, Politics and the Polls: Enfranchisement and the Burden of Responsibility' (2008) 48(3) Brit J Criminol, 31 <doi:10.1093/bjc/azn004> accessed 26 May 2021.

M12 Book reviews

Citation order:

♦ Author
♦ Review of
♦ Author and title of book being reviewed
♦ Journal citation or newspaper reference

Example in footnotes

1. John Eekelaar, Review of Anita Bernstein (ed), *Marriage Proposals: Questioning a Legal Status* (2012) 8(2) Int JLC 320.

M13 Newspaper articles

Citation order:

♦ Author or editorial or — —
♦ Article title (in single quotation marks)
♦ Title of newspaper (in italics)

If print:

♦ Place of publication and full date (in round brackets)
♦ Section (if required) and page number

If published online:

♦ Date (in round brackets)
♦ <URL> accessed date

Examples in footnotes

1. Joanne Hart, 'Tax is no burden for software firm' *Mail on Sunday* (London, 29 July 2018) 48.
2. — —, 'Pop Star Rihanna Wins Image Battle' *BBC News* (22 January 2015) <https://www.bbc.co.uk/news/entertainment-arts-30932158> accessed 26 May 2021.
3. Editorial, 'The Rise in Youth Knife Crime Should be Treated as an Emergency' *Independent* (24 June 2018). <https://www.independent.co.uk/voices/editorials/knife-crime-london-stabbing-death-police-investigations-weapons-a8413516.html> accessed 26 May 2021.

M14 Law reports (cases)

When citing a case in your text, and in footnotes, put the name of the case in italics. However, the case names should be in normal font in the table of cases.

Use abbreviations for courts: UK Supreme Court (UKSC), House of Lords (HL), Court of Appeal (CA), Chancery (Ch), Queen's Bench (QB), Family (F) or Commercial Court (Com Ct).

There are different forms for citing cases before 1865, from 1865 to 2001, and from 2002 onwards.

Pre-1865 cases

Before 1865, cases were often published by individuals (called 'nominate reporters') rather than the later series of law reports. Many pre-1865 cases were consolidated into the *English Reports*. The reference includes the location in the *English Reports* and the nominative reporter.

Citation order:

- ◆ Name of parties involved in case (in italics in text and footnote, in plain font in table of cases)
- ◆ Year of publication (in round brackets)
- ◆ Volume number
- ◆ Nominate reporter abbreviation
- ◆ First page number
- ◆ Volume number
- ◆ ER
- ◆ First page number

Example in footnotes

1. *Blenkinsopp v. Blenkinsopp* (1850) 12 Beav. 568, 50 ER 1177.

Cases from 1865 to 2001: Which case to cite?

After 1865, series of official law reports were published, but there is no single publication covering all cases heard in courts. Instead, there are many general reports (such as *All England Law Reports*) and specialist reports (such as *Industrial Relations Law Reports*) that publish selections of cases. The same case may be reported in several publications, or not reported at all.

If the case is reported in several publications, there is an order of preference for which one to cite. If possible, use a citation from one of the *Law Reports*: Supreme Court/House of Lords, Privy Council, Appeal Courts (Criminal and Civil), Chancery Division, Family Division, King or Queen's Bench. If these are not available, use the citations (in order of preference) from *Weekly Law Reports* or *All England Law Reports*. If a case is not reported in any of these, use the citation for the specialist report or newspaper. The titles of publications are abbreviated in OSCOLA. For details of the accepted abbreviations, see Cardiff University's *Cardiff Index to Legal Abbreviations* at http://www.legalabbrevs.cardiff.ac.uk.

Round or square brackets around the year?

♦ If the volumes of the law report series are independently numbered, and so can be identified without the year, place the year in round brackets
♦ If the year of publication is used to identify the volume, it should be in square brackets. If there are several volumes in one year, add the volume number after the year in square brackets

Citation order:

♦ Name of parties involved in case (in italics in text and footnote, in plain font in table of cases)
♦ Year (in square or round brackets)
♦ Volume number and abbreviation for name of report and first page of report
♦ Court abbreviation (in round brackets)

Example in footnotes: with [year]

1. *Hazell v Hammersmith and Fulham London Borough Council* [1992] 2 AC 1 (HL).

NB: Date in square brackets because the year identifies the volume required. In this instance, the 2 means that this case appeared in the second volume for the year 1992.

Example in footnotes: with (year)

1. *R v Edwards (John)* (1991) 93 Cr App R 48 (CA).

NB: Date in round brackets because there is also a volume number: this is the 93rd volume of *Criminal Appeal Reports*.

Law reports (cases) from 2002 with neutral citations

From 2002, cases were given a neutral citation that identifies the case without referring to the printed law report series in which the case was published. This helps to identify the case online, for example through the freely available transcripts of the British and Irish Legal Information Institute (www.bailii.org).

Citation order:

♦ Name of parties involved in case (in italics in footnote, in plain font in table of cases)
♦ Court abbreviation
♦ Number of case in that year
♦ Year (in square or round brackets)
♦ Volume number and abbreviation for name of report and first page of report

Example in footnotes

1. *Humphreys v Revenue and Customs* [2012] UKSC 18.

This shows that *Humphreys v Revenue and Customs* was the 18th case heard by the UK Supreme Court in 2012.

If the case was published you must add the law report citation after the neutral citation.

Example in footnotes

Humphreys v Revenue and Customs [2012] UKSC 18, [2012] 1 WLR 1545.

This shows that the case was reported in the first volume of the *Weekly Law Reports* for 2012, starting on page 1545.

If citing *several separate paragraphs*, put each in square brackets separated by a comma.

Example in footnotes

Humphreys v Revenue and Customs [2012] UKSC 18 [8], [14]

If citing *several adjacent paragraphs*, put the first and last numbers in square brackets separated by a dash.

Example in footnotes

Humphreys v Revenue and Customs [2012] UKSC 18, [15]–[21]

The use of neutral citations does not help with locating cases in printed law reports. You will need to add the citation for the law report after the neutral citation.

Example in footnotes

1. *Humphreys v Revenue and Customs* [2012] UKSC 18, [2012] 1 WLR 1545.

This shows that the case was reported in the first volume of the *Weekly Law Reports* for 2012, starting on page 1545.

Citing names of judges

If you wish to quote something said by a judge, include their name in the text associated with the source you are citing:

In *R v Jones*,[7] Williams LJ noted …

If the judge is a peer, you would write, for example, 'Lord Blackstone'. If the judge is a Mr, Mrs or Ms, you would write 'Blackstone J' (J for judge); if a Lord Justice or Lady Justice, you would write 'Blackstone LJ'.

Judge's comments in case report

If you wish to pinpoint comments, add the page number and the judge's name after the citation in your footnote.

Example in footnotes

1. *Donohue v Stevenson* [1932] AC 562, 580 (Atkin LJ).

Unreported cases

Many UK cases are not published in law reports. To cite an unreported case, give the party names, followed by the name of the court and the date in round brackets, followed by the case number if available. If the case has a neutral citation, give this after the party names.

> **Example in footnotes**
>
> 1. *R v Tom Hayes* (Southwark Crown Court, 3 August 2015) Case no. T20137308.

M15 Bills: House of Commons and House of Lords

Citation order:

- ◆ Short title
- ◆ House in which it originated
- ◆ Parliamentary session (in round brackets)
- ◆ Bill number (square brackets for Commons Bills, no brackets for Lords Bills)

> **Examples in footnotes**
>
> 1. Transport HC Bill (1999–2000) [8].
> 2. Transport HL Bill (2007–08) 1.
>
> **Examples in table of legislation**
>
> Transport HC Bill (1999–2000) [8]
>
> Transport HL Bill (2007–08) 1

M16 UK statutes (Acts of Parliament)

Before 1963, Acts were cited by the regnal year, that is, the number of years since the monarch's accession. You may see references to legislation in this format in early publications.

> **Example**
>
> 1. Act of Supremacy 1534 (26 Hen 8 c1).
>
> But this can be shortened to
>
> 1. Act of Supremacy 1534.

OSCOLA recommends that when citing all legislation (including earlier Acts), you should use the short title of the Act, with the year in which it was enacted, as shown in the example above.

For **UK statutes from 1963 to the present**, use the short title of an Act, with the year in which it was enacted.

Citation order:

- ◆ Short title of Act
- ◆ Year enacted

To cite part of an Act, add:

- ◆ s for section number
- ◆ Subsection number (in round brackets)
- ◆ Paragraph number (in round brackets)

> **Examples in footnotes**
>
> 1. Deregulation Act 2015.
> 2. Finance Act 2015, s 2(1)(a).

M17 Statutory Instruments (SIs)

Citation order:

♦ Name/title
♦ SI year/number

Example in footnotes

1. Detention Centre Rules 2001, SI 2001/238.

M18 Legislation from UK devolved legislatures

Citation order for devolved legislation:

♦ Title of legislation, including year
♦ number (in round brackets)

M18.1 Acts of the Scottish Parliament

For Acts of the post-devolution Scottish Parliament, replace the chapter number with 'asp' (meaning Act of the Scottish Parliament).

Example in footnotes

1. Scottish Elections (Reduction of Voting Age) Act 2015 (asp 7).

M18.2 Scottish Statutory Instruments (SSIs)

Note the SSI number incorporates the year.

Example in footnotes

1. Tuberculosis (Scotland) Order 2005, SSI 2005/434.

M19 Acts of the Northern Ireland Assembly

Example in footnotes

1. Budget Act (Northern Ireland) 2020.

M19.1 Statutory Rules of Northern Ireland

Note the SSI number incorporates the year.

Example in footnotes

1. Smoke Flavourings Regulations (Northern Ireland) 2005, SR 2005/76.

M20 Welsh Parliament (Sennedd Cymru) legislation

M20.1 National Assembly for Wales Measures (nawm) 2007–2011

Example in footnotes

1. NHS Redress (Wales) Measure 2008 (nawm 1).

M20.2 Acts of the National Assembly of Wales (anaw) 2012–2020

Example in footnotes

1. Legislation (Wales) Act 2019 (anaw 4).

M20.3 Acts of the Sennedd Cymru (asc) 6 May 2020 to present

Example in footnotes

2. Health and Social Care (Quality and Engagement) (Wales) Act 2020 (asc 1).

M20.4 Welsh Statutory Instruments

End with Year/SI number (W number).

Example in footnotes

1. The Bluetongue (Wales) Order 2003 Welsh Statutory Instrument 2003/326 (W 47).

M21 Command Papers

Citation order:

♦ Author
♦ Title (in italics)
♦ Paper number and year (in round brackets)

Example in footnotes

1. Lord Chancellor's Department, *Government Policy on Archives* (Cm 4516, 1999).

M22 *Hansard*

Hansard is the official record of debates, speeches, oral and written answers/ statements, petitions and Westminster Hall discussions in the Houses of the UK Parliament. A fully searchable version of *Hansard* from 1803 is available online at https://hansard.parliament.uk/.

Citation order:

♦ Abbreviation of House
♦ Deb (for debates) and date of debate
♦ Volume number, column number

Example in footnotes

1. HC Deb 19 June 2008, vol 477, col 1183.

For a pre-2014 Commons Written Answer, use the suffix W after the column number.

Example in footnotes

1. HC Deb 19 June 2008, vol 477, col 1106W.

For a pre-2014 Lords Written Answer, use the prefix WA before the column number.

Example in footnotes

1. HL Deb 19 June 2008, vol 702, col WA200.

For a pre-2014 Written Statement, use the suffix WS.

Example in footnotes

1. HC Deb 18 September 2006, vol 449, col 134WS.

For a pre-2014 debate in Westminster Hall, use the suffix WH.

Example in footnotes

1. HC Deb 21 May 2008, vol 476, col 101WH.

If quoting very old *Hansards*, it is usual, although optional, to include the series number.

Example in footnotes

1. HC Deb (5th series) 13 January 1907 vol 878, cols 69–70.

In 2007, the earlier system of Standing Committees was replaced by Public Bill Committees. Standing Committee *Hansard* should be cited as follows.

Example in footnotes

1. SC Deb (A) 13 May 1998, col 345.

The Public Bill Committees would be cited as follows.

Example in footnotes

1. Health Bill Deb 30 January 2007, cols 12–15.

But if the Bill has a long title, use the Bill number instead.

Example in footnotes

1. PBC Deb (Bill 99) 30 January 2007, cols 12–15.

Since 12 September 2014, written questions and answers are published in the Written questions, answers and statements database (https://questions-statements.parliament.uk/) instead of *Hansard*. This means that the column reference is no longer used. Questions and answers in the database are given a number to include in their citation. At the time of writing (June 2021), there was no guidance from OSCOLA for citing written questions and answers. Adapting the format for pre-September 2014 written questions and answers, we suggest the following.

Example in footnotes: written question and answer (Commons)

1. HC 9 October 2015, PQ 9236.

Example in footnotes: written question and answer (Lords)

1. HL 7 September 2015, HL 1950.

Written ministerial statements, which continue to be published in *Hansard*, are also published in the database.

Example in footnotes: Commons written statement

1. HC 25 June 2015, HCWS 55.

M23 House of Commons Library briefing papers

Citation order:

♦ Author
♦ Title (in single quotation marks)
♦ Series, number and date of publication (all in round brackets)
♦ <URL> accessed date

M24 Law Commission reports and consultation papers

Citation order:

♦ Law Commission
♦ Title of report or consultation paper (in italics)
♦ Number of report or consultation paper, and year (in round brackets)

M25 European Union (EU) legal sources

EU legislation may be legislation, directives, decisions and regulations. The most authoritative source is the *Official Journal of the European Union*.

M25.1 EU legislation

Citation order:

♦ Legislation title
♦ Year (in square brackets)
♦ *Official Journal* (OJ) series
♦ Issue/first page

M25.2 EU directives, decisions and regulations

Citation order:

♦ Legislation type
♦ Number and title
♦ Year (in square brackets)
♦ *Official Journal* (OJ) L series
♦ Issue/first page

NB: Commission decisions are cited as cases.

M25.3 Judgements of the European Court of Justice (ECJ) and General Court (GC)

Citation order:

♦ Prefix ('Case C-' for the ECJ or 'Case T-' for the GC)
♦ Case registration number
♦ Case name (in italics)

- ◆ Report citation
- ◆ If you need to pinpoint within the ECR report, use para(s) after the case number.

Examples in footnotes

1. Case C-111/03 *Commission of the European Communities v Kingdom of Sweden* [2005] ECR I-08789.
2. Case T-8/89 *DSM NV v Commission of the European Communities* [1991] ECR II-01833, para 132.

M25.4 European Case Law Identifier (ECLI)

The European Case Law Identifier (ECLI) provides a standardised descriptor for cases from the European Court of Justice, the European Court of Human Rights, the European Civil Service Tribunal and the European Patent Office.

An ECLI consists of five parts, separated by colons:

- ◆ ECLI
- ◆ The code for the country or jurisdiction
- ◆ The code for the court that made the judgement
- ◆ The year of the judgement
- ◆ An ordinal number or unique number to identify each case

Use an ECLI as you would a neutral citation in a UK case, after the party names and before the case citation.

Example in footnotes

1. Case C-111/03 *Commission of the European Communities v Kingdom of Sweden* ECLI:EU:C:2005:619, [2005] ECR I-08789.

M26 International law sources

See OSCOLA, *Citing International Law Sources* (2006) <https://www.law.ox.ac.uk/research-subject-groups/publications/oscola> accessed: 10 June 2021. Generally, cite the source as recommended in the format for that jurisdiction, but remove punctuation in abbreviations and italicisation of case names.

M26.1 United Nations documents

Citation order:

- ◆ Author
- ◆ Title
- ◆ Date (in round brackets)
- ◆ Document number

Example in footnotes

1. UNSC Res 1970 (26 February 2011) UN Doc S/RES/1970.

M26.2 International treaties

Citation order:

- ◆ Title of treaty
- ◆ Date adopted (in round brackets)
- ◆ Publication citation
- ◆ Short title (in round brackets)
- ◆ Article number

If possible, cite from the United Nations Treaty Series (UNTS).

When you mention a treaty for the first time in your text, give the formal and the short title in brackets. In subsequent references, use the short title.

Example in text

Britain supported the Convention Relating to the Status of Refugees (Refugee Convention)[1] ...

Example in footnotes

1. Convention Relating to the Status of Refugees (adopted 28 July 1951, entered into force 22 April 1954) 189 UNTS 137 (Refugee Convention) art 33.

M26.3 International Court of Justice (ICJ) cases

Citation order:

♦ Case name (in italics)
♦ Year (in square brackets)
♦ ICJ report citation *or* website and date accessed

Examples in footnotes

1. *Corfu Channel Case (UK v Albania) (Merits)* [1949] ICJ Rep 4.
2. *Maritime Dispute (Peru v Chile)* [2014] ICJ Judgement <https://www.icj-cij.org/en/case/137> accessed 26 May 2021.

M27 US legal material

See *The Bluebook: A Uniform System of Citation* (2020) 21st edn. Cambridge, MA: Harvard Law Review Association, or Martin, P.W. (2020) *Introduction to Basic Legal Citation*. Available at: http://www.law.cornell.edu/citation/ (accessed: 26 May 2021). An example of a US case, with italicisation and punctuation removed from abbreviations, is given below.

Example in footnotes

1. *John Doe Agency v John Doe Corp*, 493 US 146, 159-60 (1934) (Stevens, J., dissenting).

M28 Interviews

If you interviewed another person, use the following.

Citation order:

♦ Name, position and institution (if relevant) of the interviewee
♦ Location of the interview and date (in round brackets)

Example in footnotes

1. Interview with Jane Stephenson, Professor of International Law, Durham University (Durham 19 October 2020).

As this is unpublished, do not list it in your bibliography. You may include a transcript of the interview (with the interviewee's permission) as an appendix to your text.

For an interview conducted by someone else, use the following.

Citation order:

♦ Name of interviewer
♦ Name, position and institution (if relevant) of the interviewee
♦ Location of the interview and date (in round brackets)
♦ Add where you read, heard or saw the interview in a publication or broadcast

This interview has been published or made publically available through a broadcast, so can be referenced in your bibliography.

M29 Websites

Citation order:

♦ Author or organisation
♦ Title of webpage (in single quotation marks)
♦ Title of website (in italics) and date (all in round brackets)
♦ <URL> accessed date

M30 Blogs

Citation order:

♦ Author or username
♦ Title of post (in single quotation marks)
♦ Title of blog (in italics), full date of post (all in round brackets)
♦ <URL> accessed date

M31 Podcasts

Citation order:

♦ Author (if unavailable, use organisation providing podcast)
♦ Title of podcast (in single quotation marks)
♦ Title of website (in italics) and date (all in round brackets)
♦ <URL> accessed date

M32 Radio and television programmes

Citation order:

♦ Author (if available, if not use title)
♦ Title (in single quotation marks)
♦ Radio or television channel and date of broadcast (all in round brackets)
♦ If online, add <URL> accessed date

If you are quoting a speaker in the programme, begin the reference with their name.

M33 Speeches/lectures

Citation order:

♦ Name of speaker
♦ Title of speech (in single quotation marks)
♦ Additional information, venue and date (in round brackets)

Examples in footnotes

1. Natalie Williams, 'Privacy Law' (LAW204: Introduction to UK Law, Durham University, 8 November 2017).

M34 Conference papers

Citation order:

♦ Author
♦ Title of paper (in single quotation marks)
♦ Title, location and date of the conference (in round brackets)
♦ If a conference paper has been published, cite the publication. If available online, include <URL> accessed date

M35 Personal communications

Citation order:

♦ Form of communication
♦ Author
♦ Recipient
♦ Date (in round brackets)

Examples in footnotes

1. Email from Lord Justice Williams to George Freeman MP (28 June 2021).
2. Letter from Dr J Singh to Mrs T Collins (14 August 2021).

Don't include unpublished personal communications in your bibliography. If they are published, cite the source in which you read them, such as book or website.

Sample text

The following sample of text from an essay has footnotes and is followed by tables of cases and legislation and a bibliography.

In her summing up, Symmonds LJ noted the case of *R v Edwards*.[1] The Access to

Justice Act 1999 and the Terrorism (United Nations Measures) Order strengthened this interpretation.[2] An alternative view was suggested by Clarkson.[3] In his opinion, the Judge should have taken account of more recent cases.[4] However, Behan and O'Donnell[5] supported the Judge's view and disagreed with Clarkson's analysis.[6] They believed that the Judge had taken other cases into account in her summary.[7] Comments by Storey,[8] and by Roberts,[9] agreed with this view. They cited the 2001 Law Commission report on *Double Jeopardy*,[10] and *R v Dunlop*.[11]

Sample footnotes

1. *R v Edwards (John)* (1991) 93 Cr App R 48 (CA).
2. Terrorism (United Nations Measures) Order 2001 SI 2001/3365.
3. CMV Clarkson, *Criminal Law: Text and Materials* (7th edn, Sweet & Maxwell 2010) 47.
4. Ibid 56.
5. Cormac Behan and Ian O'Donnell, 'Prisoners, Politics and the Polls: Enfranchisement and the Burden of Responsibility' (2008) 48(3) Brit J Criminol 31, 37 <doi:10.1093/bjc/azn004> accessed 26 May 2021.
6. Clarkson (n 3) 50.
7. *R v Edwards* (n 1) 49.
8. T Storey, *Unlocking Criminal Law* (7th edn, Routledge 2020).
9. Andrew J Roberts, 'Evidence: Bad Character – Pre-Criminal Justice Act 2003 Law' (2008) 4 Crim LR, 303, 308–309.
10. Law Commission, *Double Jeopardy and Prosecution Appeals* (Law Com No 267, 2001) 42.
11. *R v Dunlop* [2006] EWCA Crim 1354, [2007] 1 WLR 1657.

Sample table of cases

R v Dunlop [2006] EWCA Crim 1354, [2007] 1 WLR 1657

R v Edwards (John) (1991) 93 Cr App R 48 (CA)

Sample table of legislation

Access to Justice Act 1999

Terrorism (United Nations Measures) Order 2001 SI 2001/3365

Sample bibliography

Behan C and O'Donnell I, 'Prisoners, Politics and the Polls: Enfranchisement and the Burden of Responsibility' (2008) 48(3) Brit J Criminol, 31 <doi:10.1093/bjc/azn004> accessed 26 May 2021

Clarkson CMV, *Criminal Law: Text and Materials* (7th edn, Sweet & Maxwell 2010)

Elliott C and Quinn F, *Criminal Law* (11th edn, Pearson Education 2016)

Law Commission, *Double Jeopardy and Prosecution Appeals* (Law Com No 267, 2001)

Roberts AJ, 'Evidence: Bad Character – Pre-Criminal Justice Act 2003 Law' (2008) 4 Crim LR, 303

Section N
Vancouver referencing style

The Vancouver referencing style is a numeric citation system used in biomedical, health and some science publications. It was first defined in 1978 at the conference of the International Committee of Medical Journal Editors (ICMJE) in Vancouver, Canada, hence its name. The authoritative source for Vancouver referencing is K. Patrias and D. Wendling, *Citing Medicine: The NLM Style Guide for Authors, Editors, and Publishers* [Internet]. 2nd ed. Bethesda (MD): National Library of Medicine (US); 2007-. Available from: https://www.ncbi.nlm.nih.gov/books/NBK7262/

Conventions when using the Vancouver referencing style

♦ Vancouver uses numeric references in the text, either numbers in brackets (1) or **superscript**[1] linked to full **citations** in **footnotes**
♦ The same citation number is used whenever a source is cited in your text
♦ These in-text numbers are matched to full, numbered **references** for each publication in a **reference list**
♦ The reference list gives publications in the order they appeared in the text, not alphabetically
♦ Very little punctuation is used

♦ Well-established abbreviations are used for journal titles

Footnote position and page numbers

The footnote can be used within the flow of your text next to where you cited the source, for example:

Research by Zhang (1) highlighted …

The footnote number can also be included at the end of the sentence. *Citing Medicine* does not indicate exactly where this should be. Some institutions prefer the footnote number to be inside the sentence punctuation, for example (1). Other institutions prefer the footnote number to be outside the punctuation, for example.(1) This is the format used in *Cite them right*. Check with your tutor if they have a preference, or choose one format and apply it consistently.

There is no agreement among citation authorities about the use of page numbers with in-text citations in Vancouver style. If you wish to use page numbers, we suggest the following format, where # is the page number in source 1.

In-text citation

Smith (1, p. #) described two examples …

If using superscript numeric references, use the following.

In-text citation

Smith[1] (p. #) described two examples …

Multiple citations

♦ If you have written a section of text based on several references, these are indicated by listing each source separated by a comma

Example

Several drug trials (3,6,9,12) proved …

Author names

♦ Authors should be cited by surname, then initials

Example

Collinton MS.

♦ There is no comma between the surname and initials, nor any full stop after the initials, or spaces between the initials. Indicate the end of the author's name with a full stop
♦ Authors should be listed in the order shown in the article or book, not alphabetically
♦ Romanise all author names
♦ Remove accents and diacritics from letters in author names; for example, ñ should be written as n, and Ø written as O

Multiple authors

♦ Many science publications are the result of collaborative work, resulting in multiple authors who require citation. If you have six authors or fewer, list all of them, separating their names with a comma. Use a full stop to indicate the end of the authors' names. If there are more than six authors, *Citing Medicine* suggests citing the first six authors followed by et al. or 'and others'

Example

Bourne AD, Davis P, Fuller E, Hanson AJ, Price KN, Vaughan JT, et al.

Organisations as authors

♦ Names of organisations are spelt out, not abbreviated

Example

General Medical Council.

No authors identified

♦ If no authors or editors are listed, use the title of the book, journal article or website

Editors

♦ The Vancouver system never abbreviates the word 'editor'

Example

Redclift N, Gibbon S, editors. Genetics: critical concepts in social and cultural theory. London: Routledge; 2017.

Edition

♦ The abbreviation ed. is used for edition

Example

Turnpenny PD, Ellard S, Cleaver R. Emery's elements of medical genetics and genomics. 16th ed. Amsterdam: Elsevier; 2021.

Dates

♦ Dates are given as 'Year' for books or 'Year month (abbreviated) day' for articles

Article titles

♦ Article titles follow immediately after the author names
♦ The article titles are in standard text and are not enclosed in quotation marks, nor italicised or underlined
♦ Capitalise the first word of the article title, **proper nouns** and initials
♦ For non-English titles, write the title as in the journal article, but give a translation in square brackets immediately after the original form
♦ Use a full stop to indicate the end of the article title

Journal titles

♦ Journal titles are abbreviated. If the correct abbreviation is not included in the journal article you have used, check the NLM Catalog: Journals referenced in the NCBI Databases (https://www.ncbi.nlm.nih.gov/nlmcatalog/journals)
♦ Use a capital letter for each word of the abbreviated title; for example, Annu Rev Cell Biol is the accepted abbreviation for Annual Review of Cell Biology

Book titles

♦ Only the first word and any **proper nouns** or acronyms are capitalised and the title is neither underlined nor italicised
♦ Book titles should be written in their original language. Non-English titles should be followed by a translation of the title in square brackets

Example

Cite them right: the essential referencing guide.

Online access

♦ When you have used information from online sources, indicate this with [Internet], the date cited in the format [cited year month day] and Available from: URL *or* DOI

Reference list and bibliography

The reference list should only include sources you have cited in your text. List any sources you read but did not cite in your work in a separate **bibliography**

How to reference common sources in your reference list

N1 Books

Citation order:

♦ Author/editor
♦ Title (capitalise only the first letter of the first word and any proper nouns)
♦ Edition (only include the edition number if it is not the first edition)
♦ Place of publication: publisher; year of publication
♦ Pagination

Example: single author

Reference list

1. Bleakley A. Patient-centred medicine in transition: the heart of the matter. Switzerland: Springer; 2014. 267 p.

Example: organisation as author

Reference list

2. Joint Formulary Committee. British national formulary. 81st ed. London: BMJ Group; 2021. 1824 p.

Example: up to six authors

Reference list

3. Nussbaum R, McInnes R, Willard H. Genetics in medicine. 8th ed. Amsterdam: Elsevier; 2015. 560 p.

Example: more than six authors

Reference list

4. Bourne AD, Davis P, Hanson AJ, Price KN, Vaughan JT, Williams V et al. Health systems. London: Fuller Ltd; 2008. 212 p.

N2 Ebooks

Citation order:

♦ Author/editor
♦ Title of ebook (capitalise only first letter of first word and any proper nouns)
♦ Edition (only include the edition number if it is not the first edition)
♦ [Internet]
♦ Place of publication: publisher; year of original publication
♦ [cited year month day]
♦ Available from: https://doi.org *or* URL

Example

Reference list

5. Rippe JM. Lifestyle medicine [Internet]. 16th ed. Boca Raton (FL): CRC Press; 2019 [cited 2021 May 12]. 141 p. Available from: https://doi.org/10.1201/9781315201108

N3 Edited books

N3.1 Whole books

Citation order:

♦ Name of editor(s) of book
♦ editor(s)
♦ Title of book
♦ [Internet] if online
♦ Place of publication: publisher; year of publication
♦ [cited year month day] if online
♦ Page numbers (preceded by p.)
♦ Available from: https://doi.org *or* URL

Example

Reference list

6. Ramirez AG, Trapido EJ, editors. Advancing the science of cancer in Latinos [Internet]. Cham: Springer; 2020 [cited 2021 Apr 30]. Available from: https://doi.org/10.1007/9783030292867

N3.2 Chapters/sections in edited books

Citation order:

♦ Author(s) of the chapter/section
♦ Title of chapter/section

- In
- Name of editor(s) of book
- editor(s)
- Title of book
- [Internet] if online
- Place of publication: publisher; year of publication
- Page numbers (preceded by p.)
- Available from: https://doi.org *or* URL

Example

Reference list

7. Garai J, Li L, Zabaleta J. Biomarkers of gastric premalignant lesions. In: Ramirez AG, Trapido EJ, editors. Advancing the science of cancer in Latinos [Internet]. Cham: Springer; 2020. p. 81–8. Available from: https://doi.org/10.1007/9783030292867

N4 Multi-volume works

Citation order:

- Author/editor (if available)
- Title
- Place of publication: publisher; year
- Number of volumes
- Number of pages (optional)

Example: whole publication

Reference list

8. British Pharmacopoeia 2018. London: The Stationery Office; 2017. 5 vols.

Example: reference to a specific volume

Reference list

9. British Pharmacopoeia 2018. Vol. 2. London: The Stationery Office; 2017.

N5 Journal articles

N5.1 Articles in print journals and magazines

Citation order:

- Author(s)
- Title of article
- Abbreviated title of journal
- Date of publication as year month day
- Volume (issue): page numbers (not preceded by p.)

Examples

Reference list

10. Consonni D, De Matteis S, Lubin JH, Wacholder S, Tucker M, Pesatori AC, et al. Lung cancer and occupation in a population-based case-control study. Am J Epidemiol. 2010 Feb 1; 171(3):323–33.
11. MD. Pandemic update. Private Eye. 2021 Apr 30–May 13; (1546):8–9.

N5.2 Articles in ejournals and online magazines

Citation order:

- Author(s)
- Title of article

- ♦ Abbreviated title of journal
- ♦ [Internet]
- ♦ Date of publication as year month day
- ♦ [cited year month day];
- ♦ Volume (issue): page numbers *or* article number *or* number of screens
- ♦ Available from: https://doi.org *or* URL

Examples

Reference list

12. Amr S, Wolpert B, Loffredo CA, Zheng YL, Shields PG, Jones R. Occupation, gender, race and lung cancer. J Occup Environ Med [Internet]. 2008 Oct [cited 2021 Feb 23]; 50(10):1167–75. Available from: https://doi.org/10.1097/JOM.0b013e31817d3639
13. Iacobellis G. COVID-19 and diabetes: Can DPP4 inhibition play a role? Diabetes Res Clin Pract [Internet]. 2020 Apr [cited 2021 Feb 23]; 162: Article number 108125. Available from: https://doi.org/10.1016/j.diabres.2020.108125
14. Kim S. Child COVID cases are highest in these states. Newsweek [Internet]. 2021 May 5 [cited 2021 May 11] [about 3 screens]. Available from: https://www.newsweek.com/coronavirus-states-highest-child-covid-cases-children-1588815

N5.3 Advance online publications

Citation order:

- ♦ Author(s)
- ♦ Title of article
- ♦ Abbreviated title of journal
- ♦ [Internet]
- ♦ Year and Advance online publication
- ♦ [cited year month day]
- ♦ Available from: https://doi.org *or* URL

Example

Reference list

15. Madan C, Spetch ML, Machado FMDS, Mason A and Ludvig EA. Encoding context denotes risky choice. Psychol Sci [Internet]. 2021 Advance online publication [cited 2021 May 4]. Available from: https://doi.org/10.1177/0956797620977516

N5.4 Article in press (forthcoming)

Citation order:

- ♦ Author(s)
- ♦ Title of article
- ♦ Abbreviated title of journal
- ♦ [Internet]
- ♦ Forthcoming
- ♦ Year
- ♦ [cited year month day]
- ♦ Available from: https://doi.org *or* URL

Example

Reference list

16. Bouman T, Steg L, Perlaviciute G. From values to climate action. Curr Opin Psychol [Internet]. Forthcoming 2021 [cited 2021 May 12]. Available from: https://doi.org/10.1016/j.copsyc.2021.04.010

N5.5 Articles in systematic reviews

Citation order:

- Author (surname followed by initials).
- Title of review
- Year month day of review
- In:
- Title of database
- [Internet]
- Place of publication: publisher year
- File size
- Available from: URL or DOI
- Record No.: CD ...

Example

Reference list

17. Pasquali S, Hadjinicolaou AV, Chiarion Sileni V, Rossi CR, Mocellin S. Systemic treatments for metastatic cutaneous melanoma. 2018 Feb 6. In: The Cochrane Database of Systematic Reviews [Internet]. Hoboken (NJ): John Wiley & Sons, Ltd. c1999-2018. 3.28MB. Available from: https://doi.org/10.1002/14651858.CD011123.pub2. Record No.: CD011123.

N6 News sources

N6.1 Articles in print newspapers

Citation order:

- Author
- Article title
- Newspaper title and edition, if applicable (in round brackets)
- Year month day
- Section (if applicable)
- Pagination

Example

Reference list

18. Vasquez T. Pharmacy company's R & D aims. Boston Globe (3rd ed.). 2018 Nov 17: C4 (col. 2).

N6.2 Articles in online newspapers

Citation order:

- Author
- Article title
- Newspaper title and edition (if applicable)
- [Internet]
- Date
- [cited year month day]
- Section (if applicable)
- Page and column *or* approximate location (number of screens in square brackets)
- Available from: URL

Example

Reference list

19. Lebrun A-L. Les rouages des troubles du comportement alimentaire [The inner workings of eating disorders]. Le Figaro [Internet]. 2021 Mar 5 [cited 2021 May 12]; Sciences [about 1 p.]. Available from https://www.lefigaro.fr/sciences/les-rouages-des-troubles-du-comportement-alimentaire-20210503

N7 Conferences and symposia

N7.1 Conference papers

Citation order:

♦ Author(s)
♦ Title of conference paper
♦ Title of conference (capitalise all initial letters, except for linking words)
♦ Date as year month day(s)
♦ Location
♦ If published, add details of place and publisher *or* journal reference

Example

Reference list

20. Valberg PA, Watson AY. Lack of concordance between reported lung cancer risk levels and occupation-specific diesel-exhaust exposure. 3rd Colloquium on Particulate Air Pollution and Human Health; 1999 Jun 6–8; Durham (NC).

N7.2 Poster presentations

Citation order:

♦ Author
♦ Title of poster
♦ [Internet] if online
♦ Poster session presented at:
♦ Name of event;
♦ Year month day(s)
♦ Location
♦ [cited year month day] if online
♦ Available from: https://doi.org *or* URL

Example

Reference list

21. Collins B. Real men get checked. Poster session presented at: American College of Surgeons Cancer Programs Conference; 2017 Sep 8–9; Chicago (IL). [cited 2021 May 10]. Available from: https://www.facs.org/~/media/files/quality%20programs/cancer/conference/2017/collins.ashx

N8 Theses or dissertations

In the Vancouver referencing style, dissertation refers to a PhD submission, while thesis refers to a Master's submission.

Citation order:

♦ Author
♦ Title
♦ Publication type (in square brackets)
♦ Place of publication: publisher; year
♦ [cited year month day]
♦ Pagination
♦ Available from: https://doi.org *or* URL

Example

Reference list

22. Beales LP. Hepatitis A virus in relation to contamination of factor VIII [dissertation on the Internet]. Milton Keynes: Open University; 1998 [cited 2021 May 21]. 242 p. Available from: http://oro.open.ac.uk/66055/

N9 Reports and working papers

Citation order:

- ♦ Author(s)
- ♦ Title of report
- ♦ [Internet]
- ♦ Place of publication: publisher; year of publication
- ♦ [cited year month day]
- ♦ Pagination
- ♦ Report series and number
- ♦ Available from: https://doi.org *or* URL

Example
Reference list

23. Basu P, Getachew Y. Redistributive innovation policy, inequality and efficiency. [Internet]. Durham: Durham University Business School; 2017 [cited 2021 May 4]. 33 p. DUBS Working Paper 2017.2. Available from: https://www.dur.ac.uk/resources/business/working-papers/RD_2017_02.pdf

N10 Government publications

Citation order:

- ♦ Jurisdiction (if using sources from more than one country)
- ♦ Author(s)
- ♦ Title of report
- ♦ [Internet]
- ♦ Place of publication: publisher; year of publication

- ♦ [cited year month day]
- ♦ Pagination
- ♦ Report series and number
- ♦ Available from: https://doi.org *or* URL

Examples
Reference list

24. United Kingdom. Department for Education. Government response to the education select committee report: extremism in schools – the Trojan Horse affair. (Cm. 9094). London: Her Majesty's Stationery Office; 2015. 20 p.
25. Australia. Department of Industry, Science, Energy and Resources. Australia's emissions projections 2020 [Internet]. Canberra: Australian Government; 2020 Jun [cited 2021 June 23]. 74 p. Available from: https://www.industry.gov.au/sites/default/files/2020-12/australias-emissions-projections-2020.pdf

N11 Legal information

N11.1 Legislation

Citation order:

- ♦ Jurisdiction (if citing more than one authority)
- ♦ Title of legislation, including year
- ♦ Number or reference

Examples

Reference list

26. Human Tissue Act 2004, c.30.

If you are citing legislation from several jurisdictions, add the country at the start of the reference:

27. United Kingdom Parliament. Fire Safety Act 2021, c.24.
28. Singapore. Vulnerable Adults Act 2018.

N11.2 Legal cases

Citing medicine notes that legal cases have established citation formats and recommends that these be used. A UK case would be cited as follows.

Citation order:

♦ Party names
♦ Legal citation
♦ Available from: URL

Example

Reference list

29. Grant & Anor v The Ministry of Justice [2011] EWHC 3379 (QB). Available from: https://www.bailii.org/ew/cases/EWHC/QB/2011/3379.html

N12 Protocols, regulations and guidelines

Citation order:

♦ Author(s)
♦ Title of report
♦ [Internet] if online
♦ Place of publication: publisher; year of publication
♦ [cited year month day] if online
♦ Pagination
♦ Report series and number
♦ Available from: https://doi.org *or* URL

Example

Reference list

30. National Institute for Health and Care Excellence. Postnatal care [Internet]. London: NICE; 2021 [cited 10 May 2021]. 61 p. [NG194]. Available from: https://www.nice.org.uk/guidance/ng194

N13 Technical standards

Citation order:

♦ Publishing organisation/institution
♦ Standard number
♦ Title
♦ [Internet] if online
♦ Place of publication: publisher; year
♦ [cited year month day]
♦ Available from: https://doi.org *or* URL

Example

Reference list

31. British Standards Institution. BS EN IEC 60068-2-13:2021. Environmental testing. Tests. Test M: Low air pressure [Internet]. London: BSI; 2021 [cited 2021 Jun 4]. Available from: https://bsol-bsigroup-com

N14 Patents

Citation order:

♦ Inventor
♦ Assignee
♦ Title
♦ Patent country and document type
♦ Country code and patent number
♦ Date issued
♦ [cited year month day]
♦ Available from: https://doi.org *or* URL

Example

Reference list

32. Padley S, inventor. Thompson Hydraulics Ltd, assignee. Radiator isolating valve. United Kingdom patent GB 2463069. 2015 Nov 21 [cited 2021 Jul 31]. Available from: https://worldwide.espacenet.com/

N15 Research datasets

Citation order:

♦ Title of data collection or programme (capitalise all initial letters, except for linking words)
♦ [Internet]
♦ Name and location of organisation
♦ [date published]
♦ Title of data series
♦ [cited year month day]
♦ Available from: https://doi.org *or* URL

Example

Reference list

33. Surveillance Epidemiology and End Results (SEER) Data 1973–2006 [Internet]. Bethesda (MA): National Cancer Institute (USA). [2021 Apr]. U.S. Mortality Data, 1969–2018; [cited 2021 Aug 23]. Available from: http://seer.cancer.gov/ resources/

N16 Tables/figures/graphs or illustrations

Cite the source in which the table, graph or figure appears, and include the number and title of the table, graph or figure after page numbers.

N16.1 Tables/figures/graphs or illustrations in books

Citation order:

♦ Author/editor of book
♦ Title of book
♦ Edition (if not first edition)
♦ Place of publication: publisher; year
♦ Figure/table number, figure/table caption
♦ Page number

Example

Reference list

34. Hocking S, Sochacki F, Winterbottom M. OCR AS/A level biology A. 2nd ed. London: Pearson; 2015. Figure 3, Calibration curve for known concentrations of glucose solution vs transmission of light; p. 77.

N16.2 Tables/figures/graphs or illustrations in journal articles

Citation order:

♦ Author(s)
♦ Title of article
♦ Abbreviated title of journal
♦ [Internet]
♦ Date of publication as year month day
♦ Volume (issue): page numbers of article
♦ Table number, caption,
♦ [cited year month day]
♦ Page number
♦ Available from: https://doi.org *or* URL

Example
Reference list

35. Ferlay J, Colombet M, Soerjomataram I, Dyba T, Randi G, Bettio M, Gavin A, Visser O, Bray F. Cancer incidence and mortality patterns in Europe: estimates for 40 countries and 25 major cancers in 2018. Eur J Cancer [Internet]. 2018 Aug 9; 103:1–32. Table 7, Estimated number of new cancer cases (hundreds) by sex, cancer site and country, 2018; [cited 2021 Aug 23]; p.8. Available from: https://doi.org/10.1016/j.ejca.2018.07.005

N16.3 Tables/figures/graphs or illustrations on website

Citation order:

♦ Author
♦ Title of internet site
♦ [Internet]
♦ Year the site was published/last updated
♦ [cited year month day]
♦ Table number, caption,
♦ Number of screens or pages
♦ Available from: URL

Example
Reference list

36. Hossain MA. Bangladesh Meteorological Department [Internet]. 2021 May 10 [cited 2021 May 10]; Table 1, Weather forecast valid for 24 hours commencing 06 PM today; [1 screen]. Available from: http://live4.bmd.gov.bd/p/Weather-Forecast/

N16.4 Chemical structure diagram on website

Citation order:

♦ Title of internet site
♦ [Internet]
♦ Place of publication: publisher; year
♦ Title of diagram
♦ [cited year month day]
♦ Available from: URL

Example
Reference list

37. PubChem [Internet]. Bethesda (MD): National Library of Medicine (US), National Center for Biotechnology Information; 2004 -. PubChem Compound Summary for CID 2244, Aspirin; [cited 2021 May 12]. Available from: https://pubchem.ncbi.nlm.nih.gov/compound/Aspirin

N16.5 Equations in a journal article

Cite equations within the source you read.

Citation order:

♦ Author
♦ Title of article
♦ Abbreviated title of journal
♦ [Internet]
♦ Date of publication
♦ Volume (issue): page numbers of article
♦ [cited year month day]
♦ Page number of equation
♦ Available from: https://doi.org *or* URL

Example

Reference list

38. Fradelizi, M, Meyer, M. Some functional inverse Santaló inequalities. Adv Math [Internet]. 2008; 218(5):1430–52 [cited 2021 Feb 23]; p.1432. Available from: https://doi.org/10.1016/j.aim.2008.03.013

N17 Software/computer programs/computer codes/computer games

Citation order:

♦ Author(s)
♦ Title of software
♦ Version
♦ [medium]
♦ Publisher
♦ Date of release
♦ [cited year month day; downloaded year month day]
♦ Available from: URL

Examples

Reference list

39. TechSmith. Camtasia 2020. Version 2021.0.0 [software]. Okemos, MI: TechSmith. 2021 Apr 27 [cited 2021 May 3; downloaded 2021 Apr 30]. Available from: https://www.techsmith.com/video-editor.html

40. 343 Industries. Halo: The Master Chief Collection [computer game]. Redmond, WA: Xbox Game Studios. 2020 Nov 17 [cited 2021 May 4; downloaded 2020 Dec 20]. Available from: https://www.xbox.com/en-GB/games/halo-the-master-chief-collection

N18 Mobile apps

Citation order:

♦ Author(s)
♦ Title of software
♦ Version
♦ [mobile app]
♦ Publisher
♦ Date of release
♦ [cited year month day; downloaded year month day]
♦ Available from: URL

41. NHS Digital. NHS COVID-19 app. Version 4.9 (185) [mobile app]. London: NHS. 2020 May 5 [cited 2021 Jan 4; downloaded 2021 Jan 3]. Available from: https://play. google.com/store/apps/ details?id=uk.nhs.covid19. production

N19 Organisation or personal internet sites

Citation order:

♦ Author/organisation
♦ Title of internet site
♦ [Internet]
♦ Year the site was published/last updated
♦ [cited year month day]
♦ [number of screens or pages]
♦ Available from: URL

42. Macmillan Cancer Support. Lung cancer [Internet]. 2018 [cited 2021 Aug 23]; [29 screens]. Available from: https://www.macmillan.org. uk/cancer-information-and-support/lung-cancer

For web pages where no author can be identified, use the title of the web page.

43. WhyQuit.com [Internet] 2021 [cited 2021 Aug 23]; [50+ screens]. Available from: http://whyquit.com/

For web pages with no date, include the cited date.

44. NHS South Tees Hospitals. What is hydrotherapy/aquatic therapy? [Internet]. Middlesbrough (UK): NHS South Tees Hospitals; [cited 2021 Jun 14]. Available from: https://www.southtees.nhs.uk/ services/physiotherapy/ community/treatments-available/ hydrotherapy-aquatic-therapy/

N20 Blogs

Citation order:

♦ Author
♦ Title
♦ [Internet]
♦ Place of publication: publisher; date
♦ [cited year month day]
♦ Available from: URL

Example

Reference list

45. Davies C. Inspiring thursday: Greta Thunberg [Internet]. Vienna: Wave Blog, 2019 [cited 2021 Aug 23]. Available from: https://blog.wave-network.org/inspiring-thursday-greta-thunberg

N21 Social media viewed on the internet

Citing medicine does not include examples of references for social media. Where social media is publicly accessible online, such as Facebook, Twitter, Instagram and Tumblr, cite as online sources. If the information is not publicly available, cite as personal communications (N25).

Citation order:

♦ Author (surname followed by initials) *or* organisation *and/or* [@username]
♦ Title or text
♦ [Internet]
♦ Year month day
♦ [cited year month day]
♦ Available from: URL

Examples

Reference list

46. AstraZeneca. Q1 2021 results [Internet]. 2021 Apr 30 [cited 2021 June 14]. Available from: https://www.instagram.com/p/COSwpyKDnW8/
47. Confederation of Indian Industry. Did you know by 2035 AI is expected to boost India's annual growth rate by 1.3%? [Internet]. 2021 May 4 [cited 2021 Aug 23]. Available from: https://www.facebook.com/FollowCII/posts/4389646397736448
48. Kuenssberg, L. [@bbclaurak]. Matt Hancock refuses to answer a question on whether ministers who break party funding rules or the law should resign [Internet]. 2021 Apr 28 [cited 2021 May 10]. Available from: https://twitter.com/bbclaurak/status/1387445378375639045
49. NASA. All about that (nucleic) base: Studying DNA aboard the International Space Station [Internet]. 2018 Apr 25 [cited 2021 Mar 4]. Available from: https://nasa.tumblr.com/post/173297824539/all-about-that-nucleic-base-studying-dna

N22 Audiovisual sources

N22.1 Radio and television programmes

Citation order:

- ◆ Title of programme
- ◆ Title of series
- ◆ [Format]
- ◆ Place of publication: channel
- ◆ Date of broadcast

Examples

Reference list

50. Complexity in biology. Inside science [Radio broadcast]. London: BBC Radio 4; 2018 Sep 6.
51. Oceans of wonder. Blue Planet II [Television broadcast]. London: BBC One; 2018 Jan 5.

N22.2 Films/movies

Citation order:

- ◆ Title
- ◆ [motion picture]
- ◆ Place of publication: publisher; year

Example

Reference list

52. Children of men [motion picture]. New York: Universal Studios; 2006.

N22.3 Online videos and podcasts

If the video is publicly available, for example in YouTube, Vimeo, IGTV, Dailymotion, TED, use this format. If you have to be invited or log in to view it, see N24.2.

Citation order:

- ◆ Author
- ◆ Title of source
- ◆ [Internet]
- ◆ Place of publication: publisher; date of publication
- ◆ [cited year month day]
- ◆ Format: length
- ◆ Available from: URL

Examples

Reference list

53. Cambridge University Cosmology. Professor Gabriella González: Black holes and gravitational waves [Internet]. Cambridge: Cambridge University; 2017 Jul 2 [cited 2021 May 4]. Video: 39:13 min. Available from: https://www.youtube.com/watch?v=Txuq1sO8fkY
54. Orlowski J. Chasing coral [Internet]. Los Gatos, CA: Netflix; 2017 [cited 2021 Sep 8]. Streaming video: 99 min. Available from: https://www.netflix.com/gb/title/80168188
55. Williams C. Audio: unhelpful thinking [Internet]. London: NHS; 2021 Mar 2 [cited 2021 May 31]. Podcast: 9:45 min. Available from: https://www.nhs.uk/mental-health/self-help/guides-tools-and-activities/mental-wellbeing-audio-guides/#confidence

N22.4 Photographs

This is for photographic prints. If you have viewed a photograph online or in a publication, use the appropriate citation format for that source.

Citation order:

♦ Artist
♦ Title
♦ Medium (in square brackets)
♦ Place of publication: publisher; date
♦ Physical description

Example

Reference list

56. Ikhanov T. Sclerosis in human liver [Photograph]. Kiev: Ukrainian Institute of Medicine; 2015. 1 photograph: colour, 10 x 20cm.

N22.5 Maps

Citation order:

♦ Author
♦ Title or description
♦ Medium (in square brackets)
♦ Place of publication: publisher; year

If print, add:

♦ Description, including size in cms
♦ Colour/black and white
♦ Series and number

If online, add:

♦ [cited year month day]
♦ Available from: URL

Example

Reference list

57. Ordnance Survey. Kendal to Morecambe [map]. Southampton: Ordnance Survey; 1982. 1 sheet: 80 x 80cm.; colour. Landranger 1:50,000 series; 97.
58. Google maps. Directions for driving from Reading to Tiddenfoot Lake [Internet]. Mountain View, CA: Google; 2021 [cited 2021 Jul 5]. Available from: https://goo.gl/maps/hC5pUfsYCiW1Yuyw5

N22.6 Infographics

Citation order:

♦ Author/poster of video
♦ Title of video
♦ [Internet]
♦ Date of publication
♦ [cited year month day]
♦ Available from: URL

Example

Reference list

59. The Health Foundation. What does the pandemic mean for health and health inequalities? [Internet]. 2021 Feb 18 [cited 2021 May 11]. Available from: https://www.health.org.uk/news-and-comment/charts-and-infographics/what-does-the-pandemic-mean-for-health-and-health-inequaliti

N23 Interviews

N23.1 Published interview

Published interviews should be cited according to the format in which you have used them, for example as a journal or newspaper article.

N23.2 Unpublished interview

If an interview is unpublished, cite it in the text of your work and not in the reference list.

Example

In-text citation

Professor Wang discussed her research into dementia (interview with author 14 Oct 2020; unreferenced).

N24 Course materials

N24.1 Lecture notes

Citation order:

♦ Author
♦ Title
♦ [format]
♦ Place of publication: publisher;
♦ Course details, date

If online, add:

♦ [cited year month day]
♦ Available from: URL

Example

Reference list

60. Brown T. Theatre procedures [lecture notes]. Newcastle: Northumbria University; ME3187: BSc Midwifery; 2021 Feb. 4 [cited 2021 Mar 3]. Available from: https://sts.northumbria.ac.uk/

N24.2 Online lectures: Zoom, Teams, Collaborate

If the lecture recording is publicly available, cite it as an online video (N22.3). If you need to be invited or to log in to view the lecture (for example Zoom, Teams, Collaborate), use the format above and change the medium to [lecture on the Internet].

Examples

Reference list

61. Brown T. Theatre procedures [lecture notes]. Newcastle: Northumbria University; DE816: BSc Design; 2021 Feb. 4 [cited 2021 Mar 3]. Available from: https://sts.northumbria.ac.uk/
62. Cloe J. The normal distribution [lecture notes on Internet]. Melbourne: Monash University, Faculty of Medicine, Nursing and Health Sciences; 2020 [cited 2020 Apr 26]. Available from: http://moodle.vle.monash.edu

N25 Personal communications: telephone calls, letters, emails, groupchats, private messages

Citing medicine states that personal communications should usually be noted in your text and not in the reference list. Provide the author's name, the date of the message, and note that it will not be included in your reference list by including the word unreferenced. You should obtain permission from the sender of personal communications to quote them in your work.

Examples

In-text citations

In an email to this author, N. Johnson (2021 Nov 12, unreferenced) …

In her letter T. Stone (2021 Feb 1, unreferenced) …

P. Vallina Martínez private messaged (2020 Dec 11, unreferenced) that …

Sample text

More than 46,400 people are diagnosed with lung cancer every year in the UK.(1) Studies elsewhere have investigated links between occupation or socio-demographic status and cancer (2,3), but smoking is the biggest single cause of lung cancer in the UK.(1) Some researchers have analysed populations to establish incidences of tumours.(4) Hart (5, p. 280) noted that tumours may spread from the lungs to elsewhere in the body. Charities and self-help groups (1,6) provide advice and moral support to victims.

Sample reference list

1. Macmillan Cancer Support. Lung cancer [Internet]. 2021 [cited 2021 Aug 23]; [29 screens]. Available from: http://www.macmillan.org.uk/Cancerinformation/Cancertypes/Lung/Lungcancer.aspx
2. Valberg PA, Watson AY. Lack of concordance between reported lung-cancer risk levels and occupation-specific diesel-exhaust exposure. 3rd Colloquium on Particulate Air Pollution and Human Health; 1999 Jun 6–8; Durham (NC).
3. Amr S, Wolpert B, Loffredo CA, Zheng YL, Shields PG, Jones R. Occupation, gender, race and lung cancer. J Occup Environ Med [Internet]. 2008 Oct [cited 2021 Aug 23]; 50(10):1167–75. Available from: https://doi.org/10.1097/JOM.0b013e31817d3639
4. Tumour incidences, Nebraska 1973–83. Surveillance Epidemiology and End Results (SEER) Data 1973–2006. National Cancer Institute (USA) [cited 2021 Aug 23]. Available from: http://seer.cancer.gov/resources/
5. Hart I. The spread of tumours. In Knowles MA, Selby PJ, editors. Introduction to the cellular and molecular biology of cancer. Oxford: Oxford University Press; 2005. p. 278–88.
6. WhyQuit.com. [Internet] 2012 Aug 13 [cited 2018 Aug 23]; [50+ screens]. Available from: http://whyquit.com/

Glossary

Bibliography: A list of all the sources you consulted for your work arranged in alphabetical order by author's surname or, when there is no author, by title. For web pages where no author or title is apparent, the URL of the web page would be used.

Citation: The in-text reference that gives brief details (for example, author, date, page number) of the source you are quoting from or referring to. This citation corresponds with the full details of the work (title, publisher and so on) given in your reference list or bibliography so that the reader can identify and/or locate the work. End-text citations are commonly known as 'references'.

Citation surfing: Using the references in one source to identify other relevant sources and authors on the topic.

Common knowledge: Facts that are generally known.

Digital Object Identifier (DOI): A numbered tag used to identify individual digital (online) sources, such as journal articles and conference papers.

Direct quotation: The actual words used by an author, in exactly the same order as in their original work, and with the original spelling. See Section E for details of how to set out all quotations in your text.

End-text citation: An entry in the reference list at the end of your work, which contains the full (bibliographical) details of information for the in-text citation.

Et al.: (From the Latin *et alia* meaning 'and others'.) A term most commonly used for works having four or more authors (for example, Harvard author-date system). The citation gives the first surname listed in the publication, followed by *et al.*

Footnote/endnote: An explanatory note and/or source citation either at the foot of the page or end of a chapter used in numeric referencing styles (for example, MHRA). These are not used in Harvard and other author-date referencing styles.

Ibid.: (From the Latin *ibidem* meaning 'in the same place'.) A term used with citations that refer to an immediately preceding cited work. It is not used in the Harvard system, where works appear only once in the alphabetical list of references.

In-text citation: Often known as simply the 'citation', this gives brief details (for example, author, date, page number) of your source of information within your text.

Op. cit.: (From the Latin *opere citato* meaning 'in the work already cited'.) A term used with citations that refer to a previously cited work. It is not used in the Harvard system, where works appear only once in the alphabetical list of references.

Paraphrase: A restating of someone else's thoughts or ideas in your own words. You must always cite your source when paraphrasing (see Section E for details and an example).

Peer-review: A process used in academic publishing to check the accuracy and quality of a work intended for publication. The author's draft of a book or article is sent by an editor to experts in the subject, who (usually anonymously) suggest amendments or corrections. This process is seen as a guarantee of academic quality and is a major distinction between traditional forms of publishing, such as books and journals, and information on web pages, which can be written by anyone, even if they have no expertise in a subject.

Phrase searching: Putting the required phrase into double quotation marks.

Plagiarism: Taking and using another person's thoughts, writings or inventions as your own without acknowledging or citing the source of the ideas and expressions. In the case of copyrighted material, plagiarism is illegal.

Proper noun: The name of an individual person, place or organisation, having an initial capital letter.

Quotation: The words or sentences from another information source used within your text (see also *direct quotation*).

Reference: The full publication details of the work cited.

Reference list: A list of references at the end of your assignment that includes the full information for your citations so that the reader can easily identify and retrieve each work (journal articles, books, web pages and so on).

Scan reading: Looking through the text quickly to locate specific information.

Secondary referencing: Citing/referencing a work that has been mentioned or quoted in the work you are reading (see Section A for more details and an example).

Short citation: This is used in numeric referencing systems, including MHRA and OSCOLA, instead of *op. cit.* When a work is cited for the first time, all bibliographic details are included in the footnotes/endnotes and in the bibliography reference. If a work is cited more than once in the text, the second and subsequent entries in the footnotes/endnotes use an abbreviated, short citation, such as the author and title (as well as a specific page reference), so that the reader can find the full bibliographic details in the bibliography.

Sic: (From the Latin meaning 'so, thus'.) A term used after a quoted or copied word to show that the original word has been written exactly as it appears in the original text, and usually highlights an error or misspelling of the word.

Skim reading: Looking through the source to get an overview or general impression.

Summarise: Similar to paraphrasing, summarising provides a brief account of someone else's ideas or work, covering only the main points and leaving out the details (see Section E for more details and an example).

Superscript number: A number used in numeric referencing styles (including Chicago, MHRA and OSCOLA) to identify citations in the text, which is usually smaller than and set above the normal text, that is[1].

URL: The abbreviation for Uniform (or Universal) Resource Locator, the address of documents and other information sources on the internet (for example, http:// …).

Virtual learning environment (VLE): An online teaching environment that allows interaction between tutors and students, and the storage of course documents and teaching materials (see Section G7 for more details).

Works Cited: The Modern Language Association's (MLA) equivalent of a reference list that provides full details of the sources cited in your text.

References and further reading

American Psychological Association (2019) *Publication manual of the American Psychological Association*. 7th edn. Washington, DC: American Psychological Association.

American Psychological Association (2021) *APA style blog*. Available at: http://apastyle. apa.org/blog (Accessed: 16 June 2021).

The Bluebook: a uniform system of citation (2020) 21st edn. Cambridge, MA: Harvard Law Review Association.

Campbell, A. (2017) 'Cultural differences in plagiarism', *Turnitin blog*, 2 December. Available at: https://www.turnitin.com/blog/ cultural-differences-in-plagiarism (Accessed: 16 June 2021).

Chicago manual of style (2017) 17th edn. Chicago: University of Chicago Press.

Chicago manual of style online (2021) Available at: https://www. chicagomanualofstyle.org/home.html (Accessed: 16 June 2021).

Cottrell, S. (2019) *The study skills handbook*. 5th edn. London: Red Globe Press.

Gaast, K., Koenders, L. and Post, G. (2019) *Academic skills for interdisciplinary studies*. Rev. edn. Amsterdam: University of Amsterdam Press.

Gillett, A., Hammond, A. and Martala, M. (2009) *Successful academic writing*. Harlow: Longman.

IEEE (2021) *IEEE reference guide*. Available at: http://journals. ieeeauthorcenter.ieee.org/wp-content/ uploads/sites/7/IEEE-Reference-Guide-Online-v.04-20-2021.pdf (Accessed: 16 June 2021).

Learning Strategy Center, Cornell University (2021) *Cornell note taking system*. Available at: https://lsc.cornell. edu/how-to-study/taking-notes/cornell-note-taking-system/ (Accessed: 16 June 2021).

Magdalinski, T. (2013) *Study skills for sports studies*. Abingdon: Routledge.

Maier, P., Barney, A. and Price, G. (2009) *Study skills for science, engineering and technology students*. Harlow: Pearson.

Martin, P.W. (2020) *Introduction to basic legal citation*. Available at: http://www.law. cornell.edu/citation/ (Accessed: 16 June 2021).

Meredith, S. and Nolan, D. (2012) *Oxford University standard for citation of legal authorities* (4th edn). Available at: www. law.ox.ac.uk/published/OSCOLA_4th_ edn_Hart_2012.pdf (Accessed: 16 June 2021).

MLA Style Center (2021) Available at: https://style.mla.org/ (Accessed: 16 June 2021).

Modern Humanities Research Association (2013, reprinted with corrections 2015)

MHRA style guide. 3rd edn. London: Modern Humanities Research Association. Available at: http://www.mhra.org.uk/style/ (Accessed: 16 June 2021).

Modern Language Association (2021) *MLA handbook*. 9th edn. New York, NY: Modern Language Association of America.

OSCOLA FAQs. Available at: https://www.law.ox.ac.uk/oscola-faqs (Accessed: 16 June 2021).

Patrias, K. and Wendling, D. (eds) (2007–2021) *Citing medicine: the NLM style guide for authors, editors, and publishers*. 2nd edn. Available at: https://www.ncbi.nlm.nih.gov/books/NBK7262/. (Accessed: 16 June 2021).

Purdue University (2021) *Purdue online writing lab*. Available at: https://owl.purdue.edu/owl/research_and_citation/resources.html (Accessed: 17 June 2021).

Simon, D. J. (2019) 'Cross-cultural differences in plagiarism: Fact or fiction?', *Duquesne Law Review*, 57(1), pp.73–91.

Wood, G. W. (2018) *Letters to a new student*. London: Routledge.

Zigunovas, P. (2017) 'Why do students plagiarize? A cultural perspective', *Elearn*, 11 October. Available at: https://elearnmagazine.com/why-do-students-plagiarize/ (Accessed: 16 June 2021).

Index